The Rhetoric of Manipulation

The Rhetoric of Manipulation

Unmasking Semantic Perversions

Robert Harvey

BLOOMSBURY ACADEMIC

NEW YORK · LONDON · OXFORD · NEW DELHI · SYDNEY

BLOOMSBURY ACADEMIC
Bloomsbury Publishing Inc
1385 Broadway, New York, NY 10018, USA
50 Bedford Square, London, WC1B 3DP, UK
29 Earlsfort Terrace, Dublin 2, Ireland

BLOOMSBURY, BLOOMSBURY ACADEMIC and the Diana logo are
trademarks of Bloomsbury Publishing Plc

First published in the United States of America 2025

Cover design by Eleanor Rose
Cover image: "Flag Face," Circa 1890 American Flag (Infamous), 2019.
Courtesy of Andres Serrano and Galerie Nathalie Obadia, Paris/Brussels.

Bloomsbury Publishing Inc does not have any control over, or responsibility for,
any third-party websites referred to or in this book. All internet addresses given in
this book were correct at the time of going to press. The author and publisher
regret any inconvenience caused if addresses have changed or sites have ceased
to exist, but can accept no responsibility for any such changes.

Library of Congress Cataloging-in-Publication Data

Names: Harvey, Robert, 1951- author.
Title: The rhetoric of manipulation : unmasking semantic perversions / Robert Harvey.
Description: New York : Bloomsbury Academic, 2025. | Includes bibliographical references
and index. Identifiers: LCCN 2024036258 (print) | LCCN 2024036259 (ebook) |
ISBN 9798765100813 (paperback) | ISBN 9798765100806 (hardback) |
ISBN 9798765100820 (eBook) | ISBN 9798765100837 (ePDF)
Subjects: LCSH: Rhetoric. | Reliability. | Manipulative behavior. |
Language and languages–Philosophy.
Classification: LCC P301 .H275 2025 (print) | LCC P301 (ebook) |
DDC 418.001–dc23/eng/20240919
LC record available at https://lccn.loc.gov/2024036258
LC ebook record available at https://lccn.loc.gov/2024036259

ISBN: HB: 979-8-7651-0080-6
        PB: 979-8-7651-0081-3
        ePDF: 979-8-7651-0083-7
        eBook: 979-8-7651-0082-0

Typeset by Integra Software Services Pvt. Ltd.
Printed and bound in the United States of America

To find out more about our authors and books visit www.bloomsbury.com
and sign up for our newsletters.

Contents

Introduction: Handedness and Underhandedness

I owe you the truth in painting and I will tell it to you.
—Paul Cézanne

I'm right-handed and only use my left hand upon necessity.
—Andres Serrano[1]

Religion relies heavily on symbols and my job as an artist is to pursue the manipulation of that symbolism and explore its possibilities.
—Andres Serrano[2]

A photograph. A portrait. A veiled figure against a bright burst of background. Yellow and orange behind red, white, and blue … A mise-en-scène.

In preparation for the camera snap, the elements have been treated with obvious dexterity.

A worn linen patchwork of familiar design has been arranged to suggest a human head beneath. Is it a living model? A bust? A mannequin? Does it matter?

Without peepholes, the eyes of the face—if face there is—are blinded. Shoulders can be made out.

---

[1] Personal email February 12, 2024.
[2] Quoted in William H. Honan, "Artist Who Outraged Congress Lives amid Christian Symbols." *The New York Times*, August 16, 1989, section C, 13.

Not casually draped over the head, the stitched patriotic head-covering has been carefully folded and pinned in such a way as to form an apex.

That *hood* with that shape "says" something to the onlookers—especially if they're from the United States. That hood stirs them. It disturbs them.

And so does the worn patchwork from which it's formed. It's a US flag, obviously. Maybe from the late nineteenth century. A vintage stars and stripes. Old Glory inevitably, implicitly evoking the stars and bars of the Confederacy.

The figure foregrounded, meanwhile, is not all that makes up the totality of this photographic composition. What about that background?! What does that flare of fulgent flames right behind the figure tell us? The incandescence invisible behind the blinded head is yellow as it emerges outward, cooling to orange, deeper and deeper, as it approaches the edges. What might be burning back there? Or are we to recall the halo of an orthodox icon …?

Of course, we know very well to what factual elements this image refers. Hoods in that shape have haunted this country from Reconstruction to Abu Ghraib and beyond. From the white hood of Klansmen peeping out at their victims and their burning crosses to the black hood blinding Abdou Hussain Saad Faleh as he stands on a box, electrified arms outstretched as if crucified. It is an all-too-familiar shape with a shamefully terroristic history.

Yet, in a way, all the artist has done is construct and immortalize an incongruously sumptuous still-life, substituting the nation's flag for the white and black cloths of infamy. *Infamous*, incidentally, is the name of the 2019 solo exhibition of works by Andres Serrano where this photograph was featured.

With "Flag Face," Serrano confronts us with a manipulation meant to make us think. To make us think, then think again. We may think that the heyday of the Klan marks the outer limits of white supremacy: myriad events occurring every day should have us thinking again. Or we may believe that war and torture reached its outer limits in Iraq: simple perusal of the newspapers should have us believing otherwise. With "Flag Face," we are no doubt faced with a shocking manipulation, but aesthetic awe should give way to enlightenment.[3]

---

[3]Several artists have manipulated images of the KKK in order to shock the society out of endemic racism. The mundane activities engaged by the clownish Klansmen that Philip Guston featured in oil paintings like *City Limits* (1969) bring home the banal promiscuity of racial hatred. Guston's cartoonish rendering of the cloth in pink, white, and gray and of the peepholes and stitching in black leaves no

Manipulation is "the action or an act of manipulating something; handling; dexterity" (*OED*). Present as a force impelling every expressive event, every gesture, manipulation is all about how one employs one's hands, how the hands are put to work. (Of course, in the cases of speech and written discourse, our hands are "merely" *thought* to be in action. Even metaphorically—and perhaps even more powerfully as such—they are at work.) The nature of handiwork may, in the best of cases, be honest and even-handed. In such cases the speaker or writer, like the artist, is delivering as best he can the truth in painting (or speech or writing). No matter the painter's handedness—left, right, ambidextrous—the spectator receives the artist's manipulated vision as unadulterated by ideology, by arbitrary definitions of normalcy or decency, untainted by prejudice.

Manipulation may, however, also be subject to any or all of these pretexts in the service of devious subterfuge. The dictionary continues: manipulation is "the action or an act of managing or directing a person, etc., esp. in a skillful manner; the exercise of subtle, underhand, or devious influence or control over a person, organization, etc.; interference, tampering." When this occurs, the gesture is, as the definition suggests, underhanded. When malice aforethought or mere thoughtless handiwork substitutes for clear-headed brain-to-hand or brain-to-mouth activity, corrupting the noble and necessary intertwining of theory and practice, hell on earth is at hand. The effect of underhandedness on the body social is disastrous, murderous.

The kind of *salutary* manipulation, then, that I see at work in Andres Serrano's "Flag Face" serves me as forward-looking example against the backdrop of the underhanded rhetorical manipulations that this book has been conceived to denounce. Salutary manipulations seem to me to be far less uncommon in the visual arts than they are in the realms of language—speech, discourse, rhetoric, writing. Whether one thinks of Goya or Banksy, the artist's handicraft opens the spectator's mind to conditions and situations to which he might have heretofore been blinded. While works like "Saturn Devouring

---

doubt that the hoods are worn by cigar-smoking knights of white supremacy. Trenton Doyle Hancock, "SKUM: Just Beneath the Skin" (2018), which is so very explicitly inspired by Guston. Another Black artist, Gary Simmons, too uses Klan imagery—very blatantly—in his 1992 installation, "Duck, Duck, Noose."

His Son" (1820–3) or "The Banality of the Banality of Evil" (2013) denounce terror in manners that are almost completely opposed, they both prepare the spectator to do something to prevent programs like the Inquisition or the Final Solution from ever happening again. In striving to tell truths, manipulation in art affirms life—even when that manipulation reads as chilling cautionary tale.

Rhetoric, on the other hand, is particularly open to and rife with forms of underhanded manipulation. The five chapters of this book examine three rather vast realms of speech interspersed by two phenomena in which ignorance and susceptibility to voluntary servitude participate in, by falling prey to, the rhetoric of manipulation. Examinations of language inflected by war, language and behavior feeding on the false concept of race, and the jargon of a corporatized university are punctuated here by studies of the use and abuse of scare quotes and the frivolous "wars" over "wokeism" and "cancel culture."

As a species endowed with language, we, of course, manipulate linguistic elements all the time. We can't help but do so. If we have a nature, this is it. No better or more concise expression of this fact can be found than Friedrich Nietzsche's unforgettable essay "On Truth and Lying in the Extramoral Sense." Yet the will to play with the arbitrariness of the sign is what produces the power of meaning in the economy that joins adressors to adressees. Lyotard and Foucault, under whom I had the privilege of studying, at least taught me that. Having cut my methodological teeth on praxis-oriented critical theory, knowledge production, and discourse analysis, this study has benefited substantially by ideas gleaned from a wide range of critical linguists.[4]

Two heroes, in particular, play not only key roles throughout this book: they supervise, as it were, every page. One was an actual person; the other an inactual, aspirational model for thinking subjects to come. The first was named Victor Klemperer; to the second, I am lending the moniker of Critical Watch.

From scholar of romance languages, Victor Klemperer became a philologist. Life-historical circumstances would subsequently turn him into

---

[4]The reader may consult the Bibliography for titles by Jay Black, Jonathan Charteris-Black, James Dawes, Karin Dovring, Norman Faircough, Harry G. Frankfurt, Roger Fowler, Erin Steuter, Steve Thorne, Teun A. van Dijk, and Deborah Wills.

a uniquely critical linguist. Born to Jewish parents in Poland, having studied in Munich, Geneva, Paris, and Berlin, by the time Hitler took power in January 1933, Klemperer held a professorship in romance languages at the Technical University of Dresden. Though he would soon thereafter lose his job, Klemperer remained—against nearly all odds—in Dresden over the next twelve-and-a-half years, only managing with harrowing difficulty to live to tell about any of this because he was married to a so-called Aryan woman.

Victor Klemperer maintained a meticulous diary about the Nazi manipulation and impoverishment of the German language—a diary that he distilled into a magisterial 1947 work bearing the title *Lingua Tertii Imperium* or *LTI*. In that now-famous work, Klemperer strategically used Latin to mark *his* distance from "the language of the Third Reich," the toxically cynical form that German took on "thanks to" the Nazis. Less well-known than *LTI*—because profuse and far less frequently honored by thorough reading—are those diaries that Klemperer managed doggedly to maintain from one end to the other of the Third Reich. Klemperer sourced and sleuthed every form of expression that came to his attention: speeches transmitted by radio, newspapers, advertising, bulletins, signs and remarks spoken and whispered. "I am not writing a history of the times here," he wrote to himself three weeks after Hitler was appointed chancellor (I:4; I:6).[5] What he *did* compile was the most thorough and meticulous chronicle of twisted language used as a tool to ensure the voluntary servitude of a nation's entire population. Klemperer was thus a rare witness—using both ears and eyes—of the semantic perversion carried out by a specific totalitarian regime.

Although any of the five avenues studied in this book along which rhetoric is manipulated can appear anywhere in the world, the paradigmatic case under scrutiny is the United States of America. The Germany that Victor Klemperer knew in the prime of his life and career serves as a binding backdrop. The France that I have known serves as occasional counterpoint. Already in his *Tagesbücher*—that priceless compilation of raw material that would become

---

[5]*"Ich schreibe hier nicht Zeitgeschichte."*

LTI and that he feared at the outset was "terribly frivolous"[6]—Klemperer had pinpointed and dissected every aspect of semantic perversion that I see in insidious operation today. And while I'm not going to claim that we live under some twenty-first-century avatar of the Third Reich, I *will* argue that if we don't open our eyes to the surreptitious power of language to form our thoughts, opinions, and outlook, if we let our critical faculties slip into slumber, those monsters can and will reappear.

This is where my other ever-vigilant figure comes into play. Inspired by the "*veilleur critique*" to whom Jean-François Lyotard refers, primarily in the preface to *The Differend*, I lend the name of Critical Watch to my other hero.[7] The Critical Watch does not merely accompany us but is a subject position to which we must—in my view—*aspire.* Confronted with the denial of truth in the form of negationism, in criminal times when witnesses are eliminated or silenced, Lyotard endeavors to envision an attitude that can "save the honor of thinking" (10; xii). The "*veilleur critique*" or Critical Watch is that position. From a position of deep pessimism, Lyotard's wager is that freeing criteria for judgment from pre-defined rules may enable the Critical Watch to attend to the admissibility of testimony beyond reality as defined by and admissible according to the law. In broader and far more direct terms, the Critical Watch would be tantamount to how Foucault saw Nietzsche responding to Kant's famous fourth question, "What is man?" Foucault thought that answer would be the *Übermensch*—an evolutionary improvement on the "human" that we have thus far become. This "beyond man," another of whose names is the "philosopher of the future" (cf. *Beyond Good and Evil*[8]), will have honed

---

[6]"Actually it's terribly frivolous to write all this in my diary [*Eigentlich ist es furchtbar leichtsinnig, dies alles in mein Tagebuch zu schreiben*]" (I:7; I:11). Regarding the references to Klemperer's *Diaries*, the convention I adopt is to give the page(s) in the English translation first, then the page(s) in the original. The Roman numeral preceding the page numbers indicates the volume. See the Bibliography for the editions used.

[7]*Veilleur* is maddeningly difficult to translate into English. Lookout, ward, observer, I would have gone for spotter, sentry, or sentinel if not for my old hypersensitization to the language of war that permeates our usage of English.

[8]Here is just one of many quotes indicating the type of critical work that the philosopher of the future must bravely engage in: "If you'll forgive me, an old philologist who can't give up the wickedness of pointing out examples of bad interpretative practice, the 'lawfulness of nature' that you physicists speak about so proudly, as if [...] this only exists by grace of your interpretations, your bad 'philology' [...] is not a factual matter, not a 'text', but rather no more than a naïve humanitarian concoction" (22).

the ability to see through the underhandedness that pervades language, polluting our lives, ultimately enabling murder and mayhem.

Perversion, then, which for over a century[9] we obstinately and pruriently thought only named variations of and inflections to sex and sexuality, can today be seen as saturating *how we name things*. Perversion, as it operates under the sway of malicious manipulation, is infinitely more insidious and detrimental to the healthy functioning of society writ large. Just as the prolific lexicon surrounding sex and sexuality that was authorized by modern societies would heighten rather than suppress "perversion," so the semantics of war and today's corporate management underscores the fundamental indecency of these two "natural" practices. These very ironies illustrate perversion at work. From "Ground Zero," "terrorist," and "collateral damage" in the realm of perpetual war to "strategic planning," "line workers," and, of course, "excellence" in the lexicon of the neoliberal corporate management of academia, semantic perversion is pervasive and has bored into the core of consciousness, anesthetizing and emasculating thought.

As Foucault repeatedly insisted, it is difficult—nay, impossible[10]—to objectively analyze situations within which one lives, works, or thinks. And even when one's existence spans a time sufficient to position situations in the past, thus supposedly creating perspective, forgetting and the impulse to narrativize creep in and skew one's view, creating lacunae. Work in academia today redoubles this distortion and blindness.

Something that the reader will notice right away impels me to admit at the outset that swaths of this book were written in anger and frustration. I was a university professor from 1988 to 2022 and it was in the last year of my teaching career that I began writing it. That fifty-five years since my political and intellectual awakening, so little has improved, and so much injustice, inequality, hypocrisy, double standard, selfishness, and stupidity persist: these are the sources of that anger and frustration. Ironically, I was fortunate to have

---

[9]Starting with Richard Freiherr von Krafft-Ebbing's *Psychopathia Sexualis* (1886).

[10]In one of his rare television interviews just after the release of *Les Mots et les Choses*, he quipped, smiling wryly: "Of course, we could dream of some Martian who could grasp our own culture in its entirety. But this is not possible since, as far as I know, Martians don't exist." Foucault interviewed by Pierre Dumayet for *Lectures pour tous* on June 15, 1966.

been able to work in a profession ostensibly meant to ameliorate all this. But the institution overseeing the sectors of education that form critically thinking citizens ultimately impedes such healthy growth at every step. And I fear that this failing is only gaining ground. To contribute to reversing this trend is what I mean this book to do.

While my fervent hope is that these words might touch everyone, I have no illusions that any audience that *The Rhetoric of Manipulation* might garner will be constituted mainly of a high number of individuals who have benefited since birth (and by the *vagaries* of birth) by a critical education and by protection from social and economic adversity, structural racism, sexism, etc., and who have therefore been able to rise to privileged positions in society. I would simply further hope that this book will inspire them, "us," to pass on the critical impulse in a spirit of mutual aid for the benefit of all.

Along the way, I have the following people to thank: Lori Repetti, Mark Aronoff, Elizabeth Hermitt, Yanling Li, Jean-Michel Rabaté, Raiford Guins, Nikos Panou, Dennis J. Schmidt, Anne Brancky, Marie-Hélène Boblet, Robert Bloomer, Daniel Levy, Sverre Raffnsøe, and, of course, as always, Hélène Volat.

1

Fighting Words

Every word immediately becomes a concept, in as much as it is not intended to serve as a reminder of the unique and wholly individualized original experience to which it owes its birth, but must at the same time fit innumerable, more or less similar cases—which means, strictly speaking, never equal—in other words, a lot of unequal cases. Every concept originates through our equating what is unequal.

—Friedrich Nietzsche, "On Truth and Lies in the Extra-Moral Sense"

[…] if power is indeed the implementation and deployment of a relationship of force, […] shouldn't we be analyzing it first and foremost in terms of conflict, confrontation, and war?

—Michel Foucault, "Lecture, Collège de France, January 7, 1976"[1]

Naturalized, taken for granted, left uncritiqued, war metaphors drive, justify, interiorize, and generalize bellicose behavior in the practitioners of language that self-proclaimed humans are. The seeds of violent culture are planted in the humus of speech. As Victor Klemperer put it in his study of the language of the Third Reich, "Words can be like tiny doses of arsenic: they are swallowed unnoticed, appear to have no effect, and then after a little time the toxic reaction sets in after all" (2013, 14). While euphemism-driven propaganda— often creepily puritanical in tenor—anesthetizes resistance, so does the

---

[1] I have modified the translation found in *Power/Knowledge*, which is "[…] if power is properly speaking the way in which relations of forces are deployed and given concrete expression, […] should we not analyse it primarily in terms of *struggle, conflict,* and *war*?" (1980, 15, 90).

"slumber of reason" in individual citizens. And while the first may never be curtailed so long as people are governed and administered, critical vigilance applied to one's own practice of language is within every individual's grasp. A first task toward activating that vigilance would be to expose the sinister underbelly of fighting words—the semantic array that keeps the United States in a permanent state of armed conflict.

"ground zero"

Although the end of the Second World War still appeared elusive, US bombers flying over Hiroshima in 1945 didn't particularly worry the city's denizens. Air-raid sirens had sounded many times before. The warplanes would usually drone by on their way further east to pulverize Tokyo. This routine scenario appeared to be unfolding yet again on August 6, at 07:09. Twenty minutes later the alert was lifted. People went back to their morning activities. However, forty-five minutes later still, right in the center of the metropolis sprawling across the Ito delta surrounded by mountains, a colossal explosion occurred, instantaneously annihilating 75,000 individuals. A further 200,000 would perish in the following hours, days, and months. Of those who were out in the street in that early morning and less than 500 meters from the epicenter, all that was left were a few silhouette negatives cast on walls by the intense heat sustained by the vanished bodies.

"Little Boy" was meant to detonate 580 meters above ground. And it did. In the specific case of an atomic bomb—the ultimate avatar of what some today call "weapons of mass destruction"—the hypocenter is the point on the ground precisely above which discharge needs to occur for maximum effect. The bomb's developers—members of the Manhattan Project—dubbed this point "ground zero."

Commercial airplanes flying over Manhattan never particularly worried New Yorkers, except when they sometimes appeared from the ground to come awfully close to the skyscrapers. There had naturally been no warning before 08:46 on that fine morning in September, when a passenger jetliner struck the North Tower of the World Trade Center. It took seventeen more minutes before people in the street and millions of people who had by then glued themselves to the television realized, when a second one hit the South Tower, that this was no accident. Within another hour, one after the other, the two towers collapsed. At first, 6,000 were feared dead. (The subsequent precise count would make it 2,595.) By the next day, a spontaneous collective voice dubbed the footprint of the erstwhile World Trade Center "ground zero."

No one may negate the deep humanity driving the shock of people who witness thousands of other people vanish. And no one can deny the extreme rarity of such an event on US soil. No one should be unaware either of the compulsiveness that results from the endlessly repeated televised images of the strikes on the twin skyscrapers and their spectacular collapse. But a confusion arises in those minds between what is deemed to have never been *seen* and that which is deemed to have never before *occurred*. As a result, to consider the 9/11 attack as unique would be to negate mass murder, let us say, elsewhere and at other moments. The more a regime strives to reign uncontested, the more it requires belief in the unprecedented nature of heroic and horrific events—even if the price is unremitting terror applied to those whose "belief" is required. Hence, also, selective comparisons, such as the equation of September 2001 in Manhattan and December 1941 at Pearl Harbor all the while ignoring or feigning to ignore that it bears any comparison with what happened in August 1945 in Hiroshima and Nagasaki.

Two features of the semantic perversion at work in the language of war drive this homonymy: mass denial and projection. As psychoanalysis teaches us, the first of these psychic processes may be partially unconscious, while the second tends to be willful, albeit unavowed.

The consecration of "Ground Zero" in southern Manhattan is a singular and paradigmatic example of a self-inflicted and twisted assault on semantics: if general consensus recognizes the term "ground zero" as the place where attacks on US soil occurred on September 11, 2001, virtually no one recognizes in this placename the epicenter for the US-made bomb that devastated Hiroshima of August 6, 1945.[2] In agreeing to use "ground zero" to indicate the location

---

[2] After visiting the Hiroshima Peace Memorial Museum and noticing that "epicenter" is the nomenclature used for the displays, I attempted repeatedly in email correspondence with Ms. Rie of the museum administration to determine whether "ground zero" had ever at some point in the museum's history

where the Twin Towers collapsed, people recognize that places so named are those where heinous crimes were committed. However, to not recognize the moral equivalence between two places based on their synonymity is either quite simply perverse or denial produced by collective amnesia.

In the more than twenty years since the 9/11 attacks, "Ground Zero" has become not only the official term memorializing martyrdom in Manhattan but the creepily manipulated misnomer has also caught on as catchphrase for large-scale destruction anywhere. Anywhere in the Empire of Virtue, that is. At the mundane level of everyday speech "ground zero" routinely points to the "center" of anything perceived as bad for "us": "Denver is ground zero for America's migrant crisis"[3] and so on. Ever awkward in his attempts to deflect blame for his failures, George W. Bush, for example, would compare the devastation left in the wake of Hurricane Katrina to the mayhem that "ground zero" encapsulates.[4] Such and such US state might be dubbed "ground zero of the economic crisis" or Greenland might be reported as "ground zero of global warming." Such promiscuous overuse of the term only further buries in oblivion its origin in a singularly spectacular act of state terror carried out by the United States.

Less than two years after atomic atrocity was wrought on Japanese citizens, the Truman Doctrine would officially open the two-generation long era of tensions that pit the United States and the USSR in a faceoff, ready to engage in a third twentieth-century world war. Less than ten years after the dissolution of the Soviet Union, the attacks in Manhattan rekindled the lust for war. It matters little that a phrase coined for the epicenter of an atomic *explosion* came to designate the location of *implosions* such as that which occurred in Manhattan's financial district. This simply demonstrates, once again, the wonderful elasticity and oft-horrific manipulability of language. What *does* matter is that the phrase made its way, over the course of the Cold War, from

---

been used. I never got a straight answer. It crossed my mind that US authorities—perhaps during the period of Occupation—prohibited them from doing so.

[3]Myah Ward, Lauren Egan, and Ben Johansen, "Ground Zero for America's Migrant Crisis." *Politico*, January 5, 2024. https://www.politico.com/newsletters/west-wing-playbook/2024/01/05/ground-zero-for-americas-migrant-crisis-00134117 (accessed January 16, 2024). El Paso and Phoenix have also been dubbed "ground zeroes" in this particular war.

[4]Simon Schama, "Sorry Mr President, Katrina Is Not 9/11." *The Guardian*, September 11, 2005.

the lexicon of military engineering to the vocabulary of victimhood and of vengeance to be taken against a diffuse and omnipresent enemy: the Terrorist.

In an earlier era of global tension, after having survived—in succession—dismissal from his professorship, racist humiliation, imprisonment, ghettoization, and imminent threat of extermination, Victor Klemperer's beloved Dresden was finally bombed a couple of short months before the fall of Berlin clinched the fall of the Third Reich. In that month of February 1945, the Allies had finally done to Dresden what the Luftwaffe had already done to Coventry during the Battle of Britain and Operation Mondscheinsonate in November 1940. Shamelessly projecting their own atrocities on civilians, Nazi propaganda had coined a handy term for bombings on "Aryan" soil. With eyes and ears whose critical acumen far surpasses even that displayed by W. G. Sebald in *The Natural History of Destruction*, the Dresden linguist noted in *LTI* that "the verb *coventrieren* lies buried under the rubble of German cities" (131).

Victor Klemperer had distilled *Lingua Tertii Imperii*, which appeared in 1947, from the raw material he had accumulated to form the mass of diaries he kept with dogged determination from 1933 until 1945—from one end to the other, that is, of the Nazi dictatorship. Encyclopedic and obsessive, Klemperer's *Tagebücher* open our eyes to myriad examples of linguistic manipulation that instituted governmental power is capable of carrying out. Not a week went by over that twelve-year period where Klemperer didn't reflect on how semantic perversion brings an uncritical population completely under biopower's sway. Systematic "militarization of language" (I:293; I:378) was perhaps the most insistent and insidious practice deployed from the top of the Third Reich.[5] It is a practice with a long and unfortunate history in the United States as well—one whose necessary critique has thus far failed to materialize.

Before returning to the historical watershed of 9/11 to further observe how the fighting words used in this country had evolved just as the twenty-first century got under way, we need to explore how the militarized language that circulates in the US political establishment, coupled with terminology fostered

---

[5]By January 1939, Klemperer was seeing war words everywhere. He muses in his diary, "Do the words 'cold weather front' in the weather report reflect the militarization of language (*Wortmilitarisierung*) in the Third Reich? I almost believe it." Extant already in the context of armed conflict in the fourteenth century, "front" became a meteorological metaphor in English in the early twentieth.

by the Pentagon, infiltrates the minds of citizens, inflecting their thought by infecting their language.

war within, war without

War occupies a place of privilege as supplier of metaphors for the English language as this language is routinely used in the United States. A few quick examples may corroborate this claim if not convince of its veracity. Successive federal administrations have waged "war on drugs," and while the Johnson era initiated a War on Poverty, Ford's War on Inflation was singularly unimpressive. If credence be granted news or social media, the United States is forever on the verge of "race war." Since 9/11 we have been engaged in a diffuse, promiscuous, open-ended "war on terrorism." Meanwhile, borrowing from White House military jargon, every corporate firm true to its gigantism has its "war room." Richard Nixon declared War on Cancer. Bill O'Reilly deplored the so-called left's so-called War on Christmas. Wars and weapons are real in every realm of so-called life in the United States.

While funding research toward cures for disease and taking all possible measures to ensure that all citizens may live with adequate shelter and sustenance are laudable aims and endeavors, the insistence that warfare wording is the best path to welfare is questionable, to say the least.[6] To the objection that "struggle" and "action" are less forceful, less impactful than "war," one could respond that in a society where violence—gun-toting if possible—is the norm, "war" is not only a default choice resulting from critical lethargy but that this choice listlessly confirms the norm. In the summer of 1934, as "the language of the 3rd Reich [...] increasingly preoccupied" him and he began to read *Mein Kampf* to explore the origins of the language of war that would come to dominate the German language under the Nazis, Victor Klemperer's wife Eva drew his attention to the "battle for work" (I:77; I:106–7) experienced by the population. Metaphorical choices of such extreme banality were symptoms of a society primed for battles of another

---

[6]"Blanket statements about whether or not a war frame is useful are misguided or overly constraining" (Flusberg, 1).

nature: extermination of "undesirable" humans, genocide. Who, on the other hand, could have taken Woodie Guthrie's "this machine kills fascists" painted on his guitar for anything other than a powerful metaphor extolling the power of *words* (i.e., lyrics) over *swords*?

Official US military terminology is itself replete with and thrives on indirect language. While this may come as no surprise, given the eerie parallels, it should give pause, at the very least. Rather than blithely pass over the oft-times-strained cleverness of rhetorical manipulation, we might ask ourselves what effect pervasive and insidious war terminology may have on the way people acquit themselves of their role as citizens. Forged to deceive the public that pays for it, this governing language lulls the populace into complacency, ensuring its compliance in the politics of perpetual war. The supposedly harmless applications of fighting words should raise hair and hackles when juxtaposed with their literal counterparts.

Continuing to confine ourselves to the case of the United States, the list of names for military operations—both covert and overt—is long. Tedious even. Consider the following, selected for their more or less clever and more or less obvious references to aggressive figures and behaviors: Unleashed back in the late 1980s when the United States were allied against Iran with Saddam's Iraq, Operations Nimble Archer and Praying Mantis—deemed by the ever-ineffectual International Court of Justice as unjustified "as measures necessary to protect essential security interests"—were meant mainly to keep Kuwaiti oil flowing.

As should be amply well-known by now, if not universally accepted, it is an understatement to observe that the United States is far from immune to committing acts of terrorism, as defined by watchdog organizations. A few examples will suffice to refresh memories. Back in 1953, there was Operation Ajax, which saw the CIA conspire with British secret services to depose democratically elected Mohammed Mossadegh and replace him with the dictatorship of Shah Mohammed Reza Pahlavi. In the following year, suspecting Marxist tendencies in Jacobo Arbeuz Guzmán, the duly elected president of Guatemala, Operation PBSUCCESS, led by the CIA alone, deposed him. All the many actions—assassination plots, sabotage, psychological warfare to name a few—deployed against Cuba under Fidel Castro during Operation Mongoose are now generally recognized under the heading of international terrorism. Dozens and dozens of annihilation programs during the US-Vietnam War bore "inventive" names—including Rolling Thunder, Flaming Dart, and Barrel Roll—meant to rally the troops and impress the public. With assassinations and "disappearances" of thousands of politicians, activists, and "ordinary citizens," under the vigilant eye of National Security Advisor and eventual Nobel Prize winner Henry Kissinger, Operation Condor wreaked its havoc in more than a half-dozen South American countries during the 1970s, all ultimately resulting in right-wing dictatorships. There was Operation Urgent Fury, the cowardly invasion of Grenada in 1983, or that of Panama in 1989, dubbed Operation Just Cause. The list goes on. But who can forget that other 11 September—the one in 1973 in Chile—when yet another government just as democratically elected as those of Iran in 1953 and Guatemala in 1943— that led by Salvador Allende—was summarily eradicated to make way for the US-backed sanguinary dictatorship of Augusto Pinochet. Then, when Saddam was no longer our friend, over the course of the global War on Terror (itself baptized Operation Enduring Freedom) Desert Storm (initially called Desert Shield) became, in a burst of wishful thinking, Iraqi Freedom. Given the state of Iraq today, nearly a generation after Saddam's hanging, that lame and empty excuse for unwarranted war has a particularly cynical ring to it. Lest we think that all these names are mere window dressing; they are meant to obviate criticism of what happens under their banner, that is, the propagation, implantation, and nurturing of the lie that the operations are just, brave, legal, disinterested, justified, and promising of peace.

A special place needs to be reserved for the ways that US military nominalism "commemorates" the geno-/ethnocide of tens of millions of this land's native peoples. As Noam Chomsky has written, "Weapons of destruction are casually given names [such as] Apache, Blackhawk, Comanche helicopters; Tomahawk missiles; and so on."[7] To which, as suggested mental experiment,

---

[7]We can confidently add the UH-60 Black Hawk utility helicopter, the UH-72 Lakota utility helicopter, CH-47 Chinook heavy-lift transport helicopter, the H-34 Choctaw transport helicopter, the OH-58 Kiowa observation helicopter, the OH-6 Cayuse observation helicopter, TH-67 Creek trainer helicopter, C-12 Huron transport aircraft, the H-21 Shawnee transport helicopter, and the RU-21 Ute electronic intelligence aircraft.

he poses the wry question, "How would we react if the Luftwaffe named its lethal weapons 'Jew' and 'Gypsy'?" (2005, 11). The realm of sports, finally, and to which I will return shortly, is the paramilitary correlate of this degrading usurpation of the names of peoples eradicated to make the United States what it is today. While "Squaw" Valley has been renamed Olympic Valley, "Braves," "Indians," "Chiefs," and "Blackhawks" that have nothing to do with indigenous Americans except in mocking memory of genocidal colonial conquest still thrill fans of baseball, football, and hockey.

euphemism, antithesis, understatement

Among the "multitude of cover-up words" used by totalitarianisms—both soft and hard—are, in their seemingly endless flow, euphemisms (Klemperer 2013, 235). Not only do "terms such as these distance us further from the full horror they describe" (Thorne, 93), in distracting the target audience from factual evidence, they dull any critical faculty they might retain for maintaining some minimal grasp of truth. Klemperer registered "shot while trying to escape" as the cookie-cutter explanation "accounting" for the deaths of countless Jews and other "undesirable elements" as the Final Solution was about to get fully under way (II:151; II:204). An intensely unrelenting will to avenge willy-nilly the 9/11 attacks rejuvenated similarly casual murderous rhetoric and redoubled efforts to substitute euphemistic weasel words for plain language. Toppling foreign governments—first that of former ally Saddam Hussein, then that of the Taliban whom the United States had covertly supported for decades against the USSR—now became known as "regime change" to be achieved by "decapitating the regime" as if war were a mere game of chess. Far from a euphemism, the second of these phrases is a product of what Klemperer termed the "frenzied arrogance of the victor [*die rasende Überheblichkeit des Siegers*]" (I:344; I:440).

After straining to assemble a "coalition of the willing," the United States unleashed a veritable Blitzkrieg on Iraq with an eye to establishing "rapid dominance." Deployed along the way were, "surgical strikes" with weapons including white phosphorous munitions, cluster bombs, and "daisy cutters" that were vastly "improved" over those used in Vietnam to burn terrorist flesh to the bones and flatten forests into helicopter landing zones, freshly nicknamed—in sophomoric rhetorical tit-for-tat with Saddam—the "mother of all bombs."[8] Surgical precision by means of "smart bombs" notwithstanding and although thousands of "enemy combatants" were "neutralized," so were tens of thousands of civilians. Mere "collateral damage," callously acknowledged the powers that be. Unacknowledged, thus, is the indiscriminate murder of civilians—or "demographic targeting"—in which frenzied revenge (*rasende Rache*) is willing to engage.[9] Meanwhile, under the blanket label of "terror suspect," thousands of individuals were tortured—subjected, that is, to "enhanced interrogation techniques." Who can tell whether simple preservation of plain language in lieu of such euphemisms might have fostered a modicum of skepticism or even criticism from the US populace? Suffice it to say that weasel language sugarcoats the bitter pill of state terror.

In addition to allowing a warring party to deflect attention from horrifically death-dealing practices it perpetrates, mendaciously manipulative language can also be used to understate failings or falling apart. By late summer 1944, Klemperer was noticing that "*crisis* is the current euphemism [*Beschönigungswort*] for 'defeat'" (II:340; II:450) and that "since Stalingrad the line in the East has been *elastic*" (II:353; II:467). If "war corrupts language" (Healy, 647), language prepares, justifies, and maintains war. Language renders war palatable to the population that will provide its fodder. Just as Truman, since war was never declared as stipulated by the US Constitution (Article I, Section 8, Clause 11), felt compelled to label the Korean War a "police action,"

---

[8] In 1990, Iraq's former Revolutionary Command Council, then Saddam Hussein himself, called their conflict with the United States over Kuwait "the mother of all battles." The BLU-82 Vietnam-era bomb was superseded in the early twenty-first century by the GBU-43/B MOAB, where MOAB stands for "mother of all bombs." One of the most powerful non-nuclear weapons in the vast and varied US arsenal, it is a true "weapon of mass destruction."

[9] Since 1984, US Department of State statements on human rights utilize the tortuous circumlocution "unlawful or arbitrary deprivation of life" instead of the universally understood term killing. "Rights Survey Stops Using Word 'Killing.'" *New York Times*, February 11, 1984. And, as a current example, see "2019 Country Reports on Human Rights: Georgia." https://www.state.gov/reports/2019-country-reports-on-human-rights-practices/georgia/ (accessed April 7, 2023). Orwell would have been impressed.

so Putin insists (on penalty of imprisonment) on "special military operation" to designate Russia's invasion of Ukraine.

Warmongering fosters expertise in the manipulative semantics of antithesis. It could even be said that antithetical signifying is a fundamental principle of propaganda. When the US Strategic Air Command (SAC) proffers "Peace is our profession" as its motto, who is really impressed or convinced that this is the case? Possible recruits? Sectors of the public who might withdraw support if they were to think otherwise? By such turns of phrase or discursive strategies, the Pentagon and successive presidential administrations strain to lend an enlightened and humane hue to the deadly activities that are their cynical raison d'être. Those of us who came of age during the Vietnam War remember asking ourselves just how many "hearts and minds" (a phrase resonating weirdly with "thoughts and prayers") were won in *that* "pacification" program. Many of us suspected rightly that harassment, coercion, and Agent Orange—delivered *not* by Viet Cong but by imperialist usurpers—were singularly dubious pacifiers. Vietnamese minds could be no more duped than anyone told that the lumbering B-36 bomber manufactured by Conair to carry first-generation atomic bombs was actually a "Peacemaker."

"only a pawn in their game": war as sport, sport as war

As early as October 1933, still hanging on with his fingernails to his professorship at the Technical University of Dresden, Klemperer took note of a "sudden decree to make the whole of Tuesday afternoon and half of Thursday afternoon free for military sports." Not just sport but sport specifically adapted to the total militarization of society. Concomitant to this prioritization of martial athletics (*Wehrsportübungen*) was the catastrophic devaluation of thought: "A series of lectures was simply canceled. Scholarship is no longer essential" (I:37; I:50). Much later, shortly following Germany's debacle at Stalingrad, Klemperer registers how the "language of boxing is indispensable to Goebbels," transcribing the following quote from one of the Minister of Propaganda's weekly editorials in *Das Reich*: "In the deciding round one must still dispose of enough strength that one can easily take an opponent's every blow and reply with a harder blow" (II:210; II:279). By the summer of 1944, with Germany's situation increasingly desperate, wondering how much longer the clarion of propaganda could continue to be sounded, Klemperer's scrutiny of *Das Reich* reveals that "even in the pathos of despair, [Goebbels] cannot desist from the language of sport" (II:338; II:447–48). Finally, at the beginning of March 1945, with the fall of Berlin only weeks away, Klemperer tries his hand at a bit of indirect discourse, demonstrating for himself just how insidiously manipulative the intertwining of war rhetoric and the language of sport can be:

> The language of sport even now: We are like the marathon runner. He has put more than 20 miles behind him, he has another six miles to go. He is covered in sweat, he has severe stitches, the sun is blazing, his strength is giving out, again and again he is tempted to give up. Only the greatest willpower keeps him going, drives him on, perhaps he will collapse unconscious at the winning post, but he must reach it! … How often has a dying man overcome death through his sheer will to live!
>
> (II:425; II:561)

Klemperer formulates this imitation in full cognizance of its content and import. He can now hold it up as a pathetic pastiche of countless cases of *direct* discourse produced on and by a brainwashed and anesthetized population.

Practicing sport as training for war is as old as "civilization." Passing war off as sport has always made it palatable to a population. Elements of language, as they are prevalently put to practice, reveal the intersection of the two domains. Mock military operations are known by the expression "war games." A joint training exercise of the United States Forces Korea and the Military of South Korea held between 1974 and 1993 was named Operation *Team Spirit*. In the same spirit of attenuation, actual military operations may harken to more ludic forms of activity. Evoking the universally recognized avuncular allegory, US support for the 1964 coup that overthrew João Goulart after he rebuffed Kennedy's request that Brazil consider joining an invasion of Cuba was dubbed Operation Brother Sam.

But sport, we are assured, is just for play, recreation, physical exercise. (Admittedly, as well, considerable sums of money are at stake in sporting events!) Football and rugby matches are ostensibly only played for entertainment. (Admittedly too, intercity, interregional, and international competition with suspiciously bellicose undertones might also enter into the equation ...) What about board games? Well, there's chess, where the goal is to checkmate—that is, kill or "neutralize"—the king. And there's go, where the goal is to surround (i.e., occupy and contain) more territory than the opponent. It would seem that, here too, war is not far away—metaphorically speaking. Less subtly to the point, there are the games of strategy that "merely" simulate battle, conquest, mass murder, and the like. We are assured by their manufacturers that there is no cause-effect dynamic between *Sniper!*® and snipers or between *Spacewar!*® and the prospect of its real-world namesake or, again, between *Total War*® and total war. And any notion that the far-reaching popularity of dozens of video games with names like *Call of Duty*® or *Metal Gear Solid: Guns of the Patriots*® are stoking the minds of compliant battalions can be dismissed by their pushers and proponents as pacifist paranoia.

The dominance of perfidious vocabulary, deceptive metaphors, and rhetoric cultivates in the minds of a population with underdeveloped or non-existent critical skills the conviction that war is paradigmatic, omnipresent, inevitable, and the sole solution to whatever problems arise in any situation. The framing of civil unrest as "race war" whenever repressed frustrations issuing from the long legacy of racism resurface is a chilling example that will be examined in a subsequent chapter. In short, the pervasiveness of combat metaphors and militarized language not only reflects the bellicose mentality of a people: it inculcates and maintains that attitude as vicious cycle until it becomes atavistic.

"the curse of the superlative"

Inflationary language operates opposite to the way euphemism does on the discursive registers of truth and fact. Exaggeration, as opposed to evasive understatement, is meant to impress—even overwhelm. Yet one need only to think back to that moment in 2003 when, in front of the full UN Security Council, to make the case for invading Iraq, Colin Powell held up a tiny vial supposedly containing anthrax for us to be reminded how gross and ridiculous inflammatory exaggeration can appear. Notwithstanding that low point in political pandering to warmongers, the United States soon unleashed its "shock and awe" campaign. This pair of words—meant to convey the same idea as "lightning war" (*Blitzkrieg*) a half century earlier and which Klemperer duly added to his glossary of "frenzied triumphal language [*bei rasender Triumphsprache*]" (I:343; I:438)—is fascinating in terms of the history of philosophy. "Awe," "shock," "horror," "momentary inhibition of the vital powers" (128–9) all being key terms or expressions found in Kant's Third Critique, one cannot help wondering if the brains who dredged up "shock and awe" for the Baghdad Blitzkrieg were somehow channeling eighteenth-century aesthetic discussions of the sublime. "Terror" too, to which I'll return in a moment, is at the heart of these lexicons.

It is no secret that largely made-in-USA eugenics inspired and stoked the Nazi racial supremacism that led in a direct line to the Final Solution. Perceiving this particular transatlantic connection at work, Klemperer scoured what he called "the curse of the superlative [*der Fluch des Superlativs*]" (I:418; I:533) as manipulative rhetoric resulting from German mimicry of exaggerated expressive habits long prevalent before in the Land of Liberty. Throughout 1940 and 1941, with the Reich's war machine thus-far triumphant, the London Blitz would be reported as "the greatest bombardment in the history of the world" or "St. Bartholomew's Eve" (I:359; I:458–59) … examples, he wrote, of "depreciation of the superlative [*Abnutzung des Superlativs*]." Under that heading, Klemperer thoroughly diagnosed Hitler's New Year Order of the Day, trumpeting "victories of unparalleled dimensions," and his prediction that "1941 will see the accomplishment of the greatest victory in our history" as simple "American superlative [*amerikanische Superlativ*]" (I:366; I:467). While Operation Barbarossa was beginning that summer in the Battle of Białystok–Minsk, the Dresden linguist was feverishly noting formulations from Goebbels such as "the greatest battle of encirclement and attrition in world history" (I:419; I:533) or those from military bulletins such as "Nine million are facing one another in a battle whose scale surpasses all historical imagination" and commenting that it all made him think of P. T. Barnum (I:421; I:536). Barbarossa was of course not Stalingrad, but its outcome foreshadowed tables turning against the "eternal"[10] Reich.

Closely related to what Klemperer called "the curse of the superlative" are the extravagant comparisons that war propaganda traffics. Bruce Reidel, senior fellow at the Brookings Institution, points out that in the months building up toward Operation Iraqi Freedom, more than two-thirds of Americans believed Saddam was "personally involved in the 9/11 attack [and an] even more staggering 82% believed [he] provided assistance to Osama bin Laden." Adding, tersely, "Both were utterly false."[11] This blindness caused by the rhetoric of manipulation made it simple for George W. Bush to revive the "Hitler of Baghdad" analogy his father had concocted in the run-up to, then throughout, the Gulf War of 1991.[12] No doubt largely to impress Daddy, "W"'s very own pet obsession with Saddam Hussein would lead to death and misery for hundreds of thousands of Iraqis.[13]

All these efforts at bombast may result in diametrically opposed predispositions in the target audience. State subjects have two alternatives: either they end up like the withered docile bodies in *Discipline and Punish*, compliant, complacent, easy to enlist as supporters and soldiers or, in rare cases, a few of them refuse to be subjugated and, instead, practice skepticism, sarcasm, critique, and resistance. These latter are the true citizens: ready to put life on the line in the name of justice. With their minds clear of manipulation and their will still intact, such individuals know very well that the activities at which the United States is actually the greatest are mass incarceration, gun ownership, murder rates, and war.

---

[10]"[…] superlativism, which is a special hallmark of the language of the Third Reich, is different from the American one. The people in the USA talk big in a childlike and fresh manner, the Nazis do it in a way that is half megalomania, half frantic autosuggestion. One of their favorite words is 'eternal'" (I:248).

[11]Bruce Reidel, "9/11 and Iraq: The Making of a Tragedy."

[12]On George H. Bush's use of the analogy, see "Saddam Hussein: The Hitler of Baghdad" chapter in Pratkanis, 87–93.

[13]See the statistics compiled by the ever-vigilant, ever-reliable Watson Institute for International and Public Affairs at Brown University. https://watson.brown.edu/costsofwar/costs/human/civilians/iraqi (accessed January 17, 2024).

"hey, Pot: meet Kettle"

Whether they seriously believed the term to describe the actual case or not is irrelevant: when Goebbels or Hitler declared their relentless conquest of Europe to be the "Jewish War [*jüdische Krieg*]" (II:277, 391; II:369, 520), they absolutely meant the pliable population of Germany to believe that this perpetual armed struggle that *they and only they* had started was war of "defense" against a half-million of their own fellow citizens tipped for extermination.[14] Of all the invented enemies deemed targets of "boundless abuse [*maßlose Beschimpfung*] and vilification" (II:465; II:613), Jews were always at the top of the list. Already on the eve of outright generalized war, by which time escape from Germany and other Reich territory had become impossible and suicides of Jews had consequently become rampant and routine, Hess was screaming that "Jews and freemasons want war against us" (I:307; I:395). Persistent in perverting truth to the end, a 1944 editorial in the *Dresdener Zeitung* proclaimed "Jews in Normandy" (II:335; II:444).

Not long ago, a senior counselor to a certain US president suggested that verifiable facts could be invalidated by—get this—"alternate truth." Once propaganda achieves acceptance of such outrageous reversal of fact, once semantics is twisted in such a way as to perversely implant a psychotic rapport with factuality in the minds of a nation's people, victims of aggression can be blamed for their fate, scapegoats can safely be "neutralized," "liquidated," "exterminated," as if they were not even goats but vermin, warehoused items, figures. As we've already seen, the term "Ground Zero" consecrates the locus of the greatest war crime in history. But does the term, we ask, designate an epicenter in New York City or in Hiroshima? Similarly, one small disingenuous step is required to get from the substitution of "special operation" for unprovoked invasion to brainwashing the Russian people into believing that it's "Ukraine's war on us." And if Palestinians are not wantonly obliterated by the tens of thousands, the Shoah would inevitably rear its ugly head once again.

---

14 "Each day teaches one anew that for the 3rd Reich this war really is the *Jewish War*, that no one can experience it as acutely and tragically as the star-wearing Jew, who is held prisoner in Germany and who in his upbringing, education, and sentiments is truly German" (II:391).

A glance at Pentagon documents reveals an ethos that promotes "alternate truths" to establish and consolidate power over other nations. Such a perusal is suggestive of specific ways in which the US public gets completely confused about actual fact or is lulled into believing its opposite. For example, a *Dictionary of Military and Associated Terms* that the US Department of Defense issued five months before the 9/11 attacks defines what they call "perception management" as follows:

> Actions to convey and/or deny selected information and indicators to foreign audiences to influence their emotions, motives, and objective reasoning as well as to intelligence systems and leaders at all levels to influence official estimates, ultimately resulting in foreign behaviors and official actions favorable to the originator's objectives. In various ways, perception management combines truth projection, operations security, cover and deception, and psychological operations.[15]

Another example comes from an instruction manual entitled Military Deception issued in January 2012 by the Joint US Armed Forces. The key to tricking the enemy is founded in manipulative language. Using language for deception makes ample use of rhetoric and semantics. Putting that principle to work participates in a veritable genre of discourse, a class of speech act:

> The cornerstone of any deception operation is the deception story. The deception story is a scenario that outlines the friendly actions that will be portrayed to cause the deception target to adopt the desired perception.

Such unspecified strategies explicitly target "foreign audiences" to alter "foreign behaviors" for the benefit of "the originator." But when "the originator" consecrates "Ground Zero" in Manhattan while at the same time conveniently forgetting that it produced the first one in Hiroshima or when it vilifies a former ally and leader of a nation that it decided to preemptively invade as "the Hitler of Baghdad," is that "originator" not, in fact, manufacturing consent right here in "the homeland"? Is this hypocrisy any less deceptive than Nazi officialdom's

---

[15]Joint Publication 1-02, April 12, 2001 (as amended through December 17, 2003); archived November 8, 2009, at the Wayback Machine.

labeling Allies the "perverse coalition" (II:462; II:611) or their bombardiers "air gangsters" (II:327; II:434) and "terror bombers" (II:274; II:366)? If the pot calls the kettle black long enough, the pot knows that the kettle will begin to believe it.

"terrorist!"

Given the US record of providing safe haven (in the form, e.g., of refugee status) to Nazis who fled the collapsed Reich[16] or to paramilitary zealots passing as Cuban exiles,[17] given our First-Amendment protection of the KKK, countless "militias," and other neo-fascists, the least one can say is that George W. Bush didn't give much thought to the possibility of contradiction and double standard before proffering the warning, "those who harbor terrorists are as guilty as the terrorists themselves."[18]

I began this chapter by presenting a case of twisted and contestable naming of consecrated land. I now begin to bring the chapter to a close with an example of perverse semantic abuse in the immediate wake of that precise naming. The arc leading from "Ground Zero" to the promiscuous use of the term "terrorist" ranges across the vast spectrum of militarized language mobilized and normalized in US English. On September 11, 2001, acts deemed to be acts of war by foreign agents were committed on US soil. The chickens of terror, which the United States routinely distributes freely across the globe, had finally come home to roost.[19] Vengeance for such audacity fostered terminology to lend voice to the unspeakable. These now well-established speech acts have wrought and

---

[16]See Eric Lichtblau, *The Nazis Next Door: How America Became a Safe Haven for Hitler's Men*. Boston: Mariner Books, 2015.

[17]The stories of Brigade 2506 and Alpha 66, for example, come to mind. As do individual criminals like Orlando Bosch, responsible for the bombing of Cubana de Aviación flight 455, killing 73 people.

[18]"President Bush Outlines Iraqi Threat." Remarks by the President on Iraq. Cincinnati Museum Center, Cincinnati, Ohio, October 7, 2002. The White House Archives. https://georgewbush-whitehouse. archives.gov/news/releases/2002/10/20021007-8.html (accessed May 8, 2023).

[19]Regarding this saying, it is instructive to revisit in this regard Malcolm X's remarks about the Vietnam War and the JFK assassination, picked up by *The New York Times* on December 2, 1963, "Malcolm X Scores U.S. and Kennedy," p. 21.

justified untold death. Every single month of "our" "just"[20] War on Terror has killed as many civilians as were killed in Manhattan: over 363,000 on the one hand, 2,763 on the other.[21] Not exactly an eye for an eye even if one factors in the mandatory dehumanization of "terrorists" that always preludes genocide.

Yet another official glossary that the US Department of State issued in 2001, before the September attacks, defined terrorism as "premeditated, politically motivated violence perpetrated against noncombatant targets by subnational groups or clandestine agents, usually intended to influence an audience."[22] In designating "subnational groups or clandestine agents" as the sole population pools from which terrorism might emerge, this definition tends to exclude any US groups or agents from the realm of possible terroristic actors with which the United States need concern itself. A month to the day after the 9/11 attacks, George W. Bush proffered a populist attempt at a grandiose version of precisely this definition to bring home the point that terror always comes from elsewhere, from a dehumanized other:

> The attack took place on American soil, but it was an attack on the heart and soul of the civilized world. And the world has come together to fight a new and different war, the first, and we hope the only one, of the 21st century. A war against all those who seek to export terror, and a war against those governments that support or shelter them.[23]

Bush's new foreign policy was briefly named "The War against Terror." That phrase was then quickly revised into "The War on Terror." Why this seemingly minor revision of a preposition? Could it simply be that "on" aligns seamlessly with the whole litany of wars *on* this or *on* that or was it that someone in the

---

[20]On "just war theory," see inter alia Chomsky 1991, 22ff.

[21]Cf. the Watson Institute for International & Public Affairs at Brown University. https://watson.brown.edu/costsofwar/figures/2021/WarDeathToll (accessed May 14, 2023).

[22]The glossary vanished after January 2009. State perhaps assumed everyone had memorized the definition. See U.S. Department of State Archive, Information released online from January 20, 2001 to January 20, 2009. https://2001-2009.state.gov/s/ct/info/c16718.htm (accessed April 5, 2023) and Gary M. Jackson, *Predicting Malicious Behavior: Tools and Techniques for Ensuring Global Security*. Indianapolis: John Wiley & Sons, 2012, p. 235.

[23]Quoted in "The Global War on Terrorism: The First 100 Days." U.S. Department of State Archive. https://2001-2009.state.gov/s/ct/rls/wh/6947.htm (accessed February 10, 2019).

Bush administration thought that "against" might somehow be construed in the minds of too many addressees that the United States too has for a long time been one of "those who seek to export terror." We may never know. But Bush's formulation was clear: the United States is and never has been an entity in the set defined as "those who seek to export terror" or "support" it. Grammatically, that which operates *on* something is positioned *above* the object of the operation, somehow immune to it, whereas that which operates *against* something is in a close, albeit separate, relationship to the object. Whichever of these reasons for the alteration—or indeed some other—the Iraq War was most emphatically a war *of* terror.

Many readers might, however, contest that indictment. "Originally," Jenny Teichman notes in one of the more thorough efforts to define the term, "terrorism was thought of as a type of behaviour perpetrated *by* governments; now it is regarded, usually though not always, as a type of behaviour directed *against* governments" (508). This is the case for at least two reasons: (1) because we think of periods like the French Revolution only as relics of a distant past and (2) because established governments, with their own propaganda machines, seconded by largely sycophantic media, are perfectly positioned to posit any form of dissent as the sole source of terror. But as Teichman's temporal qualification "usually though not always" suggests, the way the "terrorist" label functions today is versatile to the point of perversion. "Turning [...] to possible remedies for the plague" of international terrorism, Noam Chomsky has written,

> The *New York Times* called upon an expert on terrorism to offer his thoughts [...]. His advice, based upon long experience, was straightforward: "The terrorists, and especially their commanders, must be eliminated." [...] The *Times* editors gave his article the title: "It's Past Time to Crush the Terrorist Monster," and they highlighted the words: "Stop the slaughter of innocents." They identify the author solely as "Israel's Minister of Trade and Industry." His name is Ariel Sharon.
>
> (1991, 34–5)[24]

---

[24]The US Department of Justice's NCJRS characterizes the volume where this Chomsky essay appeared as follows: "The Fundamental, and Controversial, Thesis on Which the Essays in This Volume Are Focused Is That Most Significant Acts of International Terrorism Are Perpetrated, or At Least

Chomsky then proceeds to review a dozen specific achievements, starting in the early 1950s, in Sharon's extensive portfolio in the domain of terrorism. If we unpack this example, stripping it of Chomsky's delightfully sardonic irony, we can clearly see how perversely "terrorism" is used: once the national power of Israel instituted, Sharon's vast experience as a terrorist himself "qualified" him singularly as expert denouncer of the crime.

Dozens of examples of this revaluation—in "common parlance"—of "terrorist" into "statesman" (or perhaps "freedom fighter") or from "terrorist organization" into instituted political power (routinely recognized and supported by the United States) come to mind: Nelson Mandela and the African National Congress (ANC) in South Africa, and Menachem Begin and Ariel Sharon in Israel are examples. If we delete "recognized and supported by the U.S." or at least bracket the condition, we obtain still others: the Algerian FLN, Gerry Adams or Martin McGuiness of the IRA, Yasser Arafat and the PLO, Ho Chi Minh … Then there are the statesmen who have been, could or (some say) should be, considered terrorists: Slobodan Milošević, Vladimir Putin, Henry Kissinger, Benjamin Netanyahu … Countless erstwhile "terrorists" (or "freedom fighters") can be credited for conducting wars of liberation and creating or trying to create nation-states: Ireland (1919–21), Kurdistan (1921–), Israel (1924–), Vietnam (1946–54 and 1955–75), Palestine (1947– or 1967–), Algeria (1954–62), Bangladesh (1971), and East Timor (1975–99). The list is immense; "terrorist" is indeed a fluid and comprehensive catchall.

In the build-up to the invasion of Iraq, the policy of "preemption" became enshrined as a keystone of the Bush Doctrine. While paying lip-service to the caution of "legal scholars and international jurists," the National Security Strategy of the United States, published exactly one year after the 9/11 attacks, warns:

> The United States has long maintained the option of preemptive actions to counter a sufficient threat to our national security. The greater the threat, the greater is the risk of inaction—and the more compelling the case for taking anticipatory action to defend ourselves, even if uncertainty remains

---

Organized, by the United States, Its Allies, and Its Client States." https://www.ojp.gov/ncjrs/virtual-library/abstracts/western-state-terrorism (accessed May 11, 2023).

as to the time and place of the enemy's attack. To forestall or prevent such hostile acts by our adversaries, the United States will, if necessary, act preemptively.[25]

While the expression "preemptive war" per se had gained initial currency when Israel started the Six-Day War by invading Egypt on June 5, 1967, Hitler's "defensive war" against Poland in September 1939 operated according to the very same perfidious logic—a reasoning, that is, by which, supposedly, "the attacker is attacking only to deter attack."[26] As Chomsky has pointed out, "anticipatory self-defense" is yet "another euphemism for aggression at will" (28).

For a very long time already, we have taken for granted that terror, terrorism, and terrorists are intrinsically foreign, other than "us," extraterritorial. But it is sobering and salubrious to recall that the first Terror—Terror with a capital "T," Terror in the political and social realm—was the name leant to a policy, a state of affairs instituted by an actual *State*. The Terror or, as it is commonly called in English, the Reign of Terror was altogether "homegrown." Attempting to defile and distance itself from the policies of the Committee for Public Safety, the Thermidorian Convention (so named for the month in which it established itself following the execution of Robespierre) plucked *la Terreur* out of the vocabulary that had been used in philosophical discussions of the sublime ranging from Dennis and Addison since the beginning of the eighteenth century, through Burke in the middle, to a Kant contemporaneous with the Revolution. Stunned, as anyone would be, by the *awful* images of the Twin Towers collapsing as thousands of people died all at once, Karlheinz Stockhausen immediately understood that the language associated with Enlightenment sublime was about to enjoy a death-dealing revival in the form of wars of even more terrifying proportions. For that sacrilege, he was universally condemned.

---

[25]The title of this section drips with the same language characteristic of the package of laws of exception called USA PATRIOT Act: V. Prevent Our Enemies from Threatening Us, Our Allies, and Our Friends with Weapons of Mass Destruction. The White House, President George W. Bush. https://georgewbush-whitehouse.archives.gov/nsc/nss/2002/nss5.html (accessed May 14, 2023).

[26]William Safire, "On Surgical Strike." *New York Times*, May 4, 1986.

Only a century was required for terror—one of the key conceptual components in Aristotle's definition of tragedy—to course its way through aesthetics, enabling philosophy to envision an experience that, while pleasurable, differed altogether from the apprehension of beauty, to end up emblematizing the worst that humans can do to other humans. The lexicographical nexus of terror/terrorism/terrorist has taken on a monstrous life of its own. The label of "terrorist" has spawned offspring. In addition to state-sponsored terrorism, domestic terrorism, and nuclear terrorism, there are bioterrorists, cyberterrorists, ecoterrorists, agroterrorism, and narcoterrorism. There is no reason to think that the prefixes will stop proliferating.

"If you're not with us, you're against us." It's even questionable as to whether you deserve to be aligned "with them" because he who is not "with us" is outside humanity. And anyone outside humanity is outside the jurisdiction of human law. In sum, "if you're not with us," you're no better than a terrorist and you deserve to die. But the wanton or indiscriminate attribution of the "terrorist" label could lead to a trap ultimately spelling doom for the entire species. The "terrorist" is the altogether other, supposedly beyond the pale of humanity. The attempt to situate the terrorist in a definitive *elsewhere* blinds itself to the fact that the terrorist can be *anywhere*, including "here." Everyone everywhere is, therefore, potentially a terrorist—a person, that is, stripped of personhood, a human stripped of humanity. Once "reduce[d] to objects, place[d] outside military rules," as Klemperer noted, all of them can be *"liquidated [liquidiert] [or] put down [niedergemacht]"* (II:331; II:438).

In the wake of 9/11, the United States sewed the scarlet letter of "terrorist" with seemingly indiscriminate wantonness onto the breast of wide swathes of humanity. If arguably justified in cases like that of Osama Bin Laden, was it necessarily so in the case of the Palestinian viscerally but peacefully opposed to Israeli colonial expansion or in the case of the ordinary US citizen who is Muslim, of Arab "origin," both or perceived as such? Circulating uncritically since 2001, such epithets—with "terrorist" at the top of the list—along with myriad abject images referencing individuals belonging to certain religious or ethnic groups simply dehumanized individuals en masse. And everyone today should know perfectly well what Victor Klemperer expressed from every rhetorical angle at his disposal, namely that dehumanization is the first prerequisite for what would soon bear the name of genocide. While Erin Steuter and Deborah Wills repeat this point (albeit all too timidly),[27] they are certainly on the right track when they affirm that the "images and language we use to discuss the war on terror have a powerful impact on the way we think about and treat other human beings" (x).

Perfectly aligned with the life and death of metaphors, according to Nietzsche, the vacuousness of "terrorist" as a signifier is proportional to the generalization of its use. The weaker the grasp that users of the language have on a term's meaning and on the appropriateness of its attribution, the easier it is for them to accept the criminal consequences of the attribution. With "terrorist" as consensual catchall for all who are purportedly not "us," instituted power can proceed to ignore internationally agreed norms, "renditioning" arbitrarily detained individuals to "black sites," applying "enhanced interrogation techniques" (i.e., torture) like walling and waterboarding, ostensibly to keep the "Homeland"[28] safe.

The antonym of choice for "terrorist"—wherever one looks in the world—would appear to be "patriot." Since they are still in force today and their spirit has justified countless acts flaunting international norms, we would do well to start by recalling the brace of veritable *laws of exception* (in the sense lent to the term by Nazi jurist Carl Schmidt) that were hurriedly passed in 2001 under the tortuously contrived backronym, USA PATRIOT Act—a string of letters standing for the following mouthful: Uniting and Strengthening America by Providing Appropriate Tools Required to Intercept and Obstruct Terrorism. Surface-to-air missiles bearing the name are, as we might have guessed, one of the featured components of the vast US arsenal. "Patriot" in this case was oh-so cleverly filled in as Phased Array Tracking Radar to Intercept on Target. (*This* backronym demonstrating that biopolitics is far

---

[27]"The dehumanization of an entire group or race of people encourages an unconscious transformation in our minds and imaginations, a transference which is metaphor's key function, and in which entire populations are collectively stripped of their humanity and thus forfeit their claim to our empathy and compassion" (xvi).

[28]Although extant as such in the English language since at least the seventeenth century, from the Old English *hamland*, "homeland" only began to be used as comforting metaphor for the United States after the 9/11 attacks. Notable prior applications of the term were Germany under the Third Reich and in South Africa under Apartheid to designate the bantustans.

better at wielding sheer force than at naming things.) Analogously, ever since China annexed Hong Kong, all candidates for the Hong Kong's legislative council must bear Beijing's "patriot" seal of approval. Akin to the more well-known Wagner Group, Патриот is the name of one of Russia's private military and security companies deployed in Ukraine, as they have been in Syria and elsewhere. Though of negligible importance, *Les Patriotes* is the party that splintered off from France's far-right National Front (now named National Rally) in 2017. The list worldwide goes on. Returning to the US "homeland," however, the term "patriot movement" designates a wide variety of proto-fascist militias and white supremacist groups.

Upton Sinclair put the depredations of patriotic fervor starkly on display in his now all-but-forgotten 1920 novel, *100%*. The book's subtitle announces it as "the story of a patriot." In a March 1941 journal entry, Victor Klemperer noted that the hyperbolic use of "100%" to quantify the very being of the true believers is "constantly used in Nazi German" (I:378; I:480). Hyperbolic bombast regarding the patriot's political essence is not enough: it even leads to ratios beyond totality. A woman reported to Klemperer a few months later, in July 1941, that her husband was "'one hundred and fifty percent' Nazi" (I:418; I:532). Our intrepid diarist attributes such inflationary mathematics not only to fascist lockstep but to popular familiarity with Sinclair's 1920 novel. Here is how the author translates his patriotic anti-hero's thought on the subject into words:

> It was the fashion [...] for orators and public men to vie with one another in expressing the extremes of patriotism, and Peter would read these phrases, and cherish them; they came to seem a part of him, he felt as if he had invented them. He became greedy for more and yet more of this soul-food; and there was always more to be had—until Peter's soul was become swollen, puffed up as with a bellows. Peter became a patriot of patriots, a super-patriot; Peter was a red-blooded American and no mollycoddle; Peter was a "he-American," a 100% American—and if there could have been such a thing as a 101% American, Peter would have been that. Peter was so much of an American that the very sight of a foreigner filled him with a fighting impulse.

(118–19)

War is not the answer. Nor has it ever been. And received wisdom notwithstanding, war is in no way inevitable. With their "survival of the fittest" thesis, Oswald Spengler, Thomas Henry Huxley, and others sent Darwinian evolution on a wildly dangerous social drift that would ultimately lead to racist eugenics. In the same period of time, and on the other hand, careful observation would lead Peter Kropotkin to conclude that "a pitiless war for life [or] to see in that war a condition of progress" is not only irrelevant to evolution within or without our species to act as if it were so seals our destruction (2). Care with language could have obviated the death-dealing deviation of social Darwinism. We owe to the gift of our linguistic abilities to do whatever we can to *not* allow language to lead us. One of Friedrich Schiller's distichs reads as follows:

> Just because you manage a verse in an educated language,
> That writes and thinks for you, do you already think you're a poet?[29]

Klemperer took these lines to heart, turning a flat "No" to that rhetorical question into his North Star as he doggedly autopsied the language of the Third Reich.

It is too simple and altogether naïve, however, to assert that "war is not the answer," since as Michel Foucault stated, in the same Collège de France lecture from which I selected my second epigraph to this chapter, that "the role of political power is perpetually to use a sort of silent war to reinscribe in institutions, economic inequalities, language, and even the bodies of individuals a relationship of force that was established in and through war" (15–16).[30] We should note the close proximity—I would like to say interpenetration—in Foucault's formulation between language and the body of subjects: subjects of language who can also, dangerously, become subjects *to* language. Earlier,

---

[29]The extant translation is in quite archaic English. This is my translation of …

    Weil ein Vers dir gelingt in einer Gebildeten Sprache,
      Die für dich dichtet und denkt, glaubst du schon Dichter zu sein?

in *Distichen III*.

[30]Without altering Foucault's words, I have adjusted the syntax in Macey's translation to make the sentence compact and readable.

in citing War on Terror death statistics, I placed the possessive "our" in scare quotes. May I presume that you will have understood that I did not want to assume that "we" all want to assume responsibility for the horrific wages of such a war? Perhaps I'm being too presumptuous now by including *you* in my own moral disassociation from it in my use of "we."

The politics of scare quoting is slippery business. A thorough exploration of semantic perversion requires an entire chapter devoted to scare quotes.

2
Scare Quotes

scare quotes n. quotation marks used to foreground a particular word or phrase, esp. with the intention of dissociating the user from the expression or from some connotation it carries.

—"scare, n.2—draft additions, September 2004." *Oxford English Dictionary*

In some remote corner of the universe [...], there was once a planet on which clever animals invented cognition. It was the most arrogant and most mendacious minute in the "history of the world."

—FRIEDRICH NIETZSCHE, "On Truth and Lies in the Extra-Moral Sense"

They twinkle. They wink. They nod. They give an elbow nudge. They can be placed where they should be or, where they should be, they're not placed. A diminutive accessory to language, the scare quote plays a huge role in the dynamics by which we discursive animals strive to link language to truth— whatever *that* might be. Bearing a name, the scare quote is also a concept if we follow Nietzsche's application in the above epigraph. In my view, we must: not only should we be endlessly grateful for Nietzsche's call to be ever vigilant to the inevitable inaccuracy—nay, *mendacity*—of language but also for his visionary vision of a future in which we presently exist where scare quotes and their ilk are rife.

Scare quotes just might be the premier punctuation mark of the twenty-first century. Graphic pincers by which the writer (or speaker) demonstrates "the intention of dissociating the user," ironic distance, that is, from the word or phrase grasped, scare quotes isolate and draw attention to hotspots in the politics of language. Akin to a mathematical function, they inflect the words in their embrace, making it understood that the writer (or speaker) has some "issue" with their tenor or, at least, holds them at bay from her (or his) putative worldview. We've even developed a double hand gesture to mime them when speaking (or not).

Yet—irony of ironies—words and phrases also crop up that the writer (or speaker) *might have* equipped with scare quotes, but for some reason or another did not. This neglect or negligence or subterfuge is even more prevalent in speech than it is in writing—speech being, of course, more evanescent than writing. Even without scare quotes, such phrases or words momentarily arrest the addressee's attention as hot-button items. Their afterglow keeps thinking stimulated. In such cases, we sense our addressor's effort to spin, even in the absence of punctuation's warning signals.

From the Nazi's "systematic use of quotation marks [*Anführungsstiche*] as a means of rendering contemptible" (I:201; I:264) to his own application of them to retain some sense of sanity in an insanely threatening world, Victor Klemperer mastered the full range of potential harbored by scare quoting. Examples of Nazi scare quoting are countless but derive from two diametrically opposed qualities of language: its "wonderful elasticity" (II:129; II:176), on the one hand, and its susceptibility to "trivialization [*Bagatellisierten*]" (I:343; I:439) and impoverishment (II:337; II:447), on the other. The "utterly sterile [...] endlessly repetitive" (II:390; II:518) appearance of the adjective "tragic" in death notices and military bulletins drives Klemperer toward the exhaustive analysis of the word that Terry Eagleton carried out in 2003. Examples of Klemperer's scare quoting remind me of the masterful irony Jonathan Swift or the linguistic survival tactics that Black people in the United States have used for centuries of generations. Following the August 1938 decree contemptuously requiring "Jews" to append "Israel" or "Sara" to their first names, Klemperer wore it discursively as a bent badge of dishonor: "Tomorrow the typed copy of the Beaumarchais. [...] I, Victor-Israel Klemperer" (I:266; I:347). The thousands of suicides among cornered and desperate people inspired in the linguist some gallows humor set off by scare quotes: a fellow inmate of Dresden's "Jewish house" had "shrunk away to nothing after serious ill-treatment and, threatened with Theresienstadt, is now contemplating suicide (I said, Veronal should now be called 'Jewish drops')" (II:103; II:140).

Of course, what today gets qualified as scare quoting is a special function of quoting *tout court*. As one nutshell description goes, "Quotation marks essentially indicate reported speech (quotes, words spoken) and distancing" (76). The distancing to which linguist Nina Catach refers is the essence of the function we assign to this punctuation sign in general. Setting aside for a short moment the special function of distancing, however, the principal purpose of quotation marks—that of "indicating reported speech"—is to inoculate us against accusations of plagiarism. Whether I am reproducing someone else's words spoken or written, quoting is essential for indicating the dialogical components of fiction and nonfiction alike. It is fundamental too—along with bibliographic referencing—to writing deemed academic, journalistic, scientific, critical, serious, and so forth, as exemplified by what I just did in the second sentence of this very paragraph. Among strategies—verbal and gestural—to indicate quotation when speaking are:

- "quote" (or "I quote") [reported discourse] "unquote" (or "end of quote");

- air quotes with fingers of both hands while reporting discourse;

- "he said," "she said," "they said" (or any synonymous verb) introducing reported discourse;

- "I go," "he goes" or "I'm like," "he's like."

The written sign formally used can vary—at least in the English language. While most writers use double inverted commas for the opening scare quote and double commas to indicate closure—both sets suspended at the top of the adjacent letters—some writers reserve these symbols only for quotations in relation to which they feel rather neutral and single commas to indicate the scare quote function. A perfect example of this is to be found in an article by a linguist especially interested in scare quotes. On the same page where Stefano Predelli quotes a word in one of his test sentences, he writes:

> Typical scenarios for (1), for instance, involve an attachment to the effect that "proofs" is improperly employed.

Yet further down on that same page, referring to other test sentences, Predelli writes:

[…] the handy label of "scare quotes" or "apologetic quotes" for the marks in (1) or (2), but not for those in (7) or (8), is to be interpreted neither as alluding to the presence of distinct expressions, nor as defending a distinction in their conventional behavior. Speaking more appropriately, one should rather qualify cases such as (1) or (2) as sentences which, in typical settings, express an attachment pertaining to an apologetic connotation.

(14)

The reader will notice that to demonstrate my point, I had to use block indentation for the shorter first sampling, instead of quotation marks, so as to avoid the usual conversion of double suspended commas to single for quotation inside quotation.

First identified, named, and discussed "scientifically," or, more precisely, in a written and scholarly context, by Cambridge philosopher G.E.M. Anscombe in 1956, scare quotes—whether present or absent—point to the fertile grounds in language where *critique* can pursue its righteous and vital cause. By taking the pervasive use (misuse, abuse, etc.) of scare quotes in my tweezers and dissecting the body of language as it is used today, I hope that this chapter will deepen the mission I have assigned this book of making an emphatic contribution to the possibility of a world founded on *fact unadulterated*.

To that end, I want to inventory and recapitulate as many of the manifestations and effects of scare quotes that I can. Along the way, I will endeavor to do my best at speculating about what might be the intentions driving the scare quote as well as other linguistic practices that hover in the vicinity of this peculiar variety of semantic perversion. As with all discursive practices, however, it is tempting to overestimate the extent to which a speaker controls whatever intention might underlie such or such speech act. As repository of culture past and present, language and what we do with it—including the scare quoting of items—also, lest we forget, wield power over us.

naming scare quotes

Not long after Erasmus expressed regret that no written symbol existed to indicate irony, John Wilkins attempted to meet this need with an exclamation point turned on its head. That solution, however, lacked legs: the new punctuation mark failed to catch on. Then, a few decades after Rousseau renewed Erasmus's lament (but without *doing* anything about it), a quirky Belgian land surveyor by the name of Jean-Baptiste-Ambroise-Marcellin Jobard proposed a series of "emotional typographical characters," including what looks like a pine tree meant to indicate ironic intent when pointing upright. The use of this icon for irony, however, wouldn't go further than any of the rest of Jobard's repertoire as published in his own journal, *Courrier belge*. Next came Alcanter de Brahm and this vertically mirrored question mark:

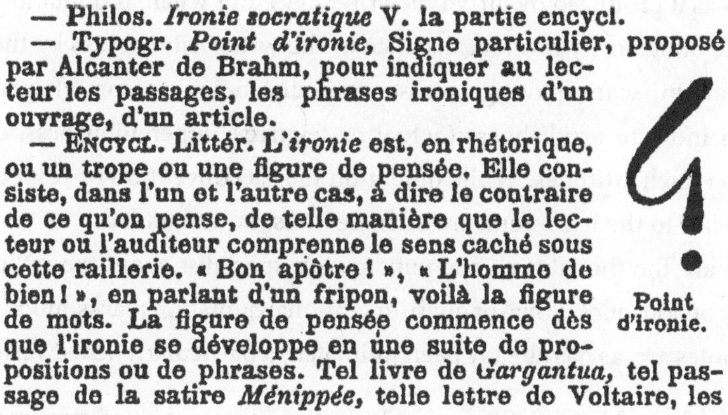

> — Philos. *Ironie socratique* V. la partie encycl.
> — Typogr. *Point d'ironie*, Signe particulier, proposé par Alcanter de Brahm, pour indiquer au lecteur les passages, les phrases ironiques d'un ouvrage, d'un article.
> — Encycl. Littér. L'*ironie* est, en rhétorique, ou un trope ou une figure de pensée. Elle consiste, dans l'un et l'autre cas, à dire le contraire de ce qu'on pense, de telle manière que le lecteur ou l'auditeur comprenne le sens caché sous cette raillerie. « Bon apôtre ! », « L'homme de bien ! », en parlant d'un fripon, voilà la figure de mots. La figure de pensée commence dès que l'ironie se développe en une suite de propositions ou de phrases. Tel livre de *Gargantua*, tel passage de la satire *Ménippée*, telle lettre de Voltaire, les

Point d'ironie.

Figure 2.1 Nouveau Larousse Illustré: Dictionnaire Universel Encyclopédique, *v. 5. Claude Augé, ed. Paris: Librairie Larousse, 1898, p. 329. Public Domain.*

Despite being baptized with a mischievous pun, the *point d'ironie* too fizzled. In the second half of the twentieth century, Hervé Bazin took the Greek *psi*, perched it on a period (full stop), suggesting that this combination looked like "an arrow in the bow [anticipating] the sound of the arrow in flight." In vain did he confidently add, "How better to denote irony?" But that arrow too, as one writer put it, "missed the target and suffered the same fate as its predecessors, perishing in obscurity."[1]

Scare quotes are today's reigning survivors of all these attempts to introduce irony or distancing punctuation into language. Variously known as "quibble marks," "sneer" or "shudder quotes," they are familiar today to virtually

---

[1]Adapted from Houston (2014). Quotes, successively, are from Bazin (142) and Maria Popova, "Ironic Serif: A Brief History of Typographic Snark and the Failed Crusade for an Irony Mark." *Brain Pickings.* https://www.brainpickings.org/2013/09/27/shady-characters-irony/ (accessed June 17, 2019).

any practitioner of the English language. And they have caught on in other languages too. Even the *General Rules for the Usage of Punctuation Marks* issued by the rather staid Ministry of Education of the People's Republic of China stipulates that quotation marks may be used "to indicate words with special meanings, for example [...] irony."[2] In the midst of a written sentence, he who scare quotes introduces precisely the same symbols he would if he were "simply" quoting. He precedes the material he wishes to scare quote with little superscripted 66s and closes with 99s—the holes of both figures inked in as if produced by dirty typewriter keys. But whereas quotation marks mark the obligatorily reverent distance of the writer who abides by the taboo of plagiarism, scare-quoting marks moral distancing—a sort of quarantine that can indicate prudishness (actual or feigned), superciliousness, disdain, and other such attitudes. While quotation marks convention or respect, scare quotes tend to the irreverent, are often devious, underhanded.

Here are the thoughts of one punctuation specialist about the rather loose category of non-quotational or quasi-quotational quotation marks, among which scare quotes are, as has already been intimated, a particularly vexed variety:

> reserved for "distantiation" or valorization, internal quotation marks are today mostly used for the titles of articles, rare words or those considered "vulgar [*populaires*]," brand names, neologisms of form or meaning, etc.

(By the way, before I continue to quote this linguist's description, the scare quotes you've just read were installed by the describer herself.) Nina Catach continues:

> [Scare quotes] allow the writer to take her distance inside the sentence from any portion of text not entirely assumed by the locutor, to isolate it and valorize it (unusual word, example, proverb, etc.):
> (daring term) *The budget "forgets" social tourism.*
> (taking up someone else's discourse) *Why "now"?*
> (naming) *"Sophie" is the truck.*
> (Catach, 78–9)[3]

---

[2] Thanks to Yanling Li for this piece of information transmitted to me by email on May 12, 2018.
[3] My translation.

Although, as in the *OED* definition I cited epigrammatically shows, the criterion of dissociation or distantiation is prominent in this description and these examples, what we will quickly see as the perverse—that is, quite diffuse and promiscuous—world of scare quotes is only summarily and superficially glanced at here.

Another punctuation expert has sights set more specifically on the *guillemet d'ironie*. Irony marks are virtually synonymous with scare quotes, he contends. Reticent, however, to construct rules, despite authoring nothing less than a *Treatise of Punctuation*, Jacques Drillon does set out these five descriptors (the second of which, I note, echoes Nina Catach's remark about "vulgar" words). In Drillon's *Treatise*, each of these is followed by an equally lively example:

> The irony mark indicates the distance, irony or disdain that the author wants to demonstrate with regard to what he quotes.

> To take cover behind a quote allows the author to use words he considers crude or that he thinks the reader would find crude.

> Affection or teasing is situated between these extremes.

> It goes without saying that irony can be exerted at the expense of the author himself and that it derives not automatically from the word itself but from the notion that it carries.

> The irony mark may help make an unfortunate word or an awkward expression more digestible for the author.

(296–7)[4]

To encapsulate and drive home the complexity of scare quoting when several of these operations are at work simultaneously, Drillon reproduces the following bit of dialogue between Man 1 and Man 2, excerpted from Nathalie Sarraute's play *Pour un oui ou pour un non*—or *Over Nothing at All*:

> M.1: All right. I can accept that. You weren't thinking of him, but you have to admit that with the little wall, the roof, the sky above the roof ... we were smack in the middle ...

---

[4]My translation.

M.2: In the middle of what?

M.1: Oh, come now, in the middle of "poetic" matters, of "poetry."

M.2: Oh, my God! all of a sudden, everything's coming out … it's those quotation marks …

M.1: What quotation marks?

M.2: The ones you always put around words when you say them in my presence … "Poetry." "Poetic." That distance, that irony, that scorn …

M.1: *I* make fun of poetry? *I* speak scornfully of the poets?

M.2: Not the "true" poets, of course. […]

(55)[5]

Is it tone of voice? Facial expression? A conventional gesture or another? Some combination of these? How the scare quotes we just now read here on the *page* come to be indicated on *stage* by the character will be discussed in some detail later. But this drift from writing into orality and theatricality exemplifies the versatility, the fluidity—the polymorphism of scare quotes. For now, I propose that we reflect on the purpose Sarraute assigned the scare quotes in this exchange she imagined. To Drillon they "indicate, in direct discourse, that a game is being played out" (298). While perfectly accurate, this is rather evasive: it gets us no further than the disdain invoked by M.2 and the linguist himself in his first descriptor.

As mischievous as the mobilization of scare quotes may be, the game their user plays may bear evidence of sinister goals like those set out from nodes of power. Nowhere is this dimension of scare quotes more obvious than in Victor Klemperer's analysis of the ways in which the Nazis transformed the German language. When Klemperer writes, in his "Punctuation" chapter of *The Language of the Third Reich*, that "the LTI makes exhaustive use of what I would call ironic inverted commas," we understand that scare quotes had pride of place in the perversely manipulative rhetoric deployed by Nazi leadership. The Dresden linguist goes on to explain: "The simple, primary inverted comma merely denotes the exact words spoken or written by someone else." What he's describing here, of course, is the conventional function of quotation marks meant for the citation of sources. But then he continues:

---

[5]Sarraute's play has also been translated under the title, *Just for Nothing*.

The ironic inverted comma is not restricted to this neutral form of quotation, instead it questions the truth of that which is quoted, declares that the reported remark is untrue. In rendering that which in spoken language would be expressed by the mere adoption of a sarcastic tone, the ironic inverted comma is closely allied to the rhetorical character of the LTI.

It wasn't invented by it. During the First World War, when the Germans were extolling the virtues of their superior culture and looking down on Western civilization as if it were an inferior, entirely superficial achievement, the French never failed to include the ironic sixty-sixes and ninety-nines when referring to the "*culture allemande.*" And it is likely that there was an ironic use of the inverted comma alongside the neutral one right from the outset.

(75–6)

Quarantining infection and disease by the application of a punctuational *cordon sanitaire* around entities deemed indecent, decadent, and, thus, destined for destruction, reached paroxysmal proportions in the last few years of the Third Reich. In a parenthesis later in his monumental study, Klemperer writes that "Just as in the LTI—most frequently in [Alfred] Rosenberg and, likewise, in the case of Hitler and Goebbels—the word *Humanität* is never used without ironic inverted commas and is frequently reinforced with a scathing epithet" (144). No need to look for Klemperer to say it, I will: in the fascist mind, humanism was a quintessentially Jewish construct. This is why he would come to "see red" every time he would hear or read Nazi reference to "German culture" (II:393; II:522). Periphrasis and euphemism thrive in the realm of scare quotes.

Rosenberg would sneeringly hold "humanity" out with those double tongs to elicit disgust in his readers, conditioning them in advance of the Final Solution. The purpose of Rosenberg's scare quotes was not to frighten the good people in the audience as much as to orient and groom them for compliance and cooperation. So why do we call them *scare* quotes? The *OED* positions the term, as shown in my epigraph, under the second of four attested definitions of the nominal application of *scare*. (The first one—obsolete since the thirteenth century—signified scorn, derision or contempt.) *Scare* stands for "an act of scaring or a state of being scared; a sudden fright or alarm;

esp. a state of general or public alarm occasioned by baseless or exaggerated rumours; *occasionally* in generalized use, panic." We thus deduce that "scare quotes" is a compound nominal expression that was still floating in the limbo of the *OED*'s draft additions for September 2004.

These considerations notwithstanding, we still don't get much closer to understanding *why* we have developed the expression *scare quotes* for such a multifarious—one might even say mercurial—practice. Short of any evidence from spoken English, perhaps dictionary examples will help. Abiding strictly by the chronology given in the *OED*, the first occurrence would have been …

> 1956 *Mind* **65** 3 "The 'scare-quotes' are mine; Aristotle is not overtly discussing the *expression* 'whichever happens.'"

Isolated from its context, this example is largely opaque. It is lifted from an article entitled "Aristotle and the Sea Battle" penned by G.E.M. Anscombe and published, as the *OED* notes, in *Mind*, the "Quarterly Review of Psychology and Philosophy," in January 1956. As Jonathan Beale informs us, Anscombe was "perhaps [Wittgenstein's] best student" claiming that she was "considered by many to be the greatest philosopher of her generation."[6] I must confess that certain elements of this British analytic philosopher's biography left me a bit perplexed, even queasy: born in Limerick due to her father having been an officer in the Royal Welch Fusiliers during the Irish War of Independence, she grew up and remained a fervent Catholic. She hated phenomenology. She bore seven children. And she was a militant anti-abortionist. Far more palatable, on the other hand, was her opposition to Oxford's granting Truman an honorary degree based on her position that he was a mass murderer for the atomic bombings of Hiroshima and Nagasaki.

Oddly, in becoming the first person to get the term scare quotes[7] out in print in reference to something that she had just added to an excerpt of a short, enigmatic passage from Aristotle, Anscombe was not doing what we usually

---

[6]Jonathan Beale, "Wittgenstein's Confession" (The Stone). *The New York Times*, September 18, 2018. https://www.nytimes.com/2018/09/18/opinion/wittgensteins-confession-philosophy.html?action=clic k&module=Opinion&pgtype=Homepage (accessed December 30, 2018).
[7]Anscombe links the words making up the term with a hyphen.

are today when we use scare quotes or what the Nazis were doing when they deployed their debased version of the German language that Klemperer called lingua tertii imperii. Far from taking authorial distance from the scare-quoted material by indicating irony in its regard, Anscombe would seem to be simply holding forth the words thus held out, highlighting them, as it were. I say "simply," but on a full read of Anscombe's study, one learns that the phrase "whichever happens" that she sets off are the nucleus of the demonstration she presents. To be clearer, here is what transpires in her article: "Aristotle and the Sea Battle" is a rigidly philological discussion of §9 of *De interpretatione*, the second text of the *Organon*, where Aristotle—anticipating modal logic as applied to time and possibility—examines propositions in regard to events past, present, and future by means of a mental experiment about a sea battle that might or might not occur. In conducting this discussion, Anscombe offers her own translation of the entire section. Aristotle proceeds, as usual, syllogistically. Here is how Anscombe phrases his first conclusion:

> So nothing is or comes about by chance or "whichever happens." Nor will it be or not be, but everything of necessity and not "whichever happens." For either someone saying something or someone denying it will be right. For it would either be happening or not happening accordingly. For whichever happens is not more thus or not thus than it is going to be.
>
> (3)

For the sake of comparison, Harold P. Cooke's 1938 translation of the same passage for today's extant Loeb Classics volume goes as follows:

> Now, if all this is so, there is nothing that happens by chance or fortuitously; nothing will ever so happen. Contingency there can be none; all events come about of necessity. Either the man who maintains that a certain event will take place or the man who maintains the reverse will be speaking the truth on that point. Things could just as well happen as not, if the one or the other assertion is not of necessity true. For as that term is used in regard to both present and future events, the contingent is that which could just as well happen in this way or that.
>
> (133–5)

When I asked my erudite colleague Nikos Panou about why, in his opinion, Anscombe's version reads so awkwardly compared to Cooke's, he responded as follows:

> [Cooke's] translation is more polished and explanatory, but it is Anscombe who provides a literal, word-for-word translation of Aristotle's dense and unpolished original. "Whichever happens" is as close as it gets to ὁπότερ᾽ ἔτυχεν, both semantically and syntactically (relative pronoun + verb). I also agree with the remarks that follow her translation. "Fortuitously" is certainly more elegant and it does work, but only insofar as there are no positive connotations of the "by lucky chance" type.

If anything, then, if we are to follow Panou, Anscombe intended her scare quotes to demonstrate and underscore her *proximity* in modern English to Aristotle's ancient Greek, even if in doing so she had to sacrifice a certain elegance and flow. Not a drop of irony or sarcasm here. Somehow, though, since then, we have twisted this function to do quite the opposite… Or have we? Are we absolutely sure we are always distancing and denigrating the words set off by the little suspended and ink-filled 66s and 99s? In using (and abusing) scare quotes are we not also sometimes doing what the old Greeks meant when they'd apply the *diple periestigmene* to textual margins? The diple, which some punctuation specialists consider an ancestor of scare quotes, was a philological device designed to indicate either quoted or dubious passages: close to the vague stuff today's scare quotes draw attention to. Ironically, then, the use to which Anscombe put scare quotes foregrounds the abuse to which they are so often subjected today.

Stefano Predelli is another linguist who has devoted as much attention as any to what we do or, rather, *think* we are doing when we use scare quotes. *Attachment* is what Predelli calls the semantic supplement that addressors clip onto words or phrases so that addressees, in harvesting them on arrival, will instantly inflect—pervert—the meaning they would normally convey. Such manipulations work similarly to the way certain adjectives like "so-called," "putative," and "supposed" or adverbs like "but" and "yet" work in most instances. In the sentence "Shaq is huge but agile," Predelli explains, "'but' is conventionally assigned the behavior of an attachment trigger" (12).

The "attachment" triggered by *scare quotes*, however, may produce deviant connotations or valences according to the critical mood of the addressee or even the tone of voice (assuming an oral delivery, rather than a written one) with which the sender delivers the sentence. This was certainly *not* G.E.M. Anscombe's intention when she added them to that crucial phrase of §9 of Aristotle's *De interpretatione*. Thinking of a completely different example, as *attached* as Abraham was to Isaac—at least the way Kierkegaard speculatively interprets the famous biblical scene in *Fear and Trembling*—perhaps his so-called *sacrifice* was the first case that ever cried out for scare quotes.

Respectful of authors' rights, as the *OED* is when quoting Anscombe, I go about setting off the verbatim words of others with the appropriate punctuation marks and, whenever possible, tag onto them a source reference in a footnote. Quoting is, all in all, quite straightforward. Not so with scare quotes. Neither their motivation nor their application is stable. When they are mobilized to communicate sarcasm, skepticism, or derision, or to elicit disgust, they are added with purpose, in the user's cognizance of his action. But this being only a partial list of tasks to which scare quotes are assigned, they fail to satisfy the purpose dreamed of for the ever-elusive irony mark. When driven by convention, they pop out unconsciously. At the very least, "every time we use or receive an expression in quotation marks" (by which this writer means scare quotes), "a familiar expression shows a shift in its meaning," it "patently deviates from its habitual sphere of use" (Gasparov 147). Scare quotes, in other words, reframe the expression in an entirely new mood. In the egregious case of "Ground Zero" which we examined in the first chapter, the original impetus for conjuring up the expression is unrecognizable once the "patent deviation" has taken place. In actuating a range of effects "from deliberate distancing to mockery," scare quoting is inherently and, as we shall continue to show, perversely volatile. Scare quotes "can convey," as Marjorie Garber reminds us, "both absolute authenticity and veracity, on the one hand, and suspected inauthenticity, irony, or doubt, on the other" (13). Without rules, this manipulative realm of communication is virtually impossible to theorize, and its manifestations elude taxonomy.

To indicate ironic intention or derision or sarcasm, variations of disavowal or bad faith, scare quotes are not the only typographical strategy writers adopt.

One can *italicize*. One can **embolden** typeface. One can underline, as in the "old days" when typewriters thus indicated italicization. Capitalization of the Key Words, as if one were nostalgic for pre-nineteenth-century English, does the trick. So does the use of all caps—the typographical equivalent of SHOUTING. In "Dominici, or the Triumph of Literature," Roland Barthes, sounding already like a Michel Foucault of some ten years later on the insidious force of language, had recourse to just such keyword capitalization in tandem with scare quotes in order to highlight the names for components making up the person named Gaston Dominici—"psychology" (48), "soul" (51), "Document" (51), "human" (51)—a personhood that institutional biopower methodically peeled away from him during his trial for triple murder. As Barthes forcefully concluded, "To steal his language from a man in the very name of language: every legal murder begins here" (52)—a sentence demonstrating how labile the term *murder* can be.

Theodor Adorno is unique among those who have tried to theorize and analyze the complex problem of scare quotes. By advocating for a strict distinction to be respected between distantiation and the drive to produce irony, Adorno lifts the veil on the manipulative promiscuousness of their use and abuse. Since for Adorno, irony reigns supreme among dialectical discursive strategies for conducting critique, irony should always be allowed to go its way alone, unadorned, unadulterated, without disguise, without crutches. Scare quotes constitute just such unnecessary prostheses: they are just the kind of device that debilitates irony's force. Adorno writes:

> Quotation marks should be used only when something is quoted and if need be when the text wants to distance itself from a word it is referring to. They are to be rejected as an ironic device. For they exempt the writer from the spirit whose claim is inherent in irony, and they violate the very concept of irony by separating it from the matter at hand and presenting a predetermined judgment on the subject.

Clearly, what irony must do is solicit the critical faculty of the addressee, thereby establishing a conspiracy of two with the addressee. For the latter to be a true ironist, she must eschew what Adorno calls "typographical cliché" and, instead, weaponize *naked* irony. Short of that, the writer risks leaving material playfully scarequoted to be twisted into her worst nightmare. Adorno continues:

> The abundant ironic quotation marks in Marx and Engels are the shadows that totalitarian methods cast in advance upon their writings, whose intention was the opposite: the seed from which eventually came what Karl Kraus called *Moskauderwelsch*.

… a mot-valise which, as the translator of this piece on "Punctuation Marks" explains within square brackets, means "Moscow double-talk, from *Moskau*, Moscow, and *Kauderwelsch*, gibberish or double-talk." The dissident Marxist Adorno's warning, though couched in his characteristically dense and allusive terms, could not be clearer:

> The indifference to linguistic expression shown in the mechanical delegation of intention to a typographic cliché arouses the suspicion that the very dialectic that constitutes the theory's content has been brought to a standstill and the object assimilated to it from above, without negotiation. Where there is something that needs to be said, indifference to literary form always indicates dogmatization of the content. The blind verdict of ironic quotation marks is its graphic gesture.
>
> (303)

In an "era of the progressive degeneration of language" (302), the Critical Watch that we must be if we are to save ourselves and a whole slew of other earthly organisms from a Holocene extinction, language must go forth *unmasked*.

Any means of setting off words—typographical, punctuational, and so on—may signal any of the polymorphous manipulative intentions I have reviewed. Freewheeling shirking of discursive responsibility may explain why some people persist in referring to "quotation marks," when they actually mean "scare quotes." Former prolific tweeter Donald J. Trump appealed promiscuously to several alternatives for snark, sarcasm, and "emphasis." As he "explains":

> After having written many best selling books, and somewhat priding myself on my ability to write [*sic*], it should be noted that the Fake News constantly

likes to pour [*sic*] over my tweets looking for a mistake. I capitalize certain words only for emphasis, not b/c they should be capitalized!

(3 July 2018)[8]

Besides his *bête noire* of "Fake News" (not to speak of the homophonic error and the dangling modifier), what the US president also puts on display here is that certain readers may detect words and expressions like "somewhat priding myself" that *should* by all rights have been adorned with scare quotes had the author been more acutely aware of their ironic value. This dimension of the scare quote universe—the one where they *should* be applied—will be more thoroughly explored in the section after next. But what the example just cited shows is how scare quotes or any of their substitutes may not only be used for the myriad purposes already named but *misused* and even *abused*. The scare quotes sometimes found in grocery ads—"Delicious 'tomatoes,'" for example—"grocer's quotes," as they have been called, are prime examples of emphasis gone awry.

Trump, of course, is one of the more prolific purveyors of semantic perversion in our times. Until being banned from Twitter and Facebook, his nonstop delivery of discursive deception and mendacity, the initial-letter capitalization of hot-button expressions, and so on, often stood in for the use of scare quotes. There should be little surprise, of course, in a twit's misuse of language: Trump reportedly rarely reads and apparently—except for his grotesquely gross signature—only writes on his "smart" phone.

For a variety of reasons—foremost among which is the distortion of fact that their "attachments" sometimes cause—scare quotes are not unanimously embraced. The obscure Australian philosopher David Stove attributed a "cult of irrationalism" to their ilk and the equally curmudgeonly Jonathan Chait has deplored their "wildly promiscuous use." Greil Marcus, whose cultural critique has gained much respect, on the other hand, laments emphatically that "scare quotes kill narrative." For Marcus, they are a prime symptom of what Georges Bataille called "the shame of a generation whose rebels are afraid of the noise of their own words" (118).

---

[8]Sarah Mervosh reported that this tweet was subsequently deleted. "Trump Uses Random Uppercase Letters, but Should You? An Issue of Capital Importance." *The New York Times*, July 4, 2018. https://www.nytimes.com/2018/07/04/us/trump-capitalization-tweets-nyt.html (accessed January 22, 2019).

Compared to quotation marks—their progenitors—scare quotes are quite untamed and elusive in both form and purpose. When veteran journalist Merrill Perlman writes, quite simply that "those written versions of 'air quotes' are called 'scare quotes,'" it is clear that experts are not quite sure whether the punctuation preceded the gesture or vice versa. And when Perlman further speculates about whether scare quoting is meant (or not) to actually *scare* the messenger's receiver, the very naming of the phenomenon is thrown into question. Misnomers themselves, as we shall see in subsequent sections, operate in the environment where scare quoting dominates communication. Even the genealogy of scare quote theorists starting with Susan Sontag (1966) leading on to Marjorie Garber (2003), Jennifer DeVere Brody (2008), and Jeff Scheible (2015) refer loosely to "quotation marks" when what they are really talking about are scare quotes. The unforgettable pathos in Rimbaud's declaration that "I is another" together with Peter Szendy's disquisition on Chekhov's short story "The Exclamation Mark" with its character, Efim Perekladin, who exclaimed "I, Efim Perekladin, I sign!" (8) drive home the infinite intensity of the speaking subject's drama concerning "their" personal use—sans scare quotes—of the first-person personal pronoun.

Scare quotes may also be used to indicate shared complicitous delight in a concept deviated from its preliminary import. Early in my knitting practice some frogging that I'd introduced into a scarf had me stymied and frustrated. I walked down to Broome Street to my favorite yarn shop to seek advice. A kind employee immediately reassured me, affirming that I shouldn't consider all mistakes "fuckups," as I'd characterized them, but rather as "design features." Ever since then, I've regularly and eagerly used this uplifting and valorizing euphemism. Without doubt, I am quoting someone else—a far more experienced knitter—when I do. But I *embrace* the expression. My "distance" from it is only to hold it out for my own delight and, perhaps, for that of whoever listens. (By the way, until I wrote this paragraph, this example had only occurred in speech. As I have "said" previously, I'll have more in the next section about scare quotes in the realm of oral communication.)

Regardless of the intention, scare quotes remain, nevertheless, *quotes*. The speaker, the writer, or the *addressee* is in some way or another *quoting*—demonstrating, that is, by means of those specific punctuation marks that the words embraced by them are not hers, that she disowns them. Quotation marks have never been as important as they are today for setting parameters for truth—especially when their specialized function as scare quotes is manifest. Take the tweeted denial "I never called Meghan Markle 'nasty.'" By applying those tweezers, the author is in perfect conformity with the *OED*'s remark that the user of scare quotes does so "with the intention of dissociating [himself] from the expression or from some implied connotation it carries."[9] Yet when this tweeter finally had to face the video-taped fact of his lie, he did so in an additional layer of twisted distancing by means of scare quotes yet again—this time around a paraphrase of his own words: "It's actually on tape. 'Wow, I didn't know she was nasty.'" As George Orwell, whom Katie Rogers quoted when reporting on this, wrote: "The party told you to reject the evidence of your eyes and ears. It was their final, most essential command."[10]

There is a seemingly inscrutable tension in the impulse that may give rise to scare quotes. Take, for example, the adjective "failing," as in "the 'failing' *New York Times*." When *I* write this, there is no way I could justify not applying those pincers indicating that *I* disown the qualifier. But when the author of this phrase writes it, he may dispense with them and, for instance, capitalize "failing" because he wants us to know that he owns the slam that he shouts. If on some occasions that same author applies the little pincers of punctuation, it's because he only has the most tenuous understanding of what they're used for. Yet again, we should defer to Adorno's wisdom and warning about "violating the very concept of irony."

To scare quote or not to scare quote: that is *not* really the question. To take semantic distance from a word or to mock the referent of a phrase, we don't really need scare quotes. In writing, there are semantic solutions for that. So too in speech, which can always be supplemented by gesture. In addition to the versatility of our voices, as Marjorie Garber points out, "'quote-unquote' often functions in this manner," adding this pair of examples: "a character in crime fiction can report to another that 'he did have quote, a jolly good reason for

---

[9] Draft addition of September 2004.

[10] Quoted in Katie Rogers, "An Orwellian Tale? Trump Denies, Then Confirms 'Nasty' Comments about Meghan Markel." *NYT*, June 5, 2019.

bumping off one special person, unquote,' while in Peter Ustinov's *Loser* we are told that someone 'expressed the personal opinion that the picture was quote great for America unquote'" (13).

Up until the preceding paragraph, I've mainly been discussing the nebulous phenomenon of scare quotes in the realm of *written* language. The examples I gleaned from Garber have allowed us to slip into the realm of *orality*. As we know, scare quotes—especially in the English-speaking world—can be signaled when spoken words are accompanied by certain gestures or inflected by certain tones of voice. This signaling is carried out by signing, as if all practitioners knew this one semantic element of ASL. It is natural, then, that we next explore air quotes and snare quotes.

sn(air) quotes

When the production of meaning becomes stealthy, when rhetoric manipulates, semantics is led down the road of perversion. Scare quotes are best at blighting meaning when they withdraw from the spotlight. If scare quotes are key to an archeology of semantic perversion, it is not their brash manifestation on the page that should preoccupy us as much as shadings of their dematerialization or our denial of their presence. That's when they operate with most effectiveness to the detriment of world peace, mutual respect, and mutual care. A short interlude exposing the practice of air quotes that snare "special" words is thus called for.

Under "physical attitudes to help delivery," James R. Arburger suggests, in his manual for voice acting, that

> [one] physical gesture that can make a big difference [...] is something commonly referred to as air quotes. When a word or phrase needs special emphasis or needs to be set apart from the rest of the copy, simply raise both hands and use your index and middle fingers to simulate making quotation marks in the air surrounding the words as you speak.
>
> (124)

Far from exclusive to acting, though, everyone nowadays is familiar with this practice and has probably indulged in it at one time or another. And while one might have a hard time imagining G.E.M. Anscombe performing the gesture to enhance an oral performance of her study of *De interpretatione*, §9, it's more than likely that people were already referring to "scare quotes" in the less formal domain of speech well before her inscription of the expression in the 1956 *Mind* article. What is unimaginable, however, is that air quotes preceded scare quotes. The very fact that in air quoting, the fingers of both hands raised imitate the printed punctuation marks is ample proof that scare quotes must have preceded their transposition off the page and into gesture.

Yet although air quotes are the pantomimic extension of scare quotes (which themselves are apparently a recently evolved convention of writing), ironic inverted commas had to have replaced earlier oral practices meant for the same purpose. Prime among these would be the application—attested in the *OED* as far back as the beginning of the nineteenth century—of the adjective *so-called* to the very same words or phrases one might today scare- or air-quote. In such contexts, "so-called" indicates that the noun, for example, thus modified by the speaker does not properly or appropriately represent (again, according to the speaker) the concept or thing the noun is meant to name. As long as "so-called" is there to signify this disqualification, the speaker is not so much engaging in the perversion of sense, but rather in denouncing it. Inversely, it is when such qualifiers as "so-called" or scare- or air-quotes *disappear* altogether that meaning begins to require vigilance and parsing so as to get to its root.

In our speech we know and use a number of equivalents to "so-called." "Alleged" might be used by lawyers, "purportedly" or "reportedly" by journalists, "putative" or "soi-disant" for those with a penchant for pedantry. But besides "so-called," the most commonly used disqualifying qualifier brought into speech is the "quote-unquote" pair. When held together in this way right in front (rather than "quote" at the beginning and "unquote" at the end) of whatever words or phrases the dyad modifies, "quote-unquote" has a withering effect on the legitimacy of said words or phrases. As Marjorie Garber puts it with delightfully dry understatement: "The mayor's quote-unquote dedication to duty means the speaker does not think the mayor is very dedicated" (13). In this example, it is the phrase "dedication to duty" that is under attack. Whose phrase could it be? Without saying as much, the speaker's disdainful "quote-unquote" leads us to deduce that it must be either the mayor or his sycophantic supporters who go on about a "dedication to duty" that those of *us* who know better find laughable. As for Stefano Predelli, our linguist at the heart of scare quote analysis, here is his example of a speaker (or writer's) supercilious stand-in for scare quotes: "this remarkable piece of so-called art consists of a large canvas covered with mud and old bus transfers" (16). Both Garber's and Predelli's examples, incidentally, point toward the *sneer* quote, which we will soon discuss. Given the centrality of *attachment* in Predelli's theory, it is refreshing and attaching, I dare add, when he uses these very expressions to serve the same function as scare quotes in certain circumstances: "I digress on certain important, only superficially unrelated issues pertaining to alleged devices of so-called conventional implicature and similar phenomena" (5).

These written or oral equivalents of air quotes are in some ways quite like what linguists call the "quotative *like.*" No one in the sphere where North American English holds sway can possibly be unaware of the massive (and massively irritating) overuse of "like" as an omnibus filler word. Some speakers interject it with seeming randomness as often as every three or four words. For addressees outside social circles where the practice is pervasive, this habit distracts decisively from capturing the speaker's actual intended meaning.

But the purpose served by "like" when it is used *quotably,* as linguists put it, is comparable to scare quoting in that it is an oral means by which the speaker may indicate that he is quoting speech by another speaker than himself. A whole dialogue may be reproduced in speech using the "quotative like." Consider the following summary of a conversation the speaker had with a third party:

> So I was like, that is like so uncool.
> And he's like, like, really?
> I'm like, duh!
> And he's like, look who's talking!

And so forth. The words I've reproduced following the "like" with a comma appended are represented as having been the content of the dialogical exchange reported. The subject pronoun modified by "like" identifies the speaker. We may note additionally that this substitute for "she stated," "he said," "they replied," and so on allows the person quoting a certain latitude in her reproduction of the exact words uttered in the exchange and even of the style or form in which they were pronounced. The "quotative like" announces without saying so that "this is a paraphrase."[11]

Continuing to bracket issues of chronological development, spoken equivalents of scare quotes are often supplemented, as we've said, by pairs of index fingers flexing in the air, as if to mimic the snaring of a word or phrase at the instant of its pronunciation. In agreement with Marjorie Garber, the gesture known as "air quotes" has become especially pervasive in academia. "How does one indicate that one is speaking in quotation?" Garber leadingly asks, adding, "Or, 'in quotation'?" as if mocking the obsessiveness of the punctuation expert community that she has joined.

> At scholarly conferences it has become conventional for a speaker to raise his or her hands above the shoulders and rapidly flex the first two fingers of each hand, miming the look of (American-style, double) quotation marks on the page. The effect is rather 'retro Rogers and Hammerstein' as one friend commented, this gesture always makes him think the speaker is auditioning for "Happy Talk."

For those readers who have forgotten or are not familiar with it, "Happy Talk" was a tune from the 1949 musical *South Pacific*, sung by Bloody Mary to Lt. Joe Cable with Liat, whom Cable courts, engaged in accompanying hand-gesture. There's a YouTube clip showing the air-quote-like motions made by France Nuyen in the role of Liat in the 1958 film version directed by Joshua Logan. Garber concludes these musings by wondering, "Do speakers from the British Isles, or others whose primary publication venue is Britain, gesture with single-finger quotation marks?" Since she leaves that question unanswered, I decided to ask several English and Irish people I know. They generally agreed that gestural practice is messy: despite the UK's prescribed use of *single* inverted commas in print for quoting, irony, and distancing, British and Irish practitioners of air quotes have recourse to double- or single-finger wiggles interchangeably, depending on the speaker's preference.

---

[11] This phenomenon is, in fact, considerably more varied and complex. "Like" may be used quotatively to express a feeling as well. See Ranger 2012.

What Garber leaves out of her hilarious romp, however, is the reciprocal effect of gesture and speech. The sign consisting of index and middle fingers of both hands being squeezed to produce air quotes not only proves that scare quotes are that sign's forebear but this genealogical succession also precludes any return influence of air quotes on scare quotes. Not the case in the relationship between air quotes and speech, which the former are designed to supplement. Air quotes not only introduce scare quotes to the theatricality of proffered communication but they also inflect it as well. "The mere gesture," Arburger writes, "almost forces you to say the words differently by separating them from the rest of the sentence with a distinctive shift of attitude" (124). The speaker may thus use his voice to demarcate the word or expression that in writing would have been set off by scare quotes. Brief guttural stops just before and just after may, for example, be combined with a slight rise or dip in pitch. What Garber dubs "the witchy gesture" impels such vocal strategies. That's why letting one's voice fall prey too often to encouragement from "the two-finger flex" (10–11) can prove detrimental to the effective delivery of speech: "excessive use of air quotes," warns the acting coach, "can result in a delivery that sounds choppy and artificial" (124).

As everyone knows, however, between what people *ought* to do and what people *actually* do, there is more often than not a gulf. Thus, the various vocal inflections that have proven successful in signaling irony, sarcasm, protestation, and so on do so with or without the gestural supplement known as air quotes. "We don't hear quotation marks themselves, as such," Peter Szendy has observed, "only in the effect their intonation has on other signs, in the differences they imprint on the pronunciation of the words they surround and demarcate" (53). Nor do we have to see them being aired for these effects to affect communication. To get themselves understood, the attitudes of distancing or disavowal listed earlier require neither the visible body nor the inscription of punctuation but only a bit of vocal virtuosity. "Implicit quotation-marking," by which Jonathan Rée meant implicit *scare-quoting*, "is typically performed by speaking the quoted material in an exaggeratedly fastidious, sniffy, arms-length voice, often with a lift at the end," not to be confused, by the way, with today's infinitely annoying pronunciation of affirmative sentences as if they were interrogatives ("uptalk" or HRT) and the speaker were unsure of everything he asserts, "especially," Rée continues, "in incredulous interrogative echoes such as Lady Bracknell's 'A handbag?' in *The Importance of Being Earnest*" (1043).

Quotes signaled with hand gestures or nonlinguistic vocal acts are not the only kind of scare quotes produced in speech. I can also modulate the tone of my voice to focus my interlocutor's attention to my skepticism with respect to the words thus inflected. If "uttering [an] expression with a particular tone" (Predelli 21) is the spoken equivalent to surrounding that expression with scare quotes, what about quotation marks more generally? Absolutely invisible as they may be in the many cases where rhetorical manipulation is at work, it has been demonstrated—and spectacularly by at least by one person— that all punctuation, including quotation marks, *may be* audible and *can* be vocalized.[12]

Let's consider further less-than-spectacular, mundane, yet still linguistic ways of indicating punctuation outside the written context. If we want commas, periods, question marks, and so on to appear on the screen when we dictate text into our "smart" phones, we can "tell" our e-appendages where to put them using their names. There's nothing so new in this practice. What's weird about it, however, is that when we do so, we are speaking to an electronic device rather than to a fellow species member. Dictation "back in the old days" required the same mediated or cumbersome procedure. But whether to a human secretary, a Dictaphone, or an iPhone, for punctuation to appear on the page, that last sentence would have to be pronounced thus: "Dictation quote back in the old days end quote required the same mediated or cumbersome procedure period."

So, what about the less-than-spectacular example that I just promised and for which Jonathan Rée gives the term: "punctuation-pronunciation" (1041)? Throughout the 1950s and beyond, an entertainer by the name of Victor Borge amused television and theatre audiences with a routine he developed during the Second World War.[13] An accomplished pianist, Victor Borge (born Børge

---

[12] I stress these modal verbs to mark difference with this statement by Peter Szendy: "Like other punctuation marks, quotation marks are inaudible and cannot be vocalized per se" (53).

[13] "Vaudeville Reviews—Roxy, New York." *Billboard*, April 29, 1944. Nielsen Business Media, Inc. p. 25 (accessed via Google Books, July 7, 2019).

Rosenbaum in Denmark) managed to flee hopelessly Nazified Europe for the United States in 1940. Having already begun to mix jokes—linguistic and musical—with his keyboard virtuosity, Borge elaborated on these, all the while learning English, in which he would quickly excel.

One of the more memorable of Victor Borge's shticks was one he would eventually refer to as "Phonetic Punctuation." I remember being delighted as a kid each time I'd see and hear this routine on our black-and-white TV. While no longer quite the youth I was, I still am (delighted). In one version that anyone can easily find on YouTube, Borge, speaking directly into and close to a camera (instead of on a stage or a television set), explains part of his system:

> Punctuation marks can be very confusing. That is why I've invented a way in which we can *hear* punctuation marks as well as see them. And here's how it works. A period sounds like this: "pwt." An exclamation point is a straight line with a period underneath: "fssss–pwt." And here's a comma: "klkik." Quotation marks are two commas: "klkuk–klkik." Or, if you happened to be left-handed, "klkik–klkuk." Question mark is rather difficult: "klklklkik–pwt."

With such a system established, it's fairly easy to guess at how Borge translated the remaining punctuation "phonetically." When applied to the reading of a text, as Borge did with deadpan application and concomitant gestures, the result on listeners is drop-dead hilarity. But while punctuation, under such treatment, *does not disappear* (far from it: it's actually even more obtrusive than when we dictate), a system such as this is neither "phonetic," as Borge put it, nor "pronounced," as Rée put it. I'm not sure the phonetic alphabet can better suggest to the mind's ear the sounds that I attempted in my quotes in the above transcription. And I'm not the first to have tried. For Marjorie Garber, "Borge's quotation marks were two commas (squeaky pop; squeaky pop)" (13), while for Rée, his apostrophe suggests "squeeeoch" (1042). Although any of us produce them, none of the sounds in Borge's system can be identified as extant onomatopoeias, like moo or woof. Unlike hiss or pish or Bronx cheer, the English language doesn't even have names for them. Neither utterances nor enunciative acts, Borge's *oral* punctuation marks are, more primitively, articulations that fail to rise to linguistic standing. Yet, as I have suggested, together and in application, they *do* form a system of equivalences for *written* punctuation marks.

As far as Rée knew in 1990, what he called punctuation-pronunciation had "not yet [been] elevated to the status of sociolinguistic concept" (1041). I'm still not sure it has. But among the shadings of scare quoting between their starkly black appearance on the white page and their total disappearance, punctuation-pronunciation constitutes a fascinating variant. While not as ethereal or fickle as air quotes—even as an Oulipean oddity—"klkuk–klkik [discursive content scare quoted] klkik–klkuk" is destined to never catch on. Rather, Victor Borge's voiced quotation marks will remain a wholly theoretical possibility in further studies of the sociological, political, and ethical ramifications of scare quoting.

I'll be the first to admit to a rather limited grasp of deconstruction. But I would be remiss in closing this interlude setting the stage for scare quotes' disappearing acts if I didn't note that they seem to me to exemplify and, I dare say, *embody* certain preoccupations essential to Jacques Derrida's methodological endeavor. It's pretty clear that from the very start, with concepts like arche-writing, supplement, and *différance*, quotation marks in general, meant, as they are, to set semantic nodes off from the rest of discourse, serve as signposts in deconstructive knots. "It's the law of quotation marks," wrote Derrida reflecting on the "spectacular" absence of scare quotes to set off *spirit* when Heidegger writes the term in his *Introduction to Metaphysics* of 1935:

> Two by two they stand guard: at the frontier or before the door, assigned to the threshold in any case, and these places are always dramatic. The apparatus lends itself to theatricalization, and also to the hallucination of the stage and its machinery: two pairs of pegs hold in suspension a sort of drape, a veil or a curtain. Not closed, just slightly open.
>
> (31)

As punctuation, scare quotes appear to be rather unique in the varied and persistent ways that their written form has been mimicked verbally and, more generally, with bodily gestures. These social or communicational phenomena tend to vindicate Derrida's otherwise counterintuitive (Searle called it "breathtakingly implausible") claim that writing preceded speech. In the case of these tiny flecks of writing that I am inflating into a major discursive phenomenon, the form of inscription on the page irrefutably inspired air quotes and their vocalized variations—whether as "quote-unquote" or "klkuk-klkik [...] klkik–klkuk."

Like any phenomenon of language, scare quotes developed organically. Bereft of prescriptive rules to set them out and resistant to any that might rein them in, their users have made of them what they will. As the drive to truth flounders and semantic perversion gains ground in today's world of manipulative rhetoric, the use, misuse, and abuse of scare quotes constitute a barometer by which we may read these changes. But they must in some fashion be *perceptible* for this instrument to serve. Unfortunately, as hypocrisy and deception advance, scare quotes are eschewed and the critical gauge becomes useless for lack of raw data. Meanwhile, the most noble of rhetorical tools—irony—withers. Fewer and fewer bold invocations of scare quotes are deployed for the sake of critique. Thus, if we are to preserve our ability to read and hear their effect and thereby keep the will to truth glimmering, we need to gain awareness of the ways in which they depart from writing into gesture and voice. Nothing even requires that their purpose—whether it be distancing or, abusively, emphasis—be signaled by quotation marks.

On the cusp of a section bearing the title ~~scare quotes~~, one additional defining practice of the Derridean enterprise comes to mind. Whereas scare quotes may, as we have seen, be used by the writer to indicate disagreement with the word or words enclosed by them, deconstruction, following Martin Heidegger's practice, would draw a line through them, thereby placing them "under erasure" while allowing the reader to see words under protest: inadequate, that is, but necessary. In the tradition that Friedrich Nietzsche inaugurated with "On Truth and Lies in the Extra-Moral Sense," this was Derrida's way of asserting the deficiency of terms like *truth* or *freedom* with respect to their supposed referent or the semantic and ethical inappropriateness of a term like *man* or *human*. In writing "scare quotes," then cancelling out the term, I, on the other hand, am asserting the dogged persistence and pervasiveness of the effects that they have been conventionally assigned, but without their *witting* or, more likely, *unwitting* practitioners bothering to make them visible or invoking them any longer.

~~scare quotes~~

*In every punctuation mark thoughtfully avoided, writing pays homage to
the sound it suppresses.*

—Theodor Adorno, "Punctuation Marks" (305)[14]

As we have seen, scare quotes emerged as a subset of quotation marks to serve the specific and specialized purposes that have been described thus far. Yet today, and with increasing frequency, they fail to appear either on the page or in the air. This disappearing act or act of omission is disorienting for the addressee unless her critical faculties are ever watchful. When on May 19, 1944, a neighbor related to Klemperer that "a German broadcast had confusedly but clearly announced that 'landings' had taken place on the west coast," systematic skepticism with respect to every single word emerging from the Nazi propaganda machine compelled him to apply scare quotes when noting this otherwise good piece of news (II:316; II:419).[15]

Scare quoting evolved out of the vast and varied world of quotation, whereas the now-familiar hashtag is a new adaptation of the pound or number sign. Though slightly "older" in this respect than the marker of metadata, the scare quote is nevertheless among the more recent functions attributed to an already existing sign of punctuation. Perhaps for this reason or perhaps because the scare quote foists distancing functions on a sign of punctuation that came to be enshrined in the venerable history of word *attribution* or perhaps, again, because its written form cleaves so closely to its oral and gestural manifestations, the purposes that the scare quote gets assigned are multiple, disparate, tending to the nebulous, the inconsistent. Worse still, since no rules—like those mobilized by the plagiarism taboo—underpin scare quotes, their practitioners may be negligent or even devious in their application. Putting your scare quotes on display reveals your game strategy. Withdrawn or relegated to the unnecessary, absent for whatever reason—conscious or

---

[14]These are the final words of Adorno's essay.

[15]Unconfirmed still two days later, Klemperer again inflects the keyword with the punctuation tool: "The news of the 'landings' in the West was again mistaken" (II:317; II:420).

unconscious—scare quoting promiscuously spreads beyond its usual domain. Under erasure, scare quotes may partake of any number of mendacious or manipulative semantic strategies.

When speakers or writers bring euphemisms, epithets, insults, slurs, or policyspeak, circumlocution, buzzwords, or weasel words into the forum of communication, unadorned by inverted commas, their deleterious effect on society, their insidiously inhuman work is redoubled. At least when scare quotes are present, the addressee is alerted to the possibility that one of these functions might be in play and that she can, consequently, adjust her understanding of the addressor's intended meaning. For the German who is a "Jew" in the eyes of eugenicist ideologues, the very word "German" becomes a lens for foreseeing an immediate future when the diarist "received a magazine with a swastika on the cover: 'The Care of the German Cat'" (I:96; I:131). The maddeningly ludicrous notion of an "Aryan" cat makes for horrified despair when the Klemperers must by Nazi decree euthanize their beloved Muschel.[16] When bunk, bullshit, buzzwords, or fuzzwords are launched incognito, without scare quotes to announce themselves, evaluating their ethical import requires redoubled critical ardor. Absent the characteristic wiggling inverted commas, we risk taking key terms at face value. In anticipation of this book's final chapters, "value" and "evaluation" need to be invoked already because this situation is not unlike that to which late nineteenth- and early twentieth-century thinkers raised alarm: namely, that while Capital relentlessly devalues the human, ensuring the compliance of its voluntary slaves, the victory of the inhuman is being proclaimed in the language of Capital's management.

Whether in print or gestured in the air, the scare quotes I mainly discussed in the first two sections all have in common the fact that they *appear*. But what about scare quotes *without* punctuation, *devoid of* vocal variant or *absent* hand gestures? What's going on when they disguise themselves or flat out hide? As potential receptors of discourse in our every waking minute, we're inevitably struck by certain words spoken or written that *ought to have been* inflected

---

[16] 15 May 1942. "Frau Ida Kreidl, whom I met while I was shopping, reported the latest decree, she then showed it to us in the *Jewish Community Newspaper*: Jews with the star and anyone who lives with them are, with immediate effect, forbidden to keep pets. [...] This is the death sentence for Muschel" (II:52).

by the little guys. Without getting into the business of prescription, one could nevertheless say that the honest scare quote player lays the inverted commas on the table, whereas the dishonest one puts on a poker face. And it's these practitioners who perversely, through their ruse, come out the winners in the semantic game.

If scare quotes no longer appear on the page, are no longer seen signed with flexing fingers, no longer vocally conjured by "quote-unquote" or "so-called," then how do we nevertheless know they're there? This is a job for the *Übermensch* of our time: the Critical Watch. For far from being a worse situation than any scare quote plague, the tendency to forego scare quoting, their very placement in hypocritical quarantine, constitutes the supreme challenge for critical thinking and possible consequent action. Was it not precisely sleuthing, sniffing out, and exposing manipulative linguistic material under ~~scare quotes~~ that most excited and drove Friedrich Nietzsche, that lover of all new ideas inflected by "*perhaps* [*vielleicht*]" who dreamt of a philosophy of quotation marks—*eine Philosophie der Gänsefüßchen*, as he called it?[17]

Molière understood this behavior and this wish. Consider, for a moment, *Les Précieuses ridicules* and Magdelon's rebuke to her father, referring to a marriage contract, that "nothing could be more hucksterish [*Marchand*] than such a procedure" (9).[18] This is an example, among dozens, not only of her and her cousin Cathos's unwillingness to use direct language—*contract*, for example, instead of "such a procedure"—but also of the distancing effect that users of scare quotes would apply to words like "hucksterish" today.[19] (It's also notable that, in print, "Marchand" is capitalized, yet in spoken delivery Molière no doubt had his actor inflect the word in a special way to indicate Magdelon's repugnance at its significance and extended implication.) Molière showed, by example, the complexity involved when the function that we assign today to

---

[17]"[…] eine Einsiedler-Philosophie, wenn sie selbst mit einer Löwenklaue geschrieben wäre, würde doch immer wie eine Philosophie der 'Gänsefüßchen' aussehen." *Die Fragmente von Frühjahr 1884 bis Herbst 1885*, Band 5—Kapitel 13; Nachlaß, Juni–Juli 1885 37 [5]. And on Nietzsche's predilection for the adverb, perhaps, see Derrida, *The Politics of Friendship*.

[18]Among English translations are the titles *Two Precious Maidens Ridiculed* and *The High-Brow Ladies*. I have used Morris Bishop's 1957 version of *The Precious Damsels*.

[19]"Encore un coup mon père, il ne se peut rien de plus Marchand que ce procédé, et j'ai mal au cœur de la seule vision que cela me fait" (10).

scare quotes is active. Again, in *Les Précieuses ridicules*, through the bantering discourse of Mascarille, we learn that holding bare meaning at arm's length can be a matter of intensity. Finally, as ridiculous, at one level, as Magdelon and Cathos are meant to appear, at another (which accounts for Molière's enduring pertinence), the ostensibly frivolous female cousins are in fact standard bearers for a feminist agenda. Magdelon may, in declaring that "the mere thought of it makes me sick to my stomach" (9), hold the "hucksterish" qualifier at a distance as if air quotes were indeed aired; she boldly and emphatically denounces Gorgibus's plans that would take women for chattel.

As Theodor Roosevelt once pointedly reminded people in reference to Woodrow Wilson's use of the twisted circumlocution "compulsion of the spirit of America" that he had concocted to stand for universal military training, the weasel "sucks all the meat out of an egg, leaving it an empty shell." Roosevelt, however, wasn't quite as original as this slam might make him appear. Aligning weasels with words by the analogy of eggs goes back, as Marjorie Garber reminds us, to Jaques in *As You Like It*.[20] However, leaving the sucking of eggs to actual weasels, adding scare quotes to terms like "tragedy" and "neoliberalism" (to whose attention I will turn mainly in a later chapter) could prove a significant step in the direction of reviving "viable resistance" to these shams. Yet, one might ask, why *should* we resist and why *should* we try to implement egalitarian alternatives to the way things are? The answer, this book is meant to pound away at, is that capitalism, now in (or perhaps beyond[21]) its neoliberal avatar, is one of the main contributors to the anthropogenic destruction that looms.

The other major contributor to the march we are on to the earth's next great die-off is our stubborn attachment to *belief* rather than a responsible and critical espousal of *science*.[22] All criminal ideologies—classism, racism, misogyny, speciesism—are founded either on the successor of superstition that we call "belief" or else on pseudoscience. Fake science and faith amount to the same thing: neither finds foundation in fact. Fake science and faith

---

[20]Cf. Garber 2001, 141. The pertinent quote from Shakespeare is, "I can suck melancholy out of a song, as a weasel sucks eggs." *As You Like It*, Act 2, Scene 5.

[21]This would be the argument laid out by Yanis Varoufakis in *Technofeudalism* (2023).

[22]See my critique of this problem in Harvey 2020.

traffic in the semantic perversion of which the disappearance of scare quotes is one of the premier indicators.

If ever scare quotes *do* get added to words inappropriately used, it is the Critical Watch who carries out this lucid and corrective operation—never the person who misuses them. Case in point: Ivanka Trump being interviewed in April 2017 by Gayle King and announcing to the world an altogether original definition of the word "complicit." King leads in with paraphrased hearsay, then elicits Trump's reaction with, "You hear the phrase 'complicit,' that 'Jared and Ivanka are "complicit" in what is happening to the White House.' Can you just weigh in on how you feel about that? [...] What do you think about that accusation?" After a prolonged pause that drips "careful pondering," Trump provides this "clever" answer: "If being complicit is wanting to ..."—here Trump turns away from King, searching mightily for the "right" words—"... is wanting to be a force for good and [squinting with seriousness] wanting to have a positive impact and to make a positive impact [cut to pained look on interviewer], then [leans forth, performs petulant back-and-forth-of-the-head-to-drill-forth-the-point and suddenly accelerated pronunciation] I'm complicit." She then babbles on a bit, extolling the "unique situation" in which she finds herself then—incredibly—says, "I don't know what it means to be—um—complicit, but [...]."[23]

She sure doesn't. And, among other things, that's because her putative mind missed the scare quotes with which her interlocutor inflected the word. Any careful listener of that exchange "hears" them. After airing a clip of this choice moment in the interview, Stephen Colbert commented: "Nope, that's not what complicit means." Colbert's set crew then handed him an *Oxford Dictionary*, from which he "reads," then *reads*: "Collaborationist, cowardly ... Here we go: *complicit.* 'Involved with others in an illegal activity or wrongdoing.'" Then resumes "reading": "Oh wait, it does have: 'being a force for good and having a positive impact' under 'complicit—comma—total opposite of.'" And then, in one of his paradigmatic analogies to demonstrate his point by absurdity: "You can't just reverse the definition to make yourself sound better! That's like

---

[23] "CBS This Morning." April 5, 2017. https://www.youtube.com/watch?v=Cw0xln927lc (accessed January 3, 2019).

saying 'If being a Nazi means fighting for civil rights, then yeah, I'm a huge Nazi.'"[24]

Ivanka's father, of course, plies trade in deceptive and deviant discourse meant to pass for face value. Here—just to remind us of that semantic nightmare—are a couple of examples with scare quotes *added* for the sake of reader sanity: that President ordered US troops pulled out of Syria because ISIS had been "defeated"; also, that President claimed to be the "least racist" person anyone has met; and so forth. These examples in what seems, still today, to be an infinite sanity-challenging series are all reminiscent of the sabotage of meaning in grocers' quotes like "'lamb chops' on sale." While fantastic misnomers and devious appropriations are rife in the era of post-truth, they are far from new, however, to political geography. Every school kid knows the enticing example of Greenland (which that President once attempted to buy), whose massive ice sheet belied its true nature, inspiring Erik the Red, who hoped thereby to attract settlers, to lend it that name without divulging his deception with scare quotes. "America" itself is a challenge to the power of scare quotes. The United States occupies less than a fourth of the western hemisphere landmass that extends from the Arctic to Tierra del Fuego. Yet the United States continues to try to lay exclusive claim to being designated "America," the land of "Americans." This is why US nationals are respectfully (and far more precisely) referred to in Latin America as *estadounidenses*. In fact, just as "Americans" ought more precisely to refer to themselves more appropriately as "Unitedstateseans," the United States is not even the only nation in the Americas composed of states united or federated: *los Estados Unidos Mexicanos* and *a República Federativa do Brasil* spring to mind.

One final term calling for scare quotes that hardly ever come is *tragedy*. Tragedy, as it is relentlessly and mindlessly used today in the United States, is an egregious case of absent scare quotes that impede paths to a sane polity. With studied neutrality,[25] Terry Eagleton writes that "[f]or most people today,

---

[24]*The Late Show with Stephen Colbert*, April 6, 2017. https://www.youtube.com/watch?v=qDWlMi14qu Y&feature=youtu.be (accessed January 3, 2019).

[25]In his justified and Herculean efforts to take "remarkably well-educated" "exponents of tragic theory" to task for ignoring "real-life tragedy," Eagleton glosses over the *preventability* of much of what passes for "tragedy in life."

tragedy means an actual occurrence, not a work of art. Indeed, some of those who nowadays use the word of actual events are probably unaware that it has an artistic sense at all" (14). Somewhere in the vicinity of euphemism or weasel word, "tragedy" misnames perfectly *preventable* horrific events that members of our species inflict on each other. But viable and implementable means toward preventive measures are emasculated by its pervasive and abusive invocation. As an example, among thousands, on May 14, 2019, a police officer in Baytown, Texas, shot an unarmed Pamela Turner five times after she resisted arrest and whacked him in the groin with his Taser. On recorded tape, Turner could be clearly heard repeatedly pleading, "I'm pregnant." "Confirming" (my scare quotes, since the autopsy report was never released) that Turner, contrary to her dying claim, was not pregnant, Lt. Steve Dorris nevertheless marshalled the "empathy" to excrete the pat statement: "It's a tragic event for everybody involved." With cookie-cutter banality, thousands of times a year, this automatism of "tragic" serves a double purpose: as in the statement just cited, it reinforces the absolute vacuousness of statements made to the victim's survivors and it attempts to render immediate extra-judiciary justice by exonerating the officer of any crime, transforming him into a poor soul ("everybody involved" includes him) who would be forever haunted by the horror. If that weren't enough, Dorris crowned his pronouncement with a weaselly variant of the pat and oxymoronic "thoughts and prayers": "Of course, our hearts go out to the family of the deceased as well as our officer." No scare quotes anywhere in any of this abject hypocrisy repeated, as I just said, thousands of times a year.

Aristotle developed his *Poetics* based on an analysis of a theatrical genre the Athenians called the "goat song," or tragedy. Taking in such representations of some legendary person's *inevitable* misfortune relieved audience members, Aristotle contended, of some of their day-to-day anxieties. He called this relief "catharsis." In today's United States, massacres of innocent citizens by firearm are considered quintessential "tragedies." That's what the hand wringers call it nearly every time one of these eminently *preventable* events occurs. No scare quotes alert the newsreader or the newslistener that the speaker or journalist is using the term advisedly or as a deviant metaphor. Remembering Aristotle, it is as if cop killings of unarmed people and massacres at the hands of "depressed loners" were driven by "fate," as if behind them were something like the blind stubbornness of a Creon or an Oedipus. Since scare quotes were lent that name when a Cambridge philosopher applied them to one of Aristotle's more arcane expressions, is it not ironic that the honor of this first thinker to inspire their use is not preserved by having them added to *tragedy* when tragedy's meaning is perverted?

Oddly, the press did not-so-systematically refer to the Valentine's Day massacre at Marjory Stoneman Douglas High School as a "tragedy." This might have become a sign that the Unitedstatesian willful self-deception about gun violence was drawing to a long-overdue close. Either that or that episodes with so many victims are just too horrific to file under the weasel category. As anyone who thinks knows, mass murders perpetrated with automatic weapons owned by socially isolated individuals—invariably white males— equipped with enough ammunition to carry out one-man wars are anything but tragedies. Yet to call such episodes *such* lulls everyone into thinking they are irremediable. This all-too-common manipulation of a perfectly good word is quite simply perverse.

These terms and phrases operate as what Victor Klemperer termed *mendacious euphemisms*. The use and abuse of scare quotes was one of the symptoms of that dimension of Nazi perversion cultivated in the fertile field of a massively compliant and largely passive population. In order to reinforce deceitfulness and ensure nefarious effect, such euphemisms must *at all costs* avoid scare quoting. Klemperer writes that "the stereotypical LTI wording reads: 'a tragic misfortune resulted in their forfeiting their lives ...'" (128). Is it not fortuitous for reinforcing the centrality of "tragedy" among examples of un-scare-quoted rhetorical operators that the Nazis' cynical circumlocution for dying uselessly is ruthlessly deemed "a tragic misfortune"? Based on this paradigmatic example, Klemperer pursues his invaluable critique: "Here my revision book registers the mendacious euphemism which played such an immense role in the make-up of the LTI" (128).

In the domain of historical fiction, Hans Fallada's 1947 novel, *Jeder stirbt für sich allein—Every Man Dies Alone—*is comparably important to Klemperer's treatise for understanding language and resistance in those horrific years under the jackboot. Fallada recounts the story of Otto and Anna Quangel, who busy themselves crafting carefully worded postcards that lambast the dictatorship and even, eventually, call for acts of resistance.[26] They only begin doing so, however, after receiving an administrative letter, driven by the same fake and empty empathy of "tragedy" misused, announcing that their beloved only son, Ottochen (little Otto), had been killed in combat. The letter reads, "died a hero's death for his Führer and his People."[27] Such boilerplate pays lip service to the elevation of hapless cannon fodder to the status of hero, when in fact all it's really about is propping up the ego of the monstrous maniac in charge. A "hero's death" can thus be seen as yet another example of the particularly pernicious practice of withholding scare quotes that Klemperer so aptly named the mendacious euphemism.

The mendacious euphemism truly deserves its place as a distinct category perversely participating in the scare quote universe. Klemperer found it operating everywhere in the discourse of the Third Reich:

> you were not imprisoned but "off travelling [*verreist*]"; you were not in a *Konzentrationslager*, and not in the KZ, to use the customary abbreviation, but rather in the "*Konzertlager.*" The verb *melden* [to present oneself] acquired a horrible new meaning. "He has to present himself" means he has been summoned to the Gestapo. And presenting oneself in this way was always associated with mistreatment, and increasingly with a one-way journey.
>
> (2013, 190)

Standing up proudly against the Nazi abuse of scare quotes, their mendacious euphemisms, and, by extension, their criminality was one Berlin worker in particular whom Klemperer had met before writing *LTI* and whose authentic heroics he said inspired him to pursue his analysis of semantic perversion. To Klemperer's question as to why she and her daughters had been imprisoned by the Gestapo, she replied in a simple circumlocution inflected by her *berlinisch* pronunciation: "Well, 'cos of certain expressions [*wejen Ausdrücken*]" (2013, 293). Those expressions that landed this tough Berliner in the cooler were

---

[26]Fallada based his novel on the actual story of Otto and Elise Hampel.

[27]*Dass er den Heldentod gestorben ist für seinen Führer und sein Volk* (14). I restored the two possessives and opted for the less alliterative but more literal "People" instead of "Fatherland."

her own, unadorned by scare quotes. They were insults hurled at the "Führer"—that egomaniacal metonymy for the criminal institutions and actors that made up the Third Reich. She may have thrust tongue into cheek with the coy "*wejen Ausdrücken*"; she had stood by those expressions, refusing to distance herself from them, even though they cost her her freedom and could easily have cost her her life.

As for the Jewish philologist who miraculously survived the Nazi era, the canny Berliner's resistance against that very same totalitarianism—resistance predicated on unabashed verbal expression—proved to be nothing less than the inspiration for converting the *Tagesbücher* into *LTI*:

> For me this was the revelation. It was this word that made me see clearly. 'Cos of certain expressions. That was the why and the wherefore of my setting to work on the diaries. I wanted to separate the balancing pole from the mass of other things, and just sketch in the hands that held it. That is how this book came about, less out of conceit, I hope, than 'cos of certain expressions.
>
> (293)

Taking to heart Jean-François Lyotard's call for us to become Critical Watches, one of the "corpses" that we must open up, to turn anatomist Xavier Bichat's admonishment[28] into a metaphor for the implementation of a *praxis*, is the body of language ravaged by semantic perversion. We must undertake this procedure in order to see if we can begin to restore language to life, to see and hear it for what it is. As horizon for semantic and rhetorical inventiveness, short of the illusion of integral truth, the establishment and maintenance of *some* justice, at the very least, would contribute fundamentally and emphatically to the possibility of a human-dominated world of which we might finally be proud.

sneer quotes

Out of the depths of this age of "alternate truth" have come more sinister variants of the scare quote than the cynical cases of their retraction foreground.

---

[28]Cf. Michel Foucault, *The Birth of the Clinic*. Translated by Alan Sheridan. London: Tavistock Publications, Ltd., 1973, chapter 8, "Open up a Few Corpses."

Exposure to ambient weasel words can conjure up a panorama of sarcasm. Feigning to address herself to one of Donald J. Trump's favorite *bêtes noires*, Arwa Mahdawi writes: "As you may have noticed, racism died out a long time ago—now people just say racially tinged or racially charged things or stumble into 'race controversies.' Sometimes they make 'inflammatory statements' or, if they're Roseanne, they take Ambien and suffer unfortunate racist-like side-effects—but they're not really racist."[29] We notice, first off, that the author generously applies the punctuation pincers called for when the speaker wishes to signal her distance from certain expressions. What group would appeal to expressions like "race controversies" and "inflammatory statements"?— Certainly not people who demonstrate with their everyday acts and speech that racism still thrives today and live, most probably, right next door. No: people who use such equivocal language believe at their core that racism, if not "dead a long time ago," is now somehow attenuated to the point of innocuousness. If racism still exists, such people contend, it no longer impels murder. The group Arwa Mahdawi mocks, of course, are the so-called progressives who perpetuate racism by other means, but just as effectively as white supremacists.

This opinion piece by Arwa Mahdawi was published in *The Guardian*. The author, as one would expect, also takes those who are patently racist to task as well. After all, the title of her parody of an open letter to the Congresswoman representing New York's fourteenth district is "Sorry Alexandria Ocasio-Cortez, your 'minority privilege' is no longer secret." In the US vocabulary of white supremacy, "minority privilege" holds pride of place alongside "socialized medicine," "single mothers," and so forth. Using linguist Stefano Predelli's analysis, we can say that "signaling her distance from such characterization[s]," Arwa Mahdawi's "use of quotation marks is accompanied by a sarcastic intent" (3). The only person Mahdawi is *not* lambasting is the letter's addressee. She is the one tasked by Mahdawi to evaluate the scare quotes and act on the basis of sober critique. What is complex, courageous, and critically useful about exercises like this is that they expose racism's perpetuity not only among

---

[29] Arwa Mahdawi, "Sorry Alexandria Ocasio-Cortez, Your 'Minority Privilege' Is No Longer Secret." *The Guardian*, January 20, 2019. https://www.theguardian.com/us-news/2019/jan/18/alexandria-ocasio-cortez-fox-news-minority-privilege (accessed January 20, 2019).

outright racists but also among so-called progressive elements complacent in their privilege and hypocrisy. Both groups ply their discursive trade in weasel words: one maliciously, the other with a nasty brew of diffidence and naivety. The combined effect is the persistent malignancy of racism and classism.

Arwa Mahdawi's double-barreled sarcasm by means of scare quotes does not quite perfectly exemplify the announced subject of this section, but almost. Intense sarcasm could, in fact, be considered the last rampart of decency before a descent into semantic perversion. Bringing back the practice of the purloined scare quote examined in previous sections, let us now, for a moment, consider the way some culture critics use certain expressions to attribute blame for the state of the world today. By doing so, we will begin to cross the threshold into the realm of the sneer quote. My first example drives an ideological position paper on the very object of this chapter: the scare quote. In an article on what she snarkily labels "Post-Sokalian Genre Theory," Swiss-US "independent scholar," Marie-Laure Ryan sees scare quotes as nothing less than the symptom par excellence of the "largely non-empirical treatment of human issues found in postmodern theory" (829, n. 23). One can feel the intensity of the snarling scare quotes hovering invisibly around several items here: "non-empirical," "human," and of course, the catch-all culprit, "postmodern theory." Her conclusion is lapidary: "As long as postmodern theory denies any validity to the concept of truth as correspondence, it will remain without impact on the practice of science" (828).

No doubt already an unfortunate choice of term when Jean-François Lyotard's report focused attention on it, "postmodernism" became and still is, to a certain extent, the catch-all scapegoat for everyone from reactionaries to critical thinkers who spend a lot of valuable time feeling guilty about their academic associations.[30] With perhaps less disdain than Ryan but all the superciliousness, Lee McIntyre couldn't be more emphatic about the blame "postmodernism" carries for the triumph of mendacity in the Trump era. For his first foray into this argument, he convokes another critic to express his

---

[30]I attempt to unravel this misunderstanding in "Jean-François Lyotard" in Michael Groden, Martin Kreiswirth, and Imre Szeman, eds. *Johns Hopkins Guide to Literary Theory and Criticism*, 2nd edition. Baltimore: Johns Hopkins University Press, 2004, pp. 618–21 and elsewhere.

position: "Stephen Marche argued that 'the post-truth condition,' in which Trumpism has flourished, has its roots in left-wing satire" (73). Satire from this sector—this "wing" as it were—is clearly seen as the product of the French theory industry and its putative sway over humanities programs in US institutions of higher learning. This is a routine procedure in the left's endless and breathless mea culpa for the ills they believe they fomented in the era of feverish theory. But then, some fifty pages on, in a bold blame-the-victim twist extending over a full fifteen pages (133–48), McIntyre details the anatomy of the nefarious tree of "right-wing postmodernism" that grew from those "roots in left-wing satire," bearing the fruit of the post-truth crisis.

These two examples (among dozens) are of course opinions—neither fact nor falsehood. In their formulation, scare quotes are sometimes employed, visibly, and sometimes not. It would of course be helpful to the extreme if the presence or absence of scare quotes were to indicate to third parties on which side of the divide between truth and lying writers and speakers positioned themselves. But that is not the case and, I fear, never will be. Though a supplement to words, scare quotes—whether actual or virtual—require interpretation as much as the utterances they inflect. With sneer quotes, we move away from a communicational economy where language and reasoning inform decision into one where emotion and prejudice dominate. Sneer quotes are scare quotes situated on the snider side of the moral spectrum of intents. The term "sneer quotes" might substitute for "scare quotes" when, rather than the subtly noble distancing of irony or the cruder distancing involved in sarcasm, the purpose of the punctuation is to jeer, slight, or scorn. With sneer quotes, we enter the dark dimension of cynicism.

While it might seem obsessively facile to keep bringing the bane of our recent political life into this discussion, the twit formerly tweeting from the White House toilet inadvertently demonstrated the complexity of scare quotes. There, I suppose I've just done it myself: to designate this aberration to beat all aberrations, I've just produced an epithet in the form of an alliterative periphrasis that perhaps, after all, deserves sneer quotes. This is not so unlike the way "progressives" and "intellectual" snobs snub the less sophisticated with expressions of their caviar-laced disdain; I too am perhaps succumbing to the temptation to denigrate. Is my "tweeting twit" analogous to the following snottily outrageous comment from a "respected" French philosopher in reaction to the news that a couple of reporters got verbally roughed up and pushed around a bit by a few *gilets jaunes* demonstrators: "The power in dictatorships locks up, tortures and kills journalists; in some democracies, like France, there is a self-declared 'people' who take care of this."[31] I hope not. Returning to Trump, however, when ideological tripe right and left becomes equally bankrupt, we can learn a great deal about this perverse world of the scare quote by recalling some of that uncritical, mindless, angry ranting devoid of grammar and syntax (let alone "proper" punctuation) that was excreted over those all-too-recent four years. Indeed, daily doses of Trump talk were what got me to the tipping point where I felt the irrepressible need to study the practice—both successful and failed—of the sneer quote.

In Trump Era I, it was easy to think that the cynically named "alternative facts" and "fake news" were new to national politics, but as *The New York Times* was already reporting in 1976, when Ronald Reagan was jumping on the "welfare queen" bandwagon to drive his campaign to victory, "The 'welfare queen' item in Mr. Reagan's repertoire is one of several that seem to be at odds with the facts. The former California Governor fairly bristles with what he calls facts, figures and statistics demonstrating what he thinks is wrong with welfare, Big Government and the United States."[32] Trump's bugaboo of "fake news" and Kellyanne Conway's audacious "alternative facts" gambit were themselves wonderful examples of bullshit emanating from twisted minds and snarling mouths of US populism. Bullshit producers never apply sneer quotes to their bullshit. We do. We do this in acts of instantaneous critical readjustment. When Conway excreted hers during the infamous January 22, 2017, *Meet the Press* interview in defending then-White-House-Press-Secretary Sean Spicer's

---

[31]Tweeted by Raphaël Enthoven on January 12, 2019. https://twitter.com/Enthoven_R/status/1084186392782036992 (accessed January 19, 2019). Danièle Sallenave was roundly mocked when with the publication of *Jojo le gilet jaune* she had the audacity not only to defend the grassroots movement but, especially, to denounce the classist disdain with which it was generally received by her fellow intellectuals.

[32]"'Welfare Queen' Becomes Issue in Reagan Campaign." *The New York Times*, February 15, 1976. https://www.nytimes.com/1976/02/15/archives/welfare-queen-becomes-issue-in-reagan-campaign-hitting-a-nerve-now.html (accessed August 5, 2019).

lies about crowd attendance at Trump's inauguration, an already shell-shocked public and press applied scare quotes to the expression as if their very sanity depended on it.

The introduction of a foreign word may be implemented to amplify the sneer of insult while deflecting responsibility for it toward an *alien* language. This procedure should not be confused, incidentally, with George W. Bush's famous (and possibly apocryphal) lament that "the problem with the French is that they don't have a word for entrepreneur." Speaking of the French, though, when a French speaker's impulse is to denigrate, but she senses that an obviously Gallic utterance might gall, she also may conjure up a foreign term—usually one from English. Whether scare quoted or not, the alien (but not alienating) term is salient and corrosive, as if italicized. But mostly, it stands as an attempt to shift blame onto a concept from "over there" for any offense perceived or taken "here." By the way, "to distance," in German, is *entfremden*—literally "to make foreign." I'll have more to say in a moment about German and scare-quoted foreign words. Back to the French, though, and the adoption of a foreign word to carry out little crimes: in May 2018, then French Secretary for European Affairs, Nathalie Loiseau, caused a stir in the Senate when she claimed that migrants from Africa had the luxury of conducting what she sneeringly termed "asylum shopping" [*shopping de l'asile*].[33] Loiseau was immediately taken to task by Green Party senator, Esther Benbassa, who took the floor at the National Assembly, saying that "there's indeed a crisis in welcoming, of which you've given an example by referring to 'shopping.'" Commonly used by the French well-to-do instead of "*courses*" or "*faire des courses*" to mark their distinction from the hoi polloi, Loiseau had used the English word in a failed attempt to alienate and preemptively exonerate herself from her own racist and classist insult. As if to say, "I didn't say that: someone foreign to me did." "How," Benbassa continued, "can you use such words in reference to people who are mired in poverty? in destitution? How? I wonder," adding, a bit later on Twitter: "Indecent vocabulary. Disdain

---

[33]Loiseau's exact words, reacting to a facial expression of protestation made by Benbassa, were: "*Madame, vous levez les yeux au ciel. Mais lorsque l'on arrive du Sud-Soudan, vous pouvez decider de faire du shopping de l'asile et trouver qu'on est mieux en Suède qu'en Italie.*"

for poverty."[34] Not to be outdone, then Interior Minister Gérard Collomb affirmed a few days later, similarly using a term in English, that "migrants engage in 'benchmarking'" when applying for asylum.[35]

Nicknaming people may be motivated by endearment. And the nicknamed may even receive it as such. Name-*calling*, however, is for belittlement, disparagement, and, ultimately, for dehumanization. As we move from pet names through innuendos and into the realm of slurs, scare quotes that snare the lexical items increasingly snarl and sneer. Despite its tediousness, Trump's childishly irrepressible branding of non-sycophants, opponents, or simply individuals he can't quite figure out—"Crooked Hillary," "Little Marco," "Lyin' Ted," "Crazy Bernie," "Sloppy Steve," "Cryin' Chuck," "Little Rocket Man," "Al Frankenstein," "Slimeball Comey," and so on—exemplified the more innocuous side of this spectrum. Snidely truncating "know-it-all commie" Alexandria Ocasio-Cortez to "Cortez" because for the monolingual and unidimensional "leader of the free world" ignorant of the way Hispanic surnames are formed,[36] "Cortez" is not quite as directly threatening to a whole phenotype of humans as the systematized Nazi practice of referring to the author of *Das Kapital* as "the Jew Marx" or the author of *Die Harzreise* as "the Jew Heine," but it moves in that direction. As the linguist known during the Third Reich as "the Jew Klemperer" explained, this is "a special technique for hammering something home stylistically" (274). The trend within the realm of the sneer quote is patent: beyond this intensely threatening and cold epithet hurling will be the deprivation of any name—even a pejorative one—that would affirm certain individuals' very belonging to the human species. We know very well how those who at first were named "vermin" ultimately ended up. Here's how Victor Klemperer tells the familiar story of semantic perversion:

---

[34] Geoffroy Clavel and Hortense de Montalivet, "La ministre Nathalie Loiseau indigne en parlant des migrants qui 'font le shopping de l'asile.'" *Huffington Post* (French edition), May 9, 2018. https://www.huffingtonpost.fr/2018/05/09/la-ministre-nathalie-loiseau-indigne-en-parlant-des-migrants-qui-font-le-shopping-de-lasile_a_23430929/?utm_hp_ref=fr-homepage (accessed December 31, 2018).

[35] In French, the perfectly good (and quite beautiful) word *étalonnage* exists for this procedure imputed to the poor, destitute, and dark-skinned.

[36] ... as well as ignoring his rather probable patriarchal bias, since the hierarchy in Hispanic surnames still dictates a preference for the first of the two, which is the father's first surname (which is his father's, and so on).

why does a palpable and undeniable brutality come to light when a female warder in Belsen concentration camp explains to the war crimes trial that on such and such a day she dealt with sixteen *"Stück" Gefangenen* ["head" of prisoners]? In both of the former cases we are dealing with the professional avoidance of reference to the person, with abstraction, *Stück*, on the other hand, involves objectification. It is the same objectification expressed by the official term "the utilization of carcasses [*Kadaververwertung*]," especially when widened to refer to human corpses: fertilizer is made out of the dead of the concentration camps and referred to in the same way as the processing of animal carcasses.

(154)

To return, once again, to the person whose emissions, either in the form of unvarnished public speech or tweets, whose every puny ejaculation made the front page of newspapers for four years is a veritable Mother Lode of linguistic monstrosities and rhetorical grotesqueries. But out of chaos, one can almost always derive some modicum of order. Those incessant excretions thus congeal, on occasion, into theoretical seedlings. It is striking that when darkness allowed any minimal light whatsoever, it was the former Tweeter-in-Chief's sneer quoting that provided it. Let us start with a less-than-(in)famous and somewhat innocuous example—one in which the writer, perhaps unwittingly, uses scare quotes properly: "We will be out for a long time," one could read during the longest US government shutdown in history, "unless the Democrats come back from their 'vacations' and get back to work." The sneer value, here, of "vacations" is multifaceted. Here are just three of those facets: stamping the term with the punctuation equivalent of "so-called" or "so they say" could translate as the implication that the Democrats were doing something other than taking time off during that congressional recess. There's disingenuousness too since the *entire* Congress—and not just the Democrats—was in recess on January 12, 2019. And let's not leave out hypocrisy: no US president took more vacation time more frequently and at extravagant tax-payer-funded expense than the current resident of Mar-a-Lago.

Two far better-known examples of presidential sneer quoting are his abiding addition of the adjective "failing" to *The New York Times* and, of course, that of "fake" to the very notion of news itself. Capitalization replaces scare quotes in the written form of this obsessive slight aimed at his hometown paper. We have seen this variant before. What is quite fascinating about "the Failing New York Times" is not that the author wields the adjective like a pin plunged repeatedly into a voodoo doll, but that the newspaper is in fact far less a failure than any number of the author's own enterprises. A fundamental purpose assigned to sneer quotes is to pawn off onto someone else a negative quality that is, in truth, one's own—the proverbial pot calling the kettle black. The corollary of this procedure, of course, is denying or depriving another of an attribute one claims exclusively and undemocratically for oneself. Sneer quotes get enlisted for this purpose too.

The informational category now known as "fake news" is my other example. A sampling of Twitter tirades reveals that when the designation first appeared, it received scare quote treatment. Then, as it took on a life of its own, the tongs were dropped in favor of initial-letter capitalization—"fake news" became Fake News. Consistency in anything is not one of Trump's primary concerns or strong suits. But whether enshrined by capitals or set off by quotation marks, the familiar function is at work: "fake news" is to be quarantined, prepared for deportation, and supplanted by "alternative facts." Sneering any and all negative media coverage of an established regime into oblivion is a policy familiar to anyone who has studied totalitarianism. And, as Adam Gabbat, among others, has argued,[37] this particular avatar of the move has become an eminently exportable made-in-USA "good." As in the case of "the Failing New York Times," however, the President's sneer quoting of "fake news" opens a deeper level of interpretation: the very presence of scare quotes (or capitalization) themselves undermines the full force of fakeness imputed to the news. As any Freudian analysis can show, the surface of dismissive distancing indicates that news critical of him is anything but fake. But until "the Donald" dons new clothes, he can maintain both his delusion and our collusion in it.

Does all this mean that Trump is a theoretician of some sort? One would be hard-pressed to assert so and I, for one, will not argue the case. Whether he

---

[37]Adam Gabbatt, "How Trump's 'Fake News' Gave Authoritarian Leaders a New Weapon." *The Guardian*, January 25, 2018. https://www.theguardian.com/us-news/2018/jan/25/how-trumps-fake-news-gave-authoritarian-leaders-a-new-weapon (accessed January 3, 2019).

knows at all what he is doing at *any* moment—beyond defending his fragile ego—contributes substantially to my reticence. What I *would* say, however, is that the intricacy that underlies these examples of "fake" and "failing" in Trump talk position him—to appeal to Molière one last time—somewhere between the Sganarelle of *Le Médecin malgré lui* and the would-be aristocrat, Monsieur Jourdain. His unwitting "abilities" situate him somewhere slightly beyond he who "for more than forty years has been speaking prose while knowing nothing of it" and not quite a linguist despite himself.

I stated earlier that sneer quotes can either censor or claim exclusive privilege. On one side of their spectrum of use, they may convey opprobrium; on the other, they may affirm supremacy. Either function occurs peremptorily. But I owe my readers a salient example beyond the train wreck that was the forty-fifth US presidency. Here is one that turns on the term you can see scare -quoted (twice) by the author. From a May 2018 *New York Times* opinion piece penned by Yossi Klein Halevi, we read:

> Every Friday for the past several weeks, the Islamist Hamas has mobilized tens of thousands of demonstrators, who have embarked on a "march of return" toward Israel. The initial goal is to destroy the fence and cross Israel's internationally recognized border. The long-term goal is to demographically destroy the Jewish-majority state through a "return" of descendants of Palestinian refugees from the 1948 war.[38]

We should probably note to begin with that, born in Borough Park, Brooklyn, and now senior fellow at the Shalom Hartman Institute in Jerusalem, this author of predictably condescending *Letters to My Palestinian Neighbor* is one of the thousands of beneficiaries of what is known officially as the Law of Return. The Law of Return, which the State of Israel promulgated in July 1950 and extended in 1970, considers any Jew who enters the territory an *oleh*, or immigrant, who can claim Israeli citizenship. Palestinians, on the other hand, whether Muslim or not, who are not somehow still dwelling on what is now

---

[38]Yossi Klein Halevi, "How Israelis See the World" (Opinion). *The New York Times*, May 4, 2018. https://www.nytimes.com/2018/05/04/opinion/how-israelis-see-the-world.html (accessed December 31, 2018).

Israeli soil and who are nominally "citizens," are unequivocally and without exception denied what *they* refer to as the "right of return." This is the case, even if they can document ancestral homes in what is currently Israel.

The reason for Halevi's careful scare quoting of "return" is obvious. The privilege was made available exclusively for Jews. Anyone else's claim to the privilege is scornfully quarantined beyond the sneer quote pale. So that whereas some readers might find other phrases like "internationally recognized border" or the term "refugees" in the expression "Palestinian refugees from the 1948 war" deserving of at least temporary scare quotes while those readers examine these words for their correspondence to the truth, Halevi only sets off those words whose import is denied non-Jews. The conclusion that may be drawn from this case of sneer quoting is that Israel, like Saudi Arabia, Iran, and so on, is indeed a theocracy—whether marginally democratic or not.[39]

It's important to remind ourselves, however, of what many of these examples show and of what I have said before: although quotes that sneer may be visible, more often than not they function at the level of *implicitness*. This often enhances their manipulative effectiveness. It's up to the receptor, the addressee, to sense or guess that they are in operation, regardless of their manifestation on the page or in voice. Sneer quoting is meant to be caustic. Their authors, therefore, dispense with the treatment that Marjorie Garber says "less eminent or reputable" sources receive.

> When [such a] figure [is] being quoted [...], the old-style "quote-unquote" is deployed, but with a lawyerly edge, casting doubt on the veracity of the person quoted or underscoring the suspicious significance of the utterance.
>
> (10–11)

The sneer quote is meant to worm its way into the heart of the referent with all the destructive virulence of a Trojan horse. Indeed, as Garber adds regarding the "quote-unquote" that sneezes at the source, "the effect is one

---

[39]As I complete this manuscript in February 2024, the untenability of the situation imposed by Israel on Palestinians is even more starkly evident. With no room to elaborate here, I would simply refer the reader to Shlomo Sand's latest and essential book, *Deux peuples pour un État ? Relire l'histoire du sionisme* [*Two Peoples for One State? Rereading the History of Zionism*]. Paris: Éditions du Seuil, 2024. The one-state solution has a long history that bears examining for the future.

of distancing rather than incorporation." This would still understate the altogether censorious aim that impels the sneer quote.

Lest the political valence of my latest examples be misconstrued, I would ask the reader to recall my first one and consider the following statement made a few years ago in the *Columbia Journalism Review*: "While *M[erriam]-W[ebster]* traces the first usage of 'scare quotes' to 1960, they have exploded in recent years, being brought to bear especially in politics, as 'liberal' and 'conservative' campaigns used their own 'scare' tactics" (Perlman). While "scare quotes" were first named, as we saw, in 1956, I want to spotlight this critic's observation that scare quoting—which includes sneer-quoting, of course—is a tool to which *all* nuances of the political spectrum avail themselves.

On a side that resonates quite well with my own thinking on the subject, Chris Lorenz (about whom I'll have more to say when I turn my attention to the corporatization of higher education) turns New Public Management's own semantic tactics against it when he writes—variously with or without the tiny tongs—of the "controlitis or evaluitis" that grips and drives NPM or of the "hegemony" of NPM's "qualispeak" and "the relative weakness of protest" (609, 625). Finally, anticipating our final analysis of power's power to pervert semantics and explaining why he himself feels the need to fire sneering salvos back, Lorenz concludes that "NPM discourse is Orwellian in nature because it redefines concepts such as quality, accountability, transparency, and professionalism and perverts them into their opposites" (625).

From the other side of the spectrum to which Perlman refers when describing the explosion of scare quotes enlisted for political strife comes Ayalet Shaked. She too tries to deflect a virulent epithet back onto its originator. Cofounder of Israel's New Right party, thought by some to be a potential future prime minister,[40] Shaked served as Minister of Justice from 2015 until 2019. In a lamentably failed attempt to counter detractors of her faction, Shaked recently played a bit too irresponsibly with the distancing effects that we assign to scare quotes. Putting her youthful "good looks" to ideological advantage, she produced a parodic commercial for a perfume branded "Fascism." Critics on

---

[40]Allison Kaplan Sommer, "Who's Afraid of Ayelet Shaked? Meet the Secular Jewish Nationalist Who Could Be Israel's Prime Minister." *Haaretz*, September 8, 2017.

the left had supposedly marked her political movement as fascistic. Filmed—perhaps ironically—in black and white, slow-motion clips of Shaked moving through luxurious interiors are overlaid with Shaked whispering putative goals or accomplishments of her ministerial activity: "scaling back judicial activism," "judicial appointments," "governance," "reining in the high court" … A pause, then cut to a close-up of her picking up the bottle labeled "Fascism." She spritzes a bit toward her neck and intones on screen to the camera, "Smells more like democracy to me." As she walks away from the camera, "The next revolution is coming" overlays the final image.

No scare quotes surround "Fascism" on the perfume bottle label. Unlike what I will do shortly with "cancel culture" and "race," Shaked doesn't mean for there to be any. Spraying herself with "fascism" while claiming that it's actually "democracy," she collapses the two systems, thus embracing indifferently one and the other as if they were equivalent. The chilling failure of her mock commercial consists in this sneer of equivalence—like the "Jewish-Bolschevist plague" that Hitler still thought he could rout in March 1945 (II:425; II:562)—predicated on the absence of scare quotes. As the byline to Roger Cohen's *Times* article on Shaked's disturbing demonstration goes, "When an Israeli minister sprays herself in Fascism to make her rightist party more popular, you know that words have achieved weightlessness."[41]

With the Third Reich's debacle well under way and Hitler's suicide only two weeks off, "It was amusing," Klemperer had a moment to observe about a minor civil servant who had also taken temporary refuge at the Gruber's, "how isolated and crumbling scraps of the LTI, which had been dutifully learned by heart, still floated around like islands in the man's disillusioned and embittered head" (II:451; II:596).[42] Amusing but disturbing. Klemperer knew that, left uncritiqued, such "crumbling scraps" can easily reemerge in future iterations of the imperfect species to which we belong.

---

[41]Roger Cohen, "A Perfume Called Fascism." *The New York Times*, March 29, 2019. https://www.nytimes.com/2019/03/29/opinion/israel-perfume-fascism-ayelet-shaked.html?smid=nytcore-ios-share (accessed May 18, 2019).

[42]Staunch opponent of the Third Reich and pacifist pastor, Heinrich Grüber sheltered Klemperer and his wife, Eva, during their flight. Klemperer's original German is worth reproducing: "*Es war nun amüsant, wie in dem desillusionierten und erbitterten Kopf des Mannes noch einzelne eingelernte und pflichtmäßige Brocken der LTI haltlos und abbröckelnder Auflösung inselhaft herumschwammen.*"

3
White Whine

> *It's an SS fantasy to believe that we have an historical mission to change species [...]. [T]his extraordinary sickness is nothing other than a culminating moment in man's history. And that means two things. First, that the solidity and stability of the species is being put to the test. Next, that the variety of relationships between men, their color, their customs, their class formation mask a truth that [...] appears with absolute clarity: namely, that there are not several human races, there is only one human race [il n'y a pas des espèces humaines, il y a une espèce humaine].*
>
> —ROBERT ANTELME

Such is the core lesson that Robert Antelme conveys toward the end of *L'Espèce humaine*[1]—his reflection on deportation and survival in Nazi-dominated Europe. The choice of "human race" in an otherwise faithful and elegant translation, where the author had carefully inscribed *espèce humaine* in the original, is both unfortunate and symptomatic. The translators missed a unique opportunity to show readers of English precisely where and why Antelme invoked the loaded term of "race" for the *one and only* time in the *entire* book. That mention of "race" comes in the conclusion of this very same paragraph where Antelme insists on the principle—and here I must again adjust the translation—that "there are not several human *species*, there is only one human *species*." The consequence of ignoring this truth produces "the canon of the species [*le canon de l'espèce*]" which is the "division into races

---

[1](219; 350–51).

[*races*] or classes [...] that sustains the axiom we're always prepared to use, the ultimate line of defense: 'Those aren't people like us.'"

Could such semantic imprecision be a contributor to the persistence of *racism* virtually everywhere? I think so. Racism is a behavioral, institutional, psychological, sociological, and economic aberration. Undergirding all dimensions and manifestations of racism is language. Racism is taken for granted because "race"—as a conceptual term—is taken for granted.

One of the first things Victor Klemperer noted in his diary was that, under the Nazis, "only race matters" (*es kommt nur auf die Rasse an*) (I:10; I:14), echoing—although in a completely different context—Benjamin Disraeli's "All is race; there is no other truth."[2] Over the course of the next twelve years, recording ample evidence of its truth, Klemperer would impute this single fundamental guiding principle for what the Nazis came very close to achieving: that is, the destruction of the European Jews.[3] Having lived mostly in the United States—first on one coast, then on the other—the majority of my own seventy-plus years, I find this also to be the case in my birth country. From what I've heard and read, I am not alone. The author of *Unusually Cruel*—a study of mass incarceration, "the real American exceptionalism"—agrees: "race plays a central role in American society and in the American criminal justice and prison systems [...] the factor of race [...] is distinctively American" (Howard, 158). What does the word "race" mean to people in the United States?—"Race" stands for a concept, an assumed truth, a touchstone, and pretext for materialization as weapon for policing, oppressing, murdering, exterminating.

A few years after the founding of the Black Panther Party in my beloved hometown, the protests in which I participated over the theories of a certain UC Berkeley professor of educational psychology named Arthur Jensen became the second big jolt in my political awakening. I was in my freshman year in that February of 1969. Jensen had just got an article on "race" published in the *Harvard Educational Review*. Its title was (and is) "How Much Can We Boost I.Q. and Scholastic Achievement?" In that 123-page screed that I patiently

---

[2] *Tancred, or The New Crusade* (1847).
[3] This is, of course, the title of Raul Hilberg's landmark book of 1961.

read (instead of focusing on integral calculus), Jensen argued that general intelligence was genetic and that it could therefore be measured by IQ testing. If, as he further asserted, so-called races were keyed to genetic difference, Blacks were consequently inferior to Whites. Therefore, he concluded, any programs such as Affirmative Action were strictly a waste of resources, effort, and time. Having read all this and having grown up in East Oakland, I agreed with those convinced that Jensen deserved no place on the university's faculty.

Later, however, I learned that Jensen hadn't always taken this position. A product of Columbia's Teachers College, within the same institution, that is, where Franz Boas and *his* students had upended physical anthropology, he had once thought environment trumped anything purportedly genetic about intelligence. However, shortly after receiving tenure at Berkeley, he had come under the sway of Stanford physicist William Shockley. Instead of sticking to his own field, this bigoted Nobel laureate dabbled in genetics to "scientifically" undergird his xenophobia. He believed firmly in and propounded the long-invalidated "science" of eugenics, for which he received generous funding from the notoriously white supremacist Pioneer Fund. Shockley was, in short, an unabashed racist and his company unleashed the latent racism in Jensen. Together, Jensen and Shockley were instrumental in turning old-fashioned miscegenation phobia into "dysgenic" phobia: the fear that "racial" mixture reverses evolution.[4] (More about so-called "dysgenics" later, when we get to the eugenics boom in the United States and elsewhere.)

whine

Exposing the roots of convict leasing in the Deep South, Marc Howard reminds us that, once the Civil War ended and the slaves were freed, the former Africans and their descendants outnumbered "English" and other whites in at least three states. Of Mississippi, Howard writes: "whites were petrified by the lawlessness that they thought would result from coexistence with

---

[4]"Shockley's and Jensen's main worries were that race mixture was causing dysgenics, or racial reverse evolution. One of their major goals was to force the NAS [National Academy of Sciences] and members of Congress to study this question in an attempt to solve our 'national Negro illness'" (Sussman 238).

impoverished, uneducated, but now-free former slaves" (153). The operative words here are "petrified," or scared out of their wits, and "thought," meaning *believed* or *imagined* in this context. When male humans with light skin suspect that their millennial reign over the rest of humankind is threatened, they are overcome by hysteria.[5] There is no other way to characterize Lindsay Graham's lip-curled shriek during the Brett Kavanagh confirmation hearings that "I know I'm a single white man [*sic*] from South Carolina and I've been told to shut up but I will not shut up," as anything other than a whiny performance of "victimization anxiety."[6] The senior senator's shrill duplicates that "strained voice [of] a drunken and paranoid laborer" that once led Germany.[7] Such displays of nervous disorder underlie a whole spectrum of social phenomena produced when white supremacy is perceived to be under threat. The so-called "Great Replacement" "theory," erections of monuments to enslavement, biased policing, and racism in sport are only a few examples of its manifestations.

Underlying the pale eligible bachelor's strident complaint is the same perverse thinking that gave birth to the illusory phenomenon of "reverse discrimination"—the notion that light-skinned "regular Americans" are being deprived of educational or professional opportunity by policies meant to rectify and compensate for systemic racism. The "silent majority" trope of the Nixon era participates of the same twisted economy. So did the reactionary political posturing in the form of handwringing over the "forgotten" (i.e., white blue-collar) people of East Palestine, Ohio. It's not the quasi-enslaved wage earners who wring hands and whine but the populist white power brokers who trump up the demagoguery. Whenever the pillar of "race" alone undergirding white privilege is chipped away at, the pot immediately calls the kettle black, as it were. Such was the logic in the expression "Jewish War" that Klemperer heard relentlessly to qualify the Nazis' expansionist war.

---

[5]Already, in the first year under Nazi rule, Klemperer noted symptoms of the neurosis: e.g., "How hysterical all the words and deeds of the government are!" (I:26; I:36); "Contemporary history on film! This time the Nürnberg rally of the Nazi Party. What stage direction of the crowds and what hysteria!" (I:34; I:47).

[6]Charles M. Blow, "White Male Victimization Anxiety." *The New York Times*, October 10, 2018.

[7]*"Der Mann schreit mit überanstrengter Stimme wie ein Besoffener undverfolgungswahnsinniger Arbeiter"* (Klemperer I:230; I:302–03).

While some manifestations of white whine[8] may today be more specific to or acute in the United States, they can be found rearing their ugly heads wherever the legacy of imperial and colonial white supremacy still rules the day. The hysterical notion—closely associated with the neo-Nazi notions of "race" or "white suicide"—that a conspiracy is afoot to replace light-skinned Europeans by dark-skinned Europeans was propagated in the early 2010s by the mediocre French novelist Renaud Camus. "Replacement" "theory" has since, and for now, taken hold everywhere that pale male panic prevails. If I insist on scare quotes for "theory" here, it is because no seriously committed scientist—and certainly no Critical Watch—would dignify such crackpot thinking as worthy of the venerable term. As for racial "replacement," this too is part of the same "naked desperation [*nackte Verzweiflung*]" (II:355; II:469) that Klemperer clearly detected in the voices of Goebbels and Deputy Reich Press Spokesman, Helmut Sündermann, as the Reich's fall neared.

Science and reason render this "theory" null and void. To elaborate, I offer the following comment that I dropped a few months ago on YouTube, undoubtedly wasting my time responding to an individual who was defending a US professor of economics for promoting the old eugenicist saw that "race" determines intelligence:

> Race: a concept clearly invented to underwrite empire, colonialism, slavery, and any number of genocides. Scientific consensus—actual science, like biology or anthropology—has determined that after several tens of thousands of years of divergence due to climate variations (e.g., the Ice Age) after our treks in various directions out of Africa, we are slowly but surely *reintegrating* and that, in any case, just as with any other animal species, there is more within-group variation among phenotypes of Homo sapiens than among-group variation.

"I know," I continued,

> that "miscegenation" puts some individuals into a blind panic, but we just can't fight the natural reproductive behavior of the animal species to

---

which we all belong. The professor whom you're spending so much time and energy defending is an economist who, like so many others I've named above, merely dabbles in biology and anthropology. As such, he really has no scientific leg to stand on.

In short, nobody can "replace" something that our relentless evolution and worldwide migrations are inexorably erasing.

monumentalized racism and essentialized "race"

From the very instant the South surrendered at Appomattox, the "lost cause" (another unremitting whine over the waning of white supremacy) took myriad forms. One of them was quite literally solid: a multitude of concretizations in stone and bronze of crimes carried out in the name of "race." Statues depicting and honoring the statesmen and warriors who put their lives on the line to defend and perpetuate chattel slavery began appearing to mark territory where the system was dismantled by force. Names of great white racists began adorning schools and designating streets. As the "Whose Heritage Timeline" produced and maintained by the Southern Poverty Law Center clearly illustrates, erections of monuments to illustrious figures in the Confederacy multiplied exponentially during two key moments: when Jim Crow legislation and the rise of the Ku Klux Klan responded to Reconstruction and when the Civil Rights Era led ever-so-slowly to the desegregation of the South.[9]

In such periods of increased white panic, the canard of "race" reinforced essentialism founded on the superficial criterion of skin color and tone. I would be remiss not to emphasize that gender, nationality, and religion also rank high among factors arbitrarily justifying discrimination and its crimes. Klemperer observed all of this happening under the Third Reich: "*the* Jew, *the* Englishman—nothing but collectives, no individual counts" (I:364;

---

[9]Whose Heritage? 153 Years of Confederate Iconography. https://www.splcenter.org/sites/default/files/com_whose_heritage_timeline_print.pdf (accessed).

I:464);[10] "Is there such a thing as *the* German, is there such a thing as *the* Jew?" (II:258; II:345); "Anyone who says: *the* German, *the* Pole, *the* Jew, is always wrong" (II:435; II:573). "Where do I belong? To the 'Jewish nation' decrees Hitler" (I:134; I:181). Finally, for a moment, when he received the brochure on "The Care of the German Cat" that I mentioned earlier, the absurdity of essentialization must have given him a short, rare laugh. Yet what better proof of the absurd vacuousness of "race"?

That Nazi "blood and soil" ideology ties directly to the "race"-based glorification of a regime sustained by the enslavement of Africans is attested by the chanting of *that very phrase* by the white nationalists who protested the impending removal of a statue of Robert E. Lee in Charlottesville. Predictably, "We will not be replaced" was also clearly heard on that ugly day and night in May 2017. By perpetuating nostalgia for an economy that enslaved imported Africans and their descendants, these statues and names attempt to enshrine "race" in the pantheon of concepts. They contribute to the legitimization of the illegitimate. They are meant to normalize the aberrant and essentialize the chimeric. They appeal to populism at its basest. They are devoid of morality.

I would be shirking the compulsion to be "fair and balanced," however, if I were to omit the mention of the thousands of public signs that *counter* white whine by decrying racism and paying tribute to freedom fighters. The National Memorial for Peace & Justice that opened in April 2018 on a six-acre site Montgomery, Alabama, is exemplary. Evoking with as much nominal and geographical precision as possible the *racial terror lynchings* (the Memorial's word) that had taken place up to its inauguration, that memorial goes a long way toward invalidating complaints from cracker. Countless streets and schools also now bear the names of abolitionists, prominent freemen and descendants of slaves, and dedicated allies in anti-racism. No doubt their numbers will increase substantially while this book is being written. But to those who bear the brunt of persistent and ongoing racist behaviors and practices, there must be something bittersweet about renaming when so many of these tributes were so belated. And what can we say about respect paid to such corrective

---

[10]Original italics restored.

tributes-by-naming when we see, for example, the River Site memorial to Emmett Till regularly pock-marked with bullet holes and nighttime videos of it flanked by frat boys from Ole Miss, whose website proudly declares Robert E. Lee to be its spiritual father.[11]

To my view, one of the most intelligent responses to any and all of the efforts to enthrone "race" in some essentialized place or time is a simple, straightforward declaration about a writer's own body. "I have rape-colored skin": thus begins a *New York Times* editorial by Caroline Randall Williams entitled "You Want a Confederate Monument? My Body Is a Confederate Monument."[12] That incipit, that title, and that body say it all: not only that "the monuments […] must come down" but that "race," as biologists, geneticists, and anthropologists have been telling us for more than a hundred years, is an empty yet lethal signifier. Thus, again, let us mark these words: in the United States still today, as in the Germany of a Reich on the rise, "only race matters."

racialized policing and mass incarceration

The seemingly endless list of Black American victims of police violence attests to this. Before, between, and beyond Rodney King and Sandra Bland, every denizen of the United States identified or identifiable as having African ancestry knows harassment that starts as soon as he or she is in the public eye: the danger of being seen in *that* skin. No wonder so many suspects are riddled from behind with bullets while fleeing. And although equipped now with smartphones and bodycams eyewitnesses to racialized policing have burgeoned, surveillance cameras and facial recognition algorithms, on the other hand of technology, perpetuate it. Meanwhile, the double standard made blatant in the way suspects, terrorists, murderers with pale skin being "taken into custody without incident" seems to leave most people indifferent, rather than cause utter outrage.

In the wake of the murder of George Floyd, the Black Lives Matter movement, which had coalesced in the summer of 2013, burst onto the

---

[11] Kappa Alpha. https://www.kappaalphaorder.org/ka/history/lee/ (accessed June 29, 2023).
[12] *The New York Times*, June 26, 2020.

national and international scene. It was largely supported by the US public at large. But whiny white reaction to the demonstrations immediately responded with "blue lives matter" or the even lamer "all lives matter" to declare what the Confederate monuments do in deafening silence, namely that "white lives most matter." That catapulting event—George Floyd's murder—occurred on the very same day one Amy Cooper, illegally walking her unleashed dog in Central Park's Ramble, used a move far from unknown in the South in the days of lynching that could easily have led to gentle birdwatcher Christian Cooper (who had simply requested that she leash her rambunctious pooch) ending up dead at the hands of the police. The bird-lover is Black; the dog-lover is White. These simultaneous events—one fatal, one tragi-comic—events in stark racial Black and white—also serve to reaffirm Howard's observation that "the factor of race [...] is distinctively American" and, still more harrowing, the applicability to the United States of Klemperer's lament that "only race matters."

As the year 1938 came to a close, Klemperer noted in secret that, "The National Socialists have always talked about World Jewry: it was an idée fixe and a phantom. They have gone on talking about this phantom for so long until it has become reality" (I:282; I:368). Like Jim Crow segregation, lynching, convict leasing, anti-miscegenation laws (*Rassengesetze*), anti-passing vigilantes, forced sterilization, syphilis Guinea-pigging, and mass incarceration of Black Americans are the pure product of the conviction that "race" corresponds to some sort of reality and that on this illusory foundation, one phenotype of human may freely oppress and deny the humanity of another.

To catalog all the crimes committed in the name of "race" would require far more space than one chapter in a book on the rhetoric of manipulation and semantic perversion. The murders, the rapes, the lynchings, the deprivations of freedom, and all the injustices that have resulted and continue to result from belief in the conceptual certitude of "race" have been presented and analyzed extremely well by many specialists. Reviewing the phases of that history in reverse, however, can efficiently draw us back to the moment when the subterfuge of "race" was naked, when we should have begun in earnest, in other words, the task of deconstructing and disavowing racism.

According to World Prison Brief,[13] the United States has the world's largest prison population and ranks sixth in the number of persons imprisoned per capita. Of the approximately 1,767,200 individuals currently locked up, about 40 percent are racially categorized as Black. Blacks, however, represent 13 percent of the overall US population. The impressively high number and ratio gave rise to the expression "mass incarceration." The disproportionate representation of African Americans sheds light on the racist nature of justice in the United States.

Some readers will no doubt have raised an eyebrow at a characterization of justice in the United States as "racist." That tiny muscle might relax a bit if its owner considers that Black mass incarceration is only the latest phase of a genealogy of practices reaching back to the kernel of reasoning that led their ancestors to transport human beings from Africa to the New World in the first place. Black mass incarceration is the direct successor of convict leasing, chain gangs, and lynching.[14] Following Emancipation, this triad—whose story is perhaps best captured in Douglas A. Blackmon's now classic *Slavery by Another Name*—had taken the place of atrocities directly enabled by slavery. And this little family story of crimes against humanity is all facilitated, supported, sustained, and condoned by the specious conviction that "race" is a *fact* and, thus, a *concept*.

To the generations that grew up in the 1950s and 1960s, "race riot" is a painfully familiar term. "Race riots" would be insurrections arising from Black ghettos created by convergent factors of which the most salient are endemic economic hardship, de facto segregation, and redlining. (Of these, perhaps redlining requires a short refresher. In the wake of Black migrations out of the South, the North devised systems for keeping Blacks out of predominantly white neighborhoods. Convinced that dark-skinned people brought down property values, the National Association of Real Estate Boards quietly advocated for the mapping of cities according to home salability. Starting in 1934, when the FHA got on the bandwagon, "residential security maps"

---

[13]World Prison Brief. https://www.prisonstudies.org/ (accessed June 30, 2023).
[14]This is eloquently explained in much more detail in Howard 2017.

began being produced to help banks and realtors recognize four categories of neighborhoods so that they could better offer or deny mortgages, steer buyers, impose restrictive covenants, and so forth. The categories were "desirable," "still desirable," "declining," and "undesirable" or "hazardous" for investment. These areas were lettered and color-coded, respectively: A–green, B–blue, C–yellow, and D–red. The less formal discriminatory practice of redlining is preserved in the red coloring for areas where virtually no mortgages could be had. This was a system *for* whites, *against* Blacks. It was a racist system. It is a perfect example of systemic racism. The mentality that gave us redlining endures and should be taught about in schools.)

Any honest and thorough overview of riots driven by "race" must begin, however, with those unleashed by whites on Blacks. The first two decades of the twentieth century are riddled with them: Atlanta in 1906; Springfield in 1908; Forsyth County and Chester Pennsylvania both in 1912; Elaine, Arkansas, Chicago, and Washington, DC, in 1919; Ocoee Florida in 1920; Tulsa in 1921 to list only a few. All these deadly clashes were set off by the dominant *whites* descended from the conquerors and colonists who settled the land in the first place by virtually eradicating millions of native people. The murderous razing of Tulsa's Black Wall Street is infamous. It is now, belatedly, categorized as a "white terrorist massacre" whose human toll can easily be consulted. Still slightly obscured by convenient oblivion is the Elaine massacre whose death toll far surpasses all of the other *pogroms* carried out by frenzied "natives":[15] over 800 people of color and five people not of color.[16] True to form, official (i.e., white) discourse (i.e., propaganda) hysterically blamed the victims: on the final day of the slaughter, a headline in the *Arkansas Gazette* read blithely "Negroes Plan to Kill All Whites."

The frivolous flimsiness of pretexts for racialized murder is exemplified by the 1919 "race" riot in Chicago. Led by the city's notorious youth "athletic" clubs—the Sparklers, the Emeralds, the Hamburgers (to which a young Richard J.

---

[15] I discuss white racist usurpation of the "native" qualifier.

[16] In his 2008 book on these events, Robert Whitaker cites 856 as the number of people murdered (lynched). Robert Whitaker, *On the Laps of the Gods: The Red Summer of 1919 and the Struggle for Justice That Remade a Nation*. New York: Random House, 2008.

Daley belonged[17])—the white "wilding" (a verb Whites systematically attribute to Black behavior) that resulted in thirty-eight deaths and hundreds of injured began simply because a young Eugene Williams had had the audacity to swim in an unofficial "white only" section of Lake Michigan. When people dared to challenge Williams' drowning after being stoned by the white mob, the good old "boys" (usually a demeaning diminutive for Black men) went to work.

More recently—in the lifetime of many with us today, one might recall the dozens killed and the hundreds jailed when the FBI waged war against the Black Panther Party simply because some dark-skinned citizens had the audacity to practice what light-skinned citizens had always done: namely, to claim the right to bear arms. Fred Hampton, Mark Clark, and Bobby Hutton were among the many Panthers assassinated by federal agents, while others ended up dead or in exile due to discord planted by COINTELPRO projects. Meanwhile, with Janine and Janet Africa only released in May 2019 after forty-one years in prison, we may recall the Philadelphia anarcho-primitivist group MOVE, nine of whose members were convicted to sentences ranging from 30 to 100 years for the murder of a police officer who was quite likely shot by "friendly" fire.

eugenics

While the belief that fetishizing and essentializing "race" somehow came to the United States from Nazi Germany might delude many, quite the opposite is true. If, as Klemperer laments, "the Jewish people [were] created by Hitler" (I:375; I:476–77),[18] it was largely because, as Hitler noted himself, his "bible" was a certain volume published in 1916 and penned by amateur anthropologist Madison Grant. Extremely popular with the general public as well as being highly influential in US academia—at least until after the Second World War—

---

[17]See Don Rose, "Unholy Centennial of the 1919 Race Riots Finds a City Still Fighting for Justice." *Chicago Sun-Times*, July 24, 2019. https://chicago.suntimes.com/2019/7/24/20707500/chicago-1919-race-riots-don-rose-richard-daley-segregation (accessed June 30, 2023).

[18]See also, "It is part of the Lingua tertii imperii that the expression 'Jewish people' appears repeatedly in the *Jüdische Nachrichtenblatt*" (I:292; I:377).

The Passing of the Great Race appeared in German translation in 1925, just after Hitler's release from Landsberg Prison and the printing of the first volume of *Mein Kampf*. The message conveyed by the two semantic elements of the title is strikingly obvious: light-skinned "Nordic" humans characterized as "the Great Race" are ominously depicted as being in the process of "passing"—or, as is claimed today, being *replaced*—by inferior ones. This paranoid delusion is, of course, predicated on the false premise that our species is composed of more than one "race."

The reception of Grant's *Passing of the Great Race* and the racist eugenics that it catapulted cannot be underestimated. In his gripping account of the eugenics craze in the United States, Edwin Black observes that "eugenics rocketed through academia, becoming an institution virtually overnight" (75). To this, Robert Wald Sussman adds the astounding statistic that "[b]y 1914, some forty-four colleges and universities offered eugenics instruction" (62). Eugenics enabled and justified the mortiferous essentialization of human groups that W. E. B. DuBois, Franz Boas, Victor Klemperer, James Baldwin, and so many other courageous voices would dedicate their lives decrying and combatting. The history of eugenics spans its inception and rise to pride of place in academia all the way to its dramatic—though not thorough—discreditation in the wake of the Shoah and the Civil Rights Movement.

Just as eugenics served as core of the Nazi's "Final Solution to the Jewish Question," so all of the crimes of humanity against humanity perpetrated in and by the United States were and continue to be driven—however surreptitiously—by the very same bogus science. When modern eugenics arose in 1883, Gobineau-style racism could truly rejoice at having finally found what it thought was unassailable scientific proof. Racism crossed with subjectively biased "science" could justify the suppression and nullification of humanity in whole swathes of humanity. What had previously gone crudely in some American universities as "niggerology" was now academically "attenuated" into "raceology." Such pseudoscientific avatars of eugenics foreshadowed Alfred Ploetz's notion of *Rassenhygiene*[19] that, in turn, fed straight into the

---

[19]Ploetz's nomination—albeit unsuccessful—for the 1936 Nobel Peace Prize helps measure how different the world would feel about eugenics ten years later (cf. Sussman 112).

Nazis' infamous *Nürnberger Rassengesetze*, the racist laws passed in 1935 that set the groundwork for the Final Solution. Klemperer repeatedly but helplessly reported "race defilement trials" for those who "shamed" the German *Volk* (I:240; I:315–16). In an irony that can never be repaired, if it hadn't been for the Third Reich, the necessary and noble discreditation of this unabashedly Eurocentric "science" justifying the annihilation of "inferior races," begging all the familiar questions for colonialism, imperialism, and white supremacy, might never have finally begun.

IQ testing is perhaps the most obvious remnant today of the now widely discredited eugenics movement in the United States. Or, to put it another way, since we are not yet quite entirely free of the disease, IQ testing is one of the last ramparts of eugenics. Stealthier vestiges of racist biology persist. The Pioneer Fund, presided over until his death in 2012 by the notorious pseudo-scientist, J. Philippe Rushton and which has had close associations with elected officials, continues its insidious white supremacist work today through the JSP Educational Foundation based in Sarasota, Florida.

Another living reminder of the heyday of eugenics at its most racist, least scientific, though purporting to be the precise opposite, is the putatively "peer-reviewed" *Mankind Quarterly*. Its editor-in-chief is Gerhard Meisenberg, whose Wikipedia account is currently blocked as part of a sock-puppet investigation. As an example of the garbage that *Mankind Quarterly* disseminates, the issue I consulted for this book (v. 63, no. 2, 2022) features an article entitled "New Evidence Confirms that the IQ in Sicily Is Lower than in the Mainland" by none other than Richard Lynn, the self-described "scientific racist" who died in 2023 as I was finishing this manuscript.

white supremacy

All of these historical phenomena have been and continue to be sustained by an unwavering conviction that "race" is an unassailable given—one that science can confirm. Their cumulative effect has been to establish white supremacy and preserve it. If we can trace the beginnings of modern eugenics *by that name* to the writings that Francis Galton began secreting shortly after the appearance of his half-cousin's *Origin of the Species*, white supremacy emerged as a conviction—a "philosophy," as proponents like to "think" of it—far before it was labeled as such. In the United States, presidents as far back as Thomas Jefferson, "advanced," albeit "as a suspicion only" that "blacks are […] inferior to the whites in the endowments of body and mind," already (albeit with a modicum of hesitation) embodied the position.[20] Far more blatantly aligned with what today is widely considered unapologetic white supremacist thinking was Andrew Johnson, whose declaration that "This is a country for white men, and by God, as long as I am president, it shall be a government for white men" is now infamous. Notwithstanding recent attempts to finesse Johnson's racism by contextualization, his amnesty of 7,000 Confederates helpfully complicates the simplistic story we are told regarding slavery and racism as children of the wicked South and the virtuous North.

The fetishization of "race" for the sole purpose of establishing the domination of people equipped with more melatonin by people with less melatonin quickly led to their simplistic and overexaggerated dichotomization into the highly exaggerated color contrast between "black" and "white." Although the self-reference by the light-skinned usurpers of the territory that would become the United States of America as "white" began already to appear around 1680 in colonial laws, "white *supremacy*" only becomes manifest as official and open policy after the defeat of the slave-holding South. Today, this segregative terminology persists—even among people determined to rid the society of racism's legacy. Hence that extension of Critical Race Theory (itself a questionable heading) known as "whiteness studies." Obviously, the purport of Toni Morrison's *Playing in the Dark: Whiteness and the Literary Imagination* or Nell Irvin Painter's *The History of White People* stands at the polar opposite of titles like *The Rising Tide of Color Against White World-Supremacy* or *Into the Darkness*, both penned by Lothrop Stoddard, who, along with Madison Grant, essentially drew up the blueprints for Nazi eugenics, but the titular terminology is eerily, even creepily, close.

The story of how the now infamous "Great White Hope" moniker first got pinned on heavyweight boxer James J. Jeffries has been told many times. If

---

[20]*Notes on the State of Virginia.*

not the Ur-story of white supremacist mentality, it is memorable, emblematic, and unforgettable. It was Jack London, a firm advocate of Madison Grant's "scientific study of race," who called for Jeffries to come out of retirement to challenge Jack Johnson—the first Black world heavyweight champion. Jeffries, whom London called "the chosen representative of the white race," was roundly defeated at Johnson's able hands. Disappointing "whites" and delighting "Blacks," "race" riots naturally ensued in dozens of cities big and small, resulting in the usual deaths and destruction.

As we have seen time and time again, will to power translated into perverse semantics results in death-dealing violence. The drive of European colonists to dominate America by exploiting the spurious category of "race" resulted in many terminological aberrations; two of the most misleading were coined by Madison Grant and inscribed in his racist classic, *The Passing of the Great Race*. One was *Homo europaeus*; the other, "Native American." In establishing the Galton Society for the Study of the Origin and Evolution of Man in 1918— naming it in honor of the British polymath Francis Galton, the "father" of modern eugenics—Grant employed the term "unalloyed native American" to refer not to the indigenous peoples, who had by that time been decimated and resettled into largely infertile Bantustans, but to the "great race" of descendants of the first Thirteen Colonies. As for the fiction of a spurious new species known as *Homo europaeus*, it was Grant who finally inscribed the term that had been circulating for decades on paper in the book that inspired *Mein Kampf* and, arguably, the Shoah.[21]

Notwithstanding the doctrine of *laïcité* that enables so many proud French Republicans to affirm the country's color blindness, racism, and white privilege abound there as well. Few French are willing to remind themselves that *laïcité*—that theoretically excludes religion from public visibility—was conceived, elaborated, and enshrined exclusively by pale-skinned "native" French ideologues who, however agnostic or atheist, were nonetheless formed by Roman Catholic culture. The unquestioned faith that *laïcité* guarantees color-blindness and class-blindness every much as it guarantees religion-blindness

---

[21]For a thoroughly researched history of the term, *Homo europaeus*, see the chapter by that title in Shane Weller's *The Idea of Europe: A Critical History* (2021).

is a perfect example of near-total disconnect between theory and practice. To question the effectiveness of *laïcité* in establishing and maintaining equality is taboo—a form of white prohibition. Like so many other things, however, including a constitution that dates back to 1958, when an overly powerful presidency was thought necessary to get France beyond the "Algerian crisis," "non-white" French citizens would like to have equal say in the conception of a new, visionary, and more democratic Republic.

Returning to the United States, police harassment and residual occasional lynching are blatant impediments to peaceful existence for Black Americans. Like everyday social shunning, discrimination in housing and employment eat away "discretely" at lives, preserving poverty and depriving opportunity. From the segregated building projects created under the New Deal to "quality of life" measures, the North was adept at developing its own stealthy version of Jim Crow. Remnants of the behavior that such policies fostered are present everywhere: from Starbuck's tolerance of "race"-based customer treatment to the demonstration of white entitlement that led to Oakland's festive BBQ'n While Black party in 2018.

persistent pervasiveness of "race"

Despite being invalidated by science and reason for designating variation within a species, despite its nullity as conceptual term, "race" has continued to be lethal in its prolonged afterlife. It suffices to follow news at the global level to admit that Ali Rattansi is right when he writes that "all geo-cultural and geo-political conflicts have had the potential to be racialized" (162).

"Race" still plagues the United States, infecting everyone, every issue, discussion, policy. So fully is it engrained in minds and behavior that it seems congenital.[22] The term can be found being taken for granted even in such visionary expressions of a time and a place in our history as Oscar Micheaux's 1920 wonderful film, *Within Our Gates*. Meanwhile, as H. Rap Brown observed in 1969, "Race prejudice in america becomes color prejudice in negro america"

---

[22] See Charles Blow, "America Was Born with a Congenital Illness." *The New York Times*, July 14, 2023.

(7).[23] "Colorism" is the term coined to designate discrimination among the Black population on the basis of skin tone.[24] Wallace Thurman's essential "novel of Negro life" of 1929, entitled *The Blacker the Berry*, fearlessly goes to the heart of this strain of the American disease. Born with particularly dark skin, Emma Lou Morgan relentlessly encounters a colorism that insidiously[25] doubles the overt racism from whites, depriving her of any meaningful relationship with any other human, reducing her existence to "begin anew, always fighting, not so much for acceptance by other people, but for acceptance of herself by herself" (257). Thurman's novel deploys a veritable lexicon of *colorism*: "mulattoes," "blue-vein people," "the right sort of people," "yaller nigger," "spade," "dictys," "black mammy," "high brown," and so on—a dubious tribute to diversity, an unceasing semantic onslaught on Emma Lou Morgan's well-being.

Slavery—the corollary of fetishized "race" in the United States—was concomitantly generalized in perverse ways. Before the importation of hundreds of thousands of Africans for menial labor, indigenous people were already being enslaved by conquistadores in the Southwest. These were called *genízaros*, borrowed from the Ottoman *yeniçeri*, or janissary. In turn (almost conversely), some indigenous people hopped on the bandwagon of enslavement, indenturing Blacks who had escaped or been freed by their white owners only to be forced back into servitude by the very people the colonizers wanted gone. Memory of this bizarre chapter of US racism has led recently to "one minority group suing another minority group for inclusion in the indigenous minority group."[26] For Marx, wage labor, of course, was simply slavery by another name. Consequently, droves of working-class people, albeit descended from Europeans, were, to Marx's view, every bit as much enslaved as those descended from Africans. This argument is nowhere more stressed than in Marx's writings on the US Civil War.

---

[23]The typographical strategy of lowered cases was prevalent discursive practice in the heyday of protest.

[24]One of the best commentators is Lauren Michele Jackson, who regularly writes for *The New Yorker*.

[25]"Color-conscious … who wouldn't be color-conscious when everywhere you go people are always talking about color. If it didn't make any difference they wouldn't talk about it, they wouldn't always be poking fun, and laughing and making jokes" (210).

[26]Caleb Gayle, "The Black Americans Suing to Reclaim Their Native American Identity." *The Guardian*, November 2, 2018. https://www.theguardian.com/us-news/2018/nov/02/black-americans-native-creek-nation (accessed July 3, 2023).

The persistence of "race" as a paradigm for identity enables many confusions between or conflation of religion and "ethnicity." Anti-Jewish sentiment and behavior have weirdly been misnamed "anti-Semitism," when hailing from a wide variety of "ethnicities," the majority of Jews are not "Semites" at all and a huge number of "Semites" are not Jewish.[27] Anti-Islamic sentiment and behavior is perhaps slightly more appropriately labeled Islamophobia, but Islamophobia conflated confusingly with prejudice against "Arabs"—not all of whom are Muslim—which in turn is a catchall for anyone whose mother tongue is Arabic and not for any particular or specific "race." At bottom, it's all "race"-based prejudice.

I've heard one white academic maintain that "everyone performs their identity—even a Black." By that superficial perversion of Judith Butler's theory of performativity, a person "presenting male" in a body enveloped in dark-brown skin would have to, in addition, *perform* Black in order to be stopped and frisked. That academic goes around in skin with a color associated with racial "whiteness." That person claims they know that race is performative because if gender is performed (or if performativity is allowed in the realm of gender[28]), then it would be "racializing, biologizing, and essentialist" to deny "race" such performative powers. Consequently, I suppose, since performing Black is theoretically everyone's possibility, maybe such charlatans of "race" as Jessica Krug are Black after all. But then why is it that people with white skin performing Black suffer none of the consequences of racism? Isn't that the point of Nella Larsen's great novel? Or, conversely, the point of Wallace Thurman's?

racial terms and tropes of racialization

Returning specifically to semantics, we have already seen how the uncritical embrace of "race" leads to grouping and categorizing people on the sole basis of skin color: *the* Black, *the* Jew, *the* WASP, and so on. Racial essentialization

---

[27]See, inter alia, Shlomo Sand's *The Invention of the Jewish People* (2009).
[28]The extent of such permission is questionable. See, for example, Hallie Liberman, "It gets to you: trans comedians on transphobia and cancel culture." *The Guardian*, January 23, 2021.

also fosters the invention of altogether imaginary groups: the "Aryan,"[29] the "Semite," *und so weiter*. Whether based in some modicum of reality or in some myth, the racialization of humans has fostered pejorative synonyms, disparaging euphemisms, and whole linguistic industries for gaslighting and gassing. Words for the crimes committed in the name of "race" lose the force of their specificity when they are marshaled for use as metaphors. Humanist decorum dictates that right-minded citizens reprove and reject direct language, thereby foreclosing critique. But what if, instead of skirting them, we looked straight in the face of all the sayings, terms, and tropes that still float around in the cesspool of "race"? Are not open discussion and steady enlightenment the most intelligently dignified ways to begin seriously upending and undoing these nefarious legacies?

That genocidal extension of slavery that is universally known as *lynching* has today been metaphorized into banality. Thus, criminal accusation or even mere harsh criticism is decried by "victims" and their defenders as "lynching." This devalued application of the term for a very specific crime against humanity was repeatedly used, for example, when Clarence Thomas, Bill Cosby, and R. Kelly were, in succession, accused of harassment of women or worse.[30] In the last of these cases, the dominance of "race" and the ambient guilt for all the crimes committed in its name allowed Kelly's representatives to preach that "Since America was born, black men and women have been lynched for having sex or for being accused of it."[31] Such gross disingenuousness insults the memory of the more than 4,300 *actual* lynchings[32]—all of which have gone unpunished—since slavery was cancelled. Semantic perversion indeed produces some strange fruit.

---

[29]As part of his coping strategy, Klemperer used "Aryan" with sarcasm and irony, countering in himself Nazi efforts to have the term accepted. Here is one idea he sketched for an entry in a philosophical dictionary: "Article *race*: the invented Aryan, Nordic race (Gobineau) romanticism. Oldest, the chosen tribe, combined with modern (pseudo-) science" (I:375; I:476–77).

[30]Powerful and wealthy Black males are not the only "victims" of this loose application of the verb: when Gérard Depardieu was accused of sexual assault, his defenders also said he was being "lynched."

[31]Salamishah Tillet, "No, Bill Cosby and R. Kelly Were Not Lynched" (Opinion). *The New York Times*, May 4, 2018. https://www.nytimes.com/2018/05/04/opinion/bill-cosby-r-kelly-lynched.html?smprod=nytcore-ipad&smid=nytcore-ipad-share (accessed December 31, 2018).

[32]The Equal Justice Initiative has documented exactly 4,384 lynchings. As for the absence of punishment, we might compare this figure to the 2,976 dead at "Ground Zero" and the hugely disproportionate retribution that the attack elicited (see Chapter 2).

gaslighting

Stigmatization by insinuation, gaslighting, and dog-whistling are national pastimes among US actors deformed by "race." More than a decade before Ronald Reagan milked the Linda Taylor story for every drop of electoral advantage he could obtain from the inference that every low-income Black woman was a "welfare queen,"[33] Dick Gregory was informing the white audiences to which he appealed about the social worker who insinuated, around 1940, that his mother was "a welfare cheater" (30).

If for a few overly optimistic yet good-hearted people the election of Barack Obama heralded the dawn of a "post-racial" era for the United States, the whiny "we want our country back" crowd and even the nickname "Obamacare" soon stood as stark semantic proof that racism was very much alive and well. No less than "welfare queen" does, "Obamacare" oozes racist pus. It is a tribute to our forty-third president's patience that—like Roosevelt when critics referred sneeringly to his sweeping economic and public services program as the "Jew deal"—he held himself above it, tolerating it.[34] As for the whine, anyone familiar with the Civil Rights Era knows full well that "we" and "our" are synecdochic code for the "white race."

Convinced, somehow, that she was ever-so-hip as a dog-whistler, Sarah Palin memorably accused Obama of "palling around with terrorists" and enlisted the verbs "shuck and jive" to portray him as evasive and dishonest. Immediately chided for her little white girl's appropriation of a bit of Black vernacular, she "cleared the air" on Facebook with a quintessential bit of Freudian denial: "For the record, there was nothing remotely racist in my use of the phrase 'shuck and jive.'" About this racist discursive strategy, I'll have much more to say under the heading of "wokeism" in the next chapter.

---

[33] Inter alia, Josh Levin, "How the 'Welfare Queen' was born." *The New York Times*, May 17, 2019.

[34] "The election of an African American president in 2008 was supposed to herald a new 'post-racial' era, or at least to signal the ongoing transformation of a 'different racial America.' Yet the 2016 election of President Donald Trump on a 'law and order' platform that included racially polarizing codes and rhetoric shows how far the country remains from such an achievement. Indeed, recent psychological research on *implicit* racial discrimination has revealed an important, striking, and troubling set of findings about how Americans relate to race and racial differences and stereotypes" (Howard 157).

Examples of racist phrases of this ilk crop up constantly in US politics: Bush Jr.'s "real Americans," his daddy's "Willy Horton," erstwhile presidential wannabee DeSantis's "to monkey up." These epithets are all dredged from the same racist sewer to function as euphemisms. In the verb "wilding," which went wild in the 1989 Central Park Six case, along with the weasel word "inner-city youth" or the scarecrow "super-predator," the "race" of the individuals designated is obvious, albeit sotto voce, to all addressees.[35]

outright insults and slurs

Like radical surgery, if we are ever "to change […] a system where a white man can destroy a black man with a single word" (Gregory 223), then we need to look straight in the face of that ultimate semantic weapon in the tenacious "race" arsenal. If "N-word" is how the word *must* now appear in print, are we now to refer to Joseph Conrad's novel as *The N-word of the Narcissus*? or to Dick Gregory's autobiography as *N-word*? or to H. Rap Brown's memoir as *Die, N-word, Die*?[36] The argument for this practice is that it protects the sensibilities of the targets of the epithet. This is not unlike how we rationalize our childish self-censorship of curse words around young children. Has anyone asked an American of African descent if she has *heard* the word hidden behind the square bracket fig leaf? Has anyone asked her if she *knows* what it designates and *why* it was used? Let's get serious. About this most abject of slurs, James Baldwin was. The author of *The Fire Next Time* could be deadly serious and he often was the way one should be if one is serious about ridding the country of its centennial disease. We're not children: we know, or we *should* know, all the harm (murder, rape, economic and existential deprivation) caused by the system that invented *that* word. Until racism is finally in remission, that word—if it is ever to be said—needs to be said with that knowledge.

---

[35]Introduced by academics in the 1990s, the racial contours of "super-predator" and "inner-city youth" are thoroughly explained by Jason Stanley (2016), pp. 95–6.

[36]I've thought for decades that Jean Genet's title, *Les Nègres*, should have been translated as *The Niggers*—"Negroes" lacking the racist disdain that *nègres* harbors.

"I started off talking about schools and highways and prisons and taxes—and I couldn't make them listen. Then I began talking about niggers," one infamous Alabama governor boasted, "and they stomped the floor."[37] This quote is as good as any at showcasing "nigger" as the most abject of all racist slurs in English. But obfuscating it under the infantile "N-word" euphemism will do nothing to cure the United States of its original sickness. Everybody knows or *should* know that George Wallace was not the first white racist to embrace the debasing invective. A few years before founding what would become the University of Alabama's School of Medicine, for example, physical anthropologist, proponent of polygenism, and slaveowner Josiah Nott was in Mobile delivering what he himself termed his "lectures on niggerology."[38]

Verbal inoculation is a viable strategy in existential warfare: one that is all too often construed by non-Blacks as some imagined continuation of stereotyped subservience. Were he far better known—as he so deserves, Wallace Thurman's ironic portmanteau invention of "niggerati" to designate the young artists and writers associated with the Harlem Renaissance might in its fully spelled-out form contribute to the dismantling of our Ur-social disease. After all, Dick Gregory's experiential analysis of being the referent of the emasculating epithet as a boy growing up with a single mother made some inroads with the white audiences he had managed to reach.[39] Moving on to Carbondale as a college athlete, then to Chicago and San Francisco as a stand-up comedian, and to the deep south where he played an important role in the Civil Rights Movement, Gregory developed the ability to enlighten white audiences with withering anecdotes such as "A little cop came over. 'Nigger, you want to go to jail.' I said: 'Come here, boy, let me tell you something. I could take you to Chicago today and let you walk through my home, then come back here and walk through your home, and out of the two of us you'd know which one was the nigger'" (185).

---

[37]Quoted in Dan T. Carter, "Legacy of Rage: George Wallace and the Transformation of American Politics." *The Journal of Southern History* 62, no 1 (February 1996), p. 17.

[38]See Sussman 32 and Asim 49.

[39]As light as some of *Nigger* can be, the book parallels some of the more horrific events with the canard of racial difference at its root. The shadow of Emmett Till hovers over Gregory's memory of "One of the white men, a man who wasn't laughing, jumped off his bar stool. 'Get your hands off that white lady, you dirty nigger'" (11).

In the final essay of his 1965 collection, John Oliver Killens wrote,

> The one thing we black Americans have in common with the other colored peoples of the world is that we have all felt the cruel and ruthless heel of white supremacy. We have all been "niggerized" on one level or another. And all of us are determined to "deniggerize" the earth. To rid the world of "niggers" is the Black Man's Burden; human reconstruction is the grand objective.
>
> (171)[40]

Achieving that objective would also, hopefully, rid whites of the notion that any of them can ever be oppressed to the extent that Blacks have been. When the slur was repurposed to forge the term "white nigger," whining from the dominant group reached heights of shrillness.[41] It's more than creepy when light-skinned Europeans—be they kept down by other light-skinned Europeans—enlist "nigger" to communicate their plight, for as the contention at the core of Ku Klux Klan ideology demonstrates, the lowliest white can always convince himself he's got at least one superficial superiority over the highest Black: his skin color.[42]

James Baldwin, as I have already hinted, reigns supreme at lending penetrating expression to the crimes committed in the name of "race." Unabashedly pronouncing "nigger" in the cleverest of rhetorical gambits to condemn slave-owners and shame their wistful apologists was a specialty of his. Just as Dick Gregory invited that ignorant white cop into a mind experiment to determine who better fit into the shoe, Baldwin concluded his "Take This Hammer" interview in 1963 with a deftly calm "You're the nigger, baby, it isn't me."[43] However, the most powerful Baldwin lesson came during

---

[40]Quoted also in Kwame Ture [Stokely Carmichael] and Charles V. Hamilton, *Black Power: The Politics of Liberation*. New York: Vintage Books, 1992, p. 39.

[41]Cf. inter alia Elvis Costello's song, "Oliver's Army" ("one more widow, one less white nigger").

[42]Cf. Patrick McKenna, "When the Irish Became White: Immigrants in Mid-19th Century U.S." *The Irish Times*, February 12, 2013. www.irishtimes.com/blogs/generationemigration/2013/02/12/when-the-irish-became-white-immigrants-in-mid-19th-century-us/; Henry McDonald, "Gerry Adams Defends N-Word Tweet." *The Guardian*, May 2, 2016. https://www.theguardian.com/politics/2016/may/02/gerry-adams-defends-n-word-tweet-django-unchained (accessed July 4, 2023).

[43]KQED, San Francisco, 1963. https://youtu.be/L0L5fciA6AU.

his visit in 1968, accompanied by Dick Gregory, to the West Indian Students' Centre in London: "my entry into America is a Bill of Sale. And that stops you from going any further. At some point in our history, I became 'Baldwin's Nigger.' That's how I got my name."[44]

invalidating or "cancelling" "race"

And so, if humanity is something this species should still preserve and perhaps even honor, our task is to combine experience and reason with admeasures of common sense and compassion in thinking through our evolution within the species. Experience must be as extensive as possible; reason must be unwavering and abidingly applied to its objects. If not, as Goya warned, "the slumber of reason produces monsters." Incarnating these qualities and putting them to the task in a first fully scientific attempt at invalidating "race" as a concept was Franz Boas.[45]

The process of nullifying "race" and its toxic offspring, eugenics, could never have been initiated without Darwin's breakthrough of evolutionary biology. Living, working, thinking, and publishing in the middle of the nineteenth century, however, Darwin was not immune to the manipulative semantic perversion concomitant with the term "race." Although the tendency—even today—to consider, as my earlier discussion showed, the term "species" as synonymous with "race," it is fortuitous that Darwin entitled his watershed work *On the Origin of Species*. Unfortunately, however, the problematic term returns immediately in the rest of the long title: ... *or the Preservation of Favoured Races in the Struggle for Life*. Worse still, but predictably, given the overwhelming influence of near-contemporary Gobineau, Darwin repeatedly refers to a plurality of "races of man" in the text.[46] Given that he held *Homo sapiens* to be one single species, this is, of course, scientifically confusing. And

---

[44]*Baldwin's Nigger*, dir. Horace Ové, 1968, 46.

[45]One of the many excellent basic presentations of Boas's life and work is "The Invention of Race" produced by National Public Radio for broadcast on November 19, 2020: https://www.npr.org/2020/11/18/936346847/the-invention-of-race.

[46]E.g., 220, 413, 456, etc.

it left the theory of evolution wide open for the whole movement of social Darwinists, like Herbert Spencer and others, that would lead straight to the development of modern eugenics. Countering the lethal default of a plurality of "races" to account for morphological difference within the species, the Danish botanist and geneticist Wilhelm Johannsen introduced the genotype-phenotype distinction in 1911. But predictably, while the lay person might accept *phenotype* as the term accounting for radical color differences in scallop shells, "race" remains to this day his way of thinking the same superficial human variation.

At the level of semantics, and even to this day, the confusion caused by the conflation of "race" and "species" and by the slippage between "race" and "races" plagues many essays, their titles, discourse, and speech. While Robert Antelme astutely entitled his 1947 memoir of survival as a political prisoner of the Nazis and reflection on our species *L'Espèce humaine*, the English translator for some reason decided to substitute the perfectly valid appropriate "species" with "race." In 1981, when the late great writer and editor Maurice Olender launched the journal *Le Genre humain* [The Human Genus] with Les Éditions du Seuil, he boldly chose "Science Versus Racism" as the theme for the first issue. The journal's title was taken from the final words in the refrain of *L'Internationale* lazily and unfortunately—again—translated into English with the default "human race."

However, also in that same year of 1911 when Johannsen unveiled the genotype-phenotype distinction, with lynching rampant in the United States, and the first iteration of the Ku Klux Klan boasting a half million members, German-Jewish émigré Franz Boas published two books—*Changes in Bodily Form of Descendants of Immigrants* and *The Mind of Primitive Man*—that would not only launch the field of cultural anthropology but blow the cover on the already well-established eugenics movement, revealing it as pure ideological bunk.[47] Like his near contemporaries, the anarchist-geographers Peter Kropotkin and Élisée Reclus and, certainly *unlike* any of the eugenicists, Boas had had vast experience living among, listening to, and attempting to understand far-flung cultures vastly different from his own. And just as

---

[47]See Sussman 147ff.

Kropotkin had concluded that mutual aid is an observable impulse common to all animals—including all humans—so Boas concluded that scientific observation cannot warrant the use of "race" as a seriously scientific factor of variation among members of our species.

Boas's article on "race" for Seligman and Johnson's massive *Encyclopedia of the Social Sciences*, published just one year before the appalling Nuremberg Laws were promulgated in his native Germany, is a perfect illustration of his patient and methodical erosion of the foundation of eugenics.[48] In that epic article, the anthropologist wastes no time making a dispassionate statement of fact followed by discreditation. It is a simple one-two punch allowing him to level a devastating critique of physical anthropology for its strict adherence to anthropometric measurement racial typology. "In recent times the belief in a close interrelation between mental behavior and bodily build has come to be a matter of great social importance. Positive evidence for such relation has never been given" (26). He then spends considerable time acknowledging the sustained efforts and interest in cranial and cephalic measurements only to dismiss them as anything remotely close to reliable indicators of racial difference: "On account of the lack of information regarding the degree of hereditary fixity of the traits dealt with, classifications based on them have no genetic value" (27). Several pages later, with dispassionate rhetoric, he drops the knockout, "It is not justifiable to identify size of brain and intelligence" (33).

Regarding IQ and other intelligence tests that still serve the remnants of eugenics today, Boas found—as he always did—that cultural environment in the form of socioeconomic and educational opportunity (and not "race") was the sole criterion of high achievement: "among groups of Europeans who had immigrated at various times and had been subjected to intelligence tests those who had stayed longest in the United States gave the best results." He reports that research had "found this to be the case among Negroes migrating from rural districts to cities. The evidence in regard to mental differences

---

[48]We need also to be cautious in overemphasizing Boas' contribution to the deconstruction of "race" as a concept. The mere fact that he concedes by writing an article on the term demonstrates his acceptance of it as a term worthy of scientific examination. See, inter alia, Bernasconi 2019.

between races has been assembled by [Thomas Russell] Garth, who reaches the conclusion that no essential differences have been proved" (33).

Working toward his closing arguments, he writes that "The only safe conclusion to be drawn is that careful tests reveal a marked dependence of mental reactions upon conditions of life and that all racial differences which have been established thus far are so much subject to outer circumstances that no proof can be given of innate racial differences" (34). In January 1939, under completely different circumstances (with no readerly audience and trapped, along with other "dysgenics," within the Reich), Victor Klemperer put it far more bluntly: "race, in the sense of pure blood, is a zoological concept, and the concept that long ago ceased to correspond to any reality, [it] is at any rate even less a reality than the old strict distinction between the spheres of man and 'wife'" (I:291–92; I:376).[49]

Boas conducted, as I said, the first fully scientific attempt at invalidating "race" as a concept. Thus, for all his daring and the convincing proof he provides for the imposture of "race," he still invokes the term as a pluralizable noun to designate possible difference within the species. Notwithstanding the emphasis he placed on the final sentence, this passage from the end of the encyclopedia article illustrates the persistence of the word:

> It must be emphasized that no proof has been given that the distribution of genetic elements which may determine personality is identical in different races. It is likely that there are differences of this kind, provided the anatomical differences between the races are sufficiently fundamental. On the other hand, the study of cultural forms shows that such differences are altogether irrelevant as compared with the powerful influence of the cultural environment in which the group lives.
>
> (34)

Despite all the diligent and carefully researched work that Boas and his many students made it their mission to carry out in the name of truth about

---

[49]"*Keinem Volk zum Schaden, den 'völkisch' im Sinn der Reinblütigkeit ist ein zoologischer Begriff und ein Begriff, dem längst keine Realität mehr entspricht, jedenfalls noch weniger Realität als der alten strikten Unterscheidung zwischen den Sphären des Mannes und 'Weibes.*" It will be noted that I've restored Klemperer's distancing scare quotes. The English translator rightly gives "race" for the term "*völkisch*," which of course had that sense for the Nazis.

our species, it was only the full revelation of the Shoah that precipitated the long overdue debunking of eugenics as justification for the concept of "race." After that, "scientific racism" was at long last revealed as bunk, a *contradictio in adjecto*, as Nietzsche said of the *Ding an sich*: a lethal absurdity. By the time the "scientific" clothes were finally stripped from the grand white supremacist wizard *racism*, it was beyond overdue. And the toxic residues persisted through postwar generations of a society poisoned by the lie that "race" is.

Ashley Montagu, a brilliant member of the Boas stable,[50] dared as early as 1942, with his masterful *Man's Most Dangerous Myth* to chip away at the aberrant word "race" by arguing that the free coupling of humans—regardless of skin color, morphology, cranial size, etc.—results, at most, in "ethnic grouping." As a result of Montagu's argument, as Painter points out, "In 1997, the American Association of Physical Anthropologists urged the American government to phase out the use of race as a data category and to substitute ethnic categories instead" (253). Montagu was also the main author of the original UNESCO document that today is entitled the "Declaration on Race and Racial Prejudice." The first statement of the first article could not be clearer: "All human beings belong to a single species and are descended from a common stock. They are born equal in dignity and rights, and all form an integral part of humanity."[51] To Montagu's great credit, he continued to question himself and adjust his conclusions based on the experience and arguments of others, including Albert Memmi and Frantz Fanon, and his notion of racialization.

Like Franz Kafka, Victor Klemperer's only experience with America was through literature. Like Franz Boas and his students (and all the more intensively for the fact that he was writing from within the Third Reich), Klemperer had people deemed Jewish primarily in mind when he reflected on the ravages of "race." Trapped in Nazi Germany, he naively believed that the United States, as "a new nation [is] *one nation, one* although mixed from a hundred races, tribes, 'cultures.'" This, in turn, misled him into concluding that Unitedstatesians "utterly contradict the racial theory of the Nazis" (I:370; I:470). Is it not telling

---

[50]Montagu studied under Boas when he first went to Columbia in 1927; his dissertation was supervised by Ruth Benedict.

[51]UNESCO, Declaration on Race and Racial Prejudice. https://en.unesco.org/about-us/legal-affairs/declaration-race-and-racial-prejudice (accessed August 10, 2023).

that Klemperer aligns the two additional terms of "tribes" and "cultures" after "race" as though to communicate discomfort with *any* conceptual term for supposed deep difference? The last of these terms joins Boas.

allyship ... and its vicissitudes

In his "Song of Myself," Walt Whitman penned a famously moving testimonial to empathy:

> The disdain and calmness of martyrs,
> The mother of old, condemn'd for a witch, burnt with dry wood, her
> children gazing on,
> The hounded slave that flags in the race, leans by the fence, blowing,
> cover'd with sweat,
> The twinges that sting like needles his legs and neck, the murderous
> buckshot and the bullets,
> All these I feel or am.
>
> I am the hounded slave, I wince at the bite of the dogs,
>
> [...]
> I do not ask the wounded person how he feels, I myself become the
> wounded person,
>
> My hurts turn livid upon me as I lean on a cane and observe.
>
> (84–5)

... demonstrating that the imagination is indeed a powerful faculty. But can it enable one person to *become*—however fleetingly and for the purpose of lending a helping hand—another person? And is the aspiration to identify even necessary in order for justice, equality, and well-being to become fundamental givens that are distributed without exception and without discrimination across the species? Is there not something presumptuous and patronizing in the claim that "I take part, I see and hear the whole" (86)?

Documented in his classic account published in 1961, John Howard Griffin's experiment in passing as Black in the Deep South, a mere couple of years before the Selma to Montgomery marches, poses these questions, albeit in a different way. Unlike Whitman, Griffin figured out a way to live for a few months within what appeared to everyone he met to be a Negro's epidermis. This white man, Griffin, managed to experience some of the despair wrought on some people by relentless racism. So much so that, in documenting it, he could hear his own "voice, as though it belonged to someone else, hollow in the empty room, detached, say[ing]: 'Nigger, what you standing up there crying for?'" (67). Pronouncing that horrid word to himself—hearing what had been a white-skinned self addressing what was now a black-skinned self—brought home to him the realization that "No one outside the Negro community could imagine the profound effect this action had in killing the Negro's hope and breaking his morale" (49). This pathos-laden statement reads as if addressed directly to Whitman: while Whitman imagines, Griffin-as-a-Black man retorts that a white man cannot imagine it.

Work across lines drawn by "race" has historically taken myriad forms, whose descriptions provide lessons to those who want to read, to listen, to learn, to improve, to correct our socioeconomic lot. In Osha Gray Davidson's *The Best of Enemies* (eventually adapted for film), and to take only one example, Ann Atwater, a single mother raising her children on welfare checks and occasional housework, befriends C. P. Ellis, a gas station attendant and leader ("Exalted Cyclops") of a Durham KKK chapter. The unlikely meeting of these two humans—one Black, one white—leads to their both becoming civil rights activists. Classic and fairy-tale-like in many ways, Davidson's account of these allies demonstrates not only that racism *can* be controlled if not cured but also that poverty is a powerful catalyst for racism. The effect that Atwater had on Ellis could multiply if only more white people would listen to relentless anti-racist pedagogical projects like that of Tim Wise and dozens of others.[52]

The ubiquity of race in the United States and the confusions it fosters can, however, turn allyship into something abject and grotesque or make it simply go haywire. In Cary, North Carolina, during a prayer walk in June 2020 advocating the end of racism, white religious leaders, seconded by white

---

[52]See, e.g., Wikipedia's page listing "American anti-racism activists." https://en.wikipedia.org/wiki/Category:American_anti-racism_activists.

police officers, could be seen washing the feet of Black pastors. Meanwhile, Whoopi Goldberg (who reportedly adopted her last name because she feels strong alliance with Jews) was suspended from "The View" in February 2022 for stating that the Shoah (she said "Holocaust") was "not about race." Despite all the handwringing and judgments like that of ABC News president, Kim Godwin, that Goldberg's comments were "wrong and hurtful," they are not altogether wrong. Jewish ancestry may well constitute a culture (actually a multiplicity of cultures) and Judaism certainly is a religion, but Jews don't belong to any particular "race." Humans have walked the earth for 180,000 years; Judaism is at most 5,784 years old. "Race," we remember Klemperer having written, "long ago ceased to correspond to any reality." Every bona fide life scientist has corroborated that position with scientific (not biblical) evidence. That the Third Reich insisted that Jews constituted a "race" and that certain "races" require eradication is proof of their wholesale espousal of the altogether fake science of eugenics developed primarily, as we saw, in the United States. Can anyone seriously object to Goldberg's observation that people would never ask her if she were "really" Jewish if she had white skin?

evolution or devolution?

If the American obsession with race is merely a disease and not a congenital defect, then what is the cure?

Henry Louis Gates, Jr., was not exaggerating when in introducing a special issue of *Critical Inquiry* on "race," he claimed that "race is the ultimate trope of difference because it is so very arbitrary in its application" (5). He was at the nub of the semantic problem when he summarized Kwame Anthony Appiah's contribution that set out to demonstrate how that little four-letter word "functions in Western culture as a metonym for muddled thinking about the relation among genetics, intention, meaning, and culture" (15). If speakers enlist a possible synonym for a whole "species" to signify parts of that species, then we have a metonym. But "race," which first signified something like lineage or breed or perceived continuity in aristocratic families, came to signify (when convenient) the whole of humanity as well. But the metonymic relationship cannot have it both ways. The double bind inherent in "race" maddened Victor Klemperer, the "dysgenic" linguist trapped in the Nazi Reich:

> Race is […] a flexible, elastic, onion concept. Race: the whole of mankind as opposed to flora and fauna; race: the nation, the tribe, the family as opposed to specific other groups. And even parts of the individual—atom splitting, irrecoverable self!—are detached as racial (also as time and milieu-bound elements!). There remains as core of the self, as personality proper, the faculté maîtresse.

(II:195; II:259)

Such inextricable ambiguity is always the indicator of a faulty concept.

Reversing the causal relationship between "race" and racism only deepens the problem. One recent example is "The Jena Declaration" of 2019. Like UNESCO's "Declaration on Race and Racial Prejudice" this one is another "effort to act against scientific legitimations of racism," as its presenters put it. "The Jena Declaration" arose from an event held at Friedrich-Schiller Universität entitled "Jena, Haeckel and the question of human races" and whose subtitle—"how racism makes race"—foreshadowed the thesis of the resulting declaration: "The concept of race is the result of racism and not its precondition."[53] Besides the obvious fact that "racism" derives grammatically from "race" by the adjunction of the "-ism" suffix, the history and analysis that we have presented in this chapter suggest a genealogy opposite to that propounded by "The Jena Declaration." Although a segregationist and elitist attitude that we *now* call racism most certainly had to have set the stage for the emergence of "race" as a bogus conceptual tool, the persistent erroneous notion that one species can consist of more than one "race" enables the perpetuation of racism. It is therefore important—notwithstanding Nell Irvin Painter's hesitation about the practice[54]—that we apply skeptical, distancing,

---

[53]Organized by Martin Fischer and Uwe Hoßfeld at Friedrich-Schiller-Universität.

[54]In her introduction to *The History of White People*, Painter writes: "I resist the temptation to put the word 'science'—even theories and assertions of the most spurious, pernicious, or ridiculous kind—in quotation marks, for the task of deciding what is sound science and what is cultural fantasy would quickly become all-consuming" (1).

and *disqualifying* scare quotes to the word "science" wherever the word is associated with "race" or eugenics.

If Ali Rattansi has one of the chapter titles in his short overview of racism pose the question, "Racism without races?," it is because the answer must be an unequivocal "yes" (86ff). Notwithstanding the dramatic and long-overdue discreditation of eugenics in the wake of Nazi collapse and despite the timorous legislative and educational measures taken in the United States to right the wrongs wrought by the concept of "race," racism persists in policing, in policy, in the polity.

teach CRT and get fired

> *Race. [...] The notion it conveys has underwritten some of the worst atrocities ever committed by one people on another [...] perceived "racial" differences have provided the rationale for the infliction of untold amounts of human misery. Clearly "race" has been a very significant component of our collective human experience.*
>
> (Tattersall/Desalle xi)

Critical Race Theory is the latest anti-racist pedagogical program to be instituted, here and there, in the United States. While we would be marginally better off adopting the practice of referring to morphologically different human groups as *phenotypes*, that conceptually problematic term of "race" still stands prominently in the phrase naming this laudable field of critical inquiry and analysis. Assuming that the proponents and practitioners of CRT are dedicated to debunking "race" as mere quackery, their struggle is a salutary and just one. And while it may be obvious that the idea driving CRT should be preserved and promoted, the articulation of "race" with "critical" and "theory" needs, at the very least, to be made explicit and obvious—especially to the unconvinced.

If CRT could only be generalized across all schooling—not only in the United States but everywhere—strides in attenuating systemic racism might eventually be made. Recognizing the semantic perversion driven by "race" should turn terms like "colorblind" into hot-button items for immediate and thorough critique in the classroom, first, and, consequently, in daily practice in the social realm. Curricula including epic debates like the 1929 head-to-head between W. E. B. DuBois and Lothrop Stoddard or the question put to William F. Buckley and James Baldwin at Cambridge University in 1965 could, and no doubt *would*, enlighten minds. Books by dozens of thinkers also come to mind: DuBois, bell hooks, Ture/Carmichael, Franz Fanon … However, it should not be surprising that, just as what happened when ethnic studies and, later, gender studies programs started to burgeon in colleges and universities in the 1970s, CRT, today, is subjected to unrelenting whiny rejection. The scientific credentials of those who have tried to block CRT from becoming a normal part of curricula are as irrelevant and unimpressive as those of the old proponents of eugenics.[55] Painting the erstwhile oppressors as victims is one of their all-too-predictable strategies. We recall that this not-so-subtle turning of tables underlay the erection of statues to the Confederacy and the cries of "reverse discrimination" as soon as Affirmative Action was legislated. According to the parents of children in schools where attempts to tell the full history of how "race" put the United States on criminally inhumane footing from the start, "white kids' feelings are more important than black kids' reality."[56] And college professors like Samuel Joeckel get fired for teaching units on racial justice which, as one concerned parent claimed, "indoctrinates students."[57]

CRT notwithstanding, racism obviously persists. And its most pernicious and tenacious avatars are institutional, economic, political, and colonial. Obviously too, every argument has its contrarians and detractors; every social movement has its reactionaries. Even science runs up against stubborn superstition and ignorance. Philosophical reasoning that appeals to sociology or economics or experiments like Critical Race Theory mounted to shape policy or even the patiently compiled findings of biologists, geneticists, cultural

---

[55]Instructive in this whole area are Tony Platt's recollections of teaching what would become CRT at UC Berkeley in the early 1970s: "The Legacies of Un-Critical Race Theory at Berkeley." *History News Network*, July 25, 2021. https://historynewsnetwork.org/article/180783.

[56]Kimberlé Crenshaw, "'Just the tip of the iceberg': Kimberlé Crenshaw warns against rightwing battle over CRT." *The Guardian*, March 4, 2023.

[57]In Joeckel's case, it was from a "Christian" institution—Palm Beach Atlantic University—which, incidentally, does not offer tenure. This firing occurred in March 2023. Joeckel had taught the same unit for many years previously.

anthropologists, and paleontologists will all be outstripped by evolution itself in erasing "race" from the mind of *Homo sapiens*. If only the reality of our evolving bodies could efface the ugly face of "race," then this pillar of racism would dissolve.

Perhaps this could happen if no plurality whatsoever could ever again be inferred by "race." In this vein, rarely has the simple word "only" been used with as much force as when Stephen Jay Gould uttered the truism that "the only living human species [is] *Homo sapiens*" (398). "Only" describes that which is utterly and properly singular. Only one species. Or, if one really insists, one "race." But one and only one. Where could Gould have got such an idea but from the bodies he studied over the full course of their existence? "Africa is most of humanity by any proper genealogical definition," Gould continued, "all the rest of us occupy a branch within the African tree. This non-African branch has surely flourished, but can never be topologically more than a subsection within an African structure" (399). Like it or not, then, we are *all* African. Only climates encountered and cultures developed in relative multiple isolations beyond Africa caused us to evolve into *looking* slightly different one from another. And this radical original isolation is fading very quickly.

If ever the term "race" *must* be used in reference to the species that we (of this very species) have named *Homo sapiens*, then it may only refer to the *entire* species as distinct from, say, *Homo erectus* or *Pan paniscus*. Nothing, however, in the 180,000-year history of "our" species has allowed for anything like "racial differentiation" to occur *within* the species. Furthermore, with rapidly advancing global movement and the new reproductive possibilities that that trend affords, any phenomenon that racists insist on calling "racial differentiation" will one day fade to naught.

Already in the mid-1930s, Franz Boas was gathering some of the elements for such a development: "There are no races of man in which no overlapping occurs," he wrote regarding "race," "Negroes and Europeans may be tall or short, round headed or long headed, large or small brained" (28). And, in addition to what, today, biological scientists, paleontologists, and anthropologists alike agree upon, that is, "that there is more within-group variation among humans than among-group variation" (Tattersall/Desalle 197), Boas was keenly focused on human migration, foreseeing the inexorable effects of reproductive intermingling. On the long historical view of the species, two migratory phenomena appeared to Boas: the first involved the spread of humans out of Africa; the second—ongoing at present and unstoppable—the global reunion of the disparate cousins. The first would account for the evolved physiological variations erroneously attributed to a plurality of "races"; the second holds the promise (notwithstanding the persistence of the fake concept) of the attenuation of these superficial differences. "Even in earliest prehistoric times migrations must have occurred," Boas wrote regarding the first. "The sudden change from the Neandertal type prevailing at the end of the older paleolithic period to the new type of the later paleolithic can be explained only by migration" (31). Regarding the second, he added that "The period of isolation must have been exceedingly remote, and it may be expected that an intermingling of types will be found almost everywhere. It is therefore particularly important that the effect of intercrossing be understood" (31).

Today, bolstered by further scientific evidence and emboldened by thinkers from Frantz Fanon and Stokely Carmichael to Cornel West and Michele Alexander, whose analyses are finally being listened to, more and more people "in the mainstream" are coming to realize that "differences among human populations that we intuitively view has racial are not only superficial in terms of import but also of astonishingly recent origin" (Tattersall/DeSalle xi). And this realization has, in turn, begun to chip away at "race" as a criterion for policy. As Nell Irwin Painter recently wrote,

> it has been obvious since the invention of racial science in the eighteenth century that skin color can change drastically from one generation to the next. All that is needed is sex between people of different colors, which has taken place as soon as people meet. Acknowledgment of the existence of people of "mixed race," as in the U.S. census, means acknowledgment of the impermanence of race.
>
> (256)

Or, as curators past and present of American Natural History Museum in New York have put it, "*Homo sapiens* is one single species: one large, interbreeding unit, freely exchanging our genes with each other and with nothing else on the planet" (Tattersall/DeSalle xii).

toward some conclusion to that which ends not

"You must begin to define yourself," H. Rap Brown once admonished his readers, "you must begin to define your Black heritage" (68). Such is what Henry Louis Gates Jr. has been helping people to do for decades and shows most dramatically with his PBS series, "Finding Your Roots." Is genealogical "closure," however, a path that will be effective in curing our minds and our way of being of "race" and its destructive consequences? In the short term, maybe. Although the Ben Affleck snafu proves once again, not only that "only race matters" but that it's still largely, as Klemperer lamented, "zoology + business." In the long term we should be looking forward to tearing down walls, building bridges, facilitating movement, retiring the notion of nation … in short, we should be looking forward to embracing, finally, *the oneness of the human species*. Nature in the form of evolution within the species will be our best ally, for as paleoanthropologist Ian Tattersall and geneticist Robert DeSalle state, "Despite cultural barriers that uniquely help slow the process down in our species, the reintegration of *Homo sapiens* is proceeding apace. And places the notion of 'races' as anything other than sociocultural constructs ever more at odds with reality. Increasingly, it seems, we are simply who we think we are" (xv).

4

"Cancel Culture"...

Of these five chapters examining how words can manipulate us into doing their worst work, the title of this one calls for scare quotes. While reactionaries and racists of all stripes frantically wave the bogeyman of "cancel culture" in the face of progressive elements, social egalitarians fret that this scarlet letter glows afresh just when the redness of "political correctness" was fading.

Indeed, the expression "cancel culture" was forged by those bent on denigrating moves to bring the powerful to account for reprehensible statements and actions directed especially toward historically least powerful individuals or groups in the society. The expression "cancel culture" emerged in the late 1980s as the latest manifestation of what those same forces dubbed the "culture wars"—yet another phrase displaying the affinity for metaphors that dog-whistle armed conflict. Squabbling about "cancel culture" and its close cousin, "wokeism," is just the latest episode in that artificial construct of which, incidentally, and as we will explore further in the final chapter, the University is crucible.

---

[1] https://trumpwhitehouse.archives.gov/briefings-statements/remarks-president-trump-south-dakotas-2020-mount-rushmore-fireworks-celebration-keystone-south-dakota/; in his Executive Order of January 18, 2021, on Building the National Garden of American Heroes, Trump labeled "cancel culture" "a dangerous anti-American extremism that seeks to dismantle our country's history, institutions and very identity." The plan to build such a garden was cancelled by President Biden.

The term "cancel culture" was forged in haughtily offended reaction when in 2006 the social media movement known by the hashtag #metoo began exposing sexual harassers, rapists, and femicides. Reactionary repulsion at "cancel culture" then amplified further into violently offended recoil before the founding in 2013 of the Black Lives Matter (BLM) movement. That the sole purpose of blurting the anathema of "cancel culture" is to stifle minoritized voices raised in the name of justice is revealed by the act of *calling out*. Victims of sexual violence call out perpetrators; survivors, demonstrators, and allies call out the names of Black people murdered by police.

Popular attempts—attempts from "below"—to deprive individual or corporate persons of power and profit can be both just and, occasionally, effective. Meanwhile, those who sneer at what they designate as deleterious consequences of "cancel culture" willfully ignore what movements like #metoo, BLM, and their ancestors have been relentlessly calling for, namely, *consequences* for nefarious behavior and *reckoning* about the conditions that foster it. If the consequences of calling out injustice remind people of the cancellation of a failed TV show, then so be it.

The whole economy in which power, knowledge, politics, and psychology intertwine in the US social fabric can never be thought independently of the puritanical traditions of shaming and the pillory, among whose current manifestations are bullying and the perp walk. But the strategy of the *boycott*— closely related to the noble tradition of nonviolent resistance and not just idiosyncratically Unitedstatesean—is also to be found in the toolbox of what is denounced as "cancel culture."

Ultimately, though, if the expression "cancel culture" is to mean what its publication on the page suggests, it is not as withering sarcasm directed at the historically weak who seek equality and justice but as a term for the wanton cancelling of peoples and cultures that have punctuated the human experience writ large. And the theoretical correlate of the expression would be the cancelling of endeavors that some humans have developed to train and exercise the critical faculties of the brain. Thus we recall that when Klemperer noted, in the first year of the Nazi régime, that "military sports" were being prioritized over study, "A series of lectures was simply canceled. Scholarship is no longer essential" (I:37; I:50).

Turning yet again, then, to the Dresden linguist, I dare say that through his diaries (and invoking another word that entered the US semantic "mainstream" simultaneously with "cancel culture"), Klemperer proves himself to be the most *woke witness* of the Third Reich. While the exact expression never appears under Klemperer's pen (or from the keys of his typewriter, before it was confiscated), through his cumulative observations we can perceive a clear distinction between the phantasm persistently named "cancel culture" and *actual* cancel culture. In addition, Klemperer's record of experience perfectly illustrates the connection between so-called race and what "cancel culture" should actually signify. As we have endeavored to show earlier, elevating "race" to the level of concept is what passes as validation for racism. In turn, racism's ultimate effect is the *cancellation* of cultures, or ethnocide.

On the one hand, the Third Reich obsessively and relentlessly justified its regime by inventing or exaggerating demographic distinctions, accusing Jews—even perfectly secular persons deemed Jewish—of tainting or even nullifying everything "purely" German. Once armed conflict appeared on the horizon, the trumped-up complaint devolved into a defensive (and, therefore, just) war against the quintessential fictitious enemy: a "Jewish war." From one end to the other of the Second World War, the whole conflagration was to be imputed to the putative Jewish plot to *cancel* German culture.

On the other hand (again to the twisted Nazi mind), that which is "German" can only be affirmed by cancelling "the Jew"—an inexorably incremental process that would culminate in genocide. The process leading to the biological cancellation of Jews across the Reich was, in the Nazis' own word, "fanatical." Thus, already in the summer of 1934, "the building regulations of the Third Reich requiring 'German' houses, flat roofs [like Klemperer's] are 'un-German'" (I:73; I:99). By the next summer, "The Jew-baiting and the pogrom atmosphere growing day by day," Klemperer is reading in "*Der Stürmer*, Goebbels' speeches ('exterminate like fleas and bedbugs!'), acts of violence" foreshadowing *actual* cancellation (I:128; I:172). In the meantime, the professor who had been "so convinced of [his own] Germanness" (I:239; I:315)[2] was removed from his

---

[2] In March 1942, with the first exterminations at Belzec well under way, Klemperer reflects thus on a remark made by another victim of cancel culture: "Recently Seliksohn said in utter seriousness: 'I

university post. Shunned by his former colleagues—"I am like a plague corpse" (I:136; I:184)—Klemperer wonders, "Is a Jewish professor allowed [...] to be 'noticeable' in any way?" (I:158; I:208). A member of the "cancelling" "race" becomes a true object of cancellation.

Opposite the shrill Nazi voices that attribute every perceived evil to the "subhumans"[3] to be "liquidated"[4] so that their hallucinated omnipotence be staunched, whispers and exchanged looks in silence are, according to rampant propaganda of fascist paranoia, the preferred means of communication among the putative culture-cancellers.[5] But just who are these whispering traitors? According to Klemperer, they are the pure paranoid construct of Nazism. The experience of surviving the Third Reich convinced him, as we saw amply in the last chapter, that "the Jewish people [were] created by Hitler" (I:375; I:476–7).[6]

David and Goliath

All this was worked through nearly eighty years ago by a German forcibly made a Jew by those claiming that Jews were "cancelling" them.[7] Here we are with the first spectacular modern case of complaints about pervasive "cancel culture" endlessly being cried out by cancellers. Just who are the individuals today who raise their voices in outraged indignation? Mario Cuomo, Dominique Strauss-Kahn, J. K. Rowling, Harvey Weinstein, Gérard Depardieu, Donald Trump, Nigel Farage, and Tucker Carlson to name just a few. Tellingly, not

---

cannot eat pork and black pudding. That's a five-thousand-year-old tradition in my blood.' His wife put in: 'But you eat ham.'—How great an effect does tradition have? [...] I *think* German, I *am* German—I did not give it to myself, I cannot clear it out of myself. What is tradition? Everything begins with *myself*. No, certainly with my parents" (II:34; II:46).

[3]In December 1940, Klemperer notes the appearance of the neologism (I:366; 466).

[4]"German civilizing work on the Lublin Ghetto" (I:331; 423).

[5]"Just at the right moment, Eva told me, that there is a new poster in town—two people whispering to each other—with the caption: 'Anyone who whispers, is lying.'" June 1, 1943 (II:234; II:312).

[6]The most extensively researched study on this issue remains Shlomo Sand's *The Invention of the Jewish People*.

[7]During his return from Munich to Dresden, though relieved that the nightmare had ended, could foresee that semantic perversion would persist and continue to threaten peaceful existence: "I [...] had the momentary feeling of having emerged from the life of the vagabond and returned to the joys (even if for the time being the most mendacious ones) of civilization" (II:512; II:672).

only can they easily be named but our recognition of them—their renown—preceded their falling "victim" of "cancel culture." Ironically, for some who have supposedly suffered the same "injustice"—Amy Cooper, Rick Santorum, Josh Hawley to name a few more—"cancellation" itself has proved to be their sole path to reaching dubious limelight. Meanwhile, the French right delights in citing the names of "leftist" intellectuals like Alain Finkielkraut, Marcel Gauchet, Elisabeth Badinter, Sylviane Agazinski, Michel Onfray, and Régis Debray—supposedly "ostracized" by Gallic "cancel culturists."[8] The civilizational discontent of "cancel culture" would be so rampant in the United States, according to the gatekeepers, as to even require defending Mr. and Mrs. Potato Head from its withering effects.[9] Ditto for thoroughbred horses owned by Saudi businessmen and trained by rednecks.[10] Roman Polanski labels it "hysterical"; Vladimir Putin compares the West's "cancelling" of Russian culture to that of poor J. K. Rowling.[11] And so on, ad nauseam.

Interestingly (and surprisingly), the grammatical dynamics of Putin's complaint suggests a bivalence or perhaps even a contradiction within the expression under examination. At first blush—with "cancel" operating as adjective modifying "culture"—the semantic unit suggests an *attitude* or *bent of mind* (no doubt thought to be growing or spreading like bacteria in a Petri dish) whose aim is to at least question and, in a few cases, to undermine the authority of individuals who abuse others: in exaggerated shorthand, to "cancel" them. In this case, the object of the act of or attempt to cancel is situated outside the expression. Ever since Fox cancelled *The O'Reilly Factor* and the show's erstwhile host forked out $32 million to cover his sexual misconduct, old Bill has continued to rail that he was a "victim" of "cancel

---

[8] See "Les nouveaux intolérants, ces juges de la pensée qui rêvent de réduire au silence ceux qui ne pensent pas comme eux." *Le Figaro*, February 18, 2022.

[9] Akin Olla, "No, Dr Seuss and Mr Potato Head Haven't Been 'Cancelled'. Here's the Difference." *The Guardian*, March 6, 2021. https://www.theguardian.com/commentisfree/2021/mar/06/dr-seuss-mr-potato-head-cancel-culture.

[10] "Trainer: Kentucky Derby Winner Faces Disqualification Due to 'Cancel Culture.'" https://www.theguardian.com/sport/2021/may/10/bob-baffert-medina-spirit-kentucky-derby-horse-racing-cancel-culture-disqualification?CMP=Share_iOSApp_Other.

[11] "Putin Says West Treating Russian Culture Like 'Cancelled' JK Rowling." https://www.theguardian.com/world/2022/mar/25/putin-says-west-treating-russian-culture-like-cancelled-jk-rowling.

culture." But when Putin, in the name of Russian people, plays victim, the culture supposedly under threat that he's referring to is a set of civilizational achievements imputed to a nation, a language, their art, their literature, and so on. In this case, "cancel" becomes a fully fledged verb for an alleged crime committed against a cultural heritage. Seen in this way, "cancel culture" might suggest cancellations of whole entities than mere efforts to confront powerful individuals with their misdeeds and hold them to consequences.

Rather than the program or policy of a troublemaking segment of the US population, "cancel culture" is the latest avatar of epithets hurled in an age-old struggle at the puny and the powerless by the pundits and the powerful. And this struggle takes place not in mythology or legend but in the everyday life led by actual persons. This is why, in addition to reflecting on how the expression's meaning changes when the grammatical functions assigned to its components are manipulated, it is extremely helpful to consider vital distinctions that can be made clear by *judicious* application of scare quotes. Closely resembling the whining of white people "threatened" by demographic changes, that of the first group justifies setting "cancel culture" off by the typographical indicators of critical distance. On the other hand, the rapist wields and exercises power overwhelmingly over the raped person. The act of rape is an act of cancellation that bears no comparison of degree to being impeached or fired for harassment. The corrupt official who suffers professional consequences as a result of work done by the investigative journalist suffers infinitely less than the journalist who has been murdered for courageously performing her work. Everyone would agree that "cancellation" in the first example is a ludicrous exaggeration compared to the loss of life. The deprivation of rights, of peace and well-being—indeed, sometimes, of existence itself—is a reality for the puny and powerless. In this regard, fretting about "cancel culture" by the powerful is mere petty distraction compared to the damage caused when lives and cultures are cancelled, and voices are muted. It would now seem to become possible to express the struggle in the following manner: what the gatekeepers label "cancel culture" is a natural, just, and perhaps inevitable dialectical reversal of the dynamics that has allowed—and still allows—hegemonic power to cancel cultures.

An important and revealing text at the heart of the "cancel culture" debate is the "Letter on Justice and Open Debate" signed by 152 individuals and published in *Harper's Magazine* on July 7, 2020. Appearing in the heat of the massive protests following the murder of George Floyd, the signatories "applaud" the "protests for racial and social justice." However, they see "cancel culture" (cannily left unnamed but alluded to by reference to "a vogue for public shaming and ostracism") as a variant of "dogma and coercion" that is as harmful as the "illiberalism" of the "right-wing demagogues." Fearing that the "stifling atmosphere will ultimately harm the most vital causes of our time," the 152 plead to be free to speak …

… As if any of them had been censored, lost their jobs or livelihood—let alone their well-being, their right to dignity, or, indeed, their culture or life. Sadly, some of the most respected luminaries of our time—Cornel West, Nell Irvin Painter, Noam Chomsky—accepted Thomas Chatterton Williams' invitation to endorse this statement. (The *actual* life of Salman Rushdie, who also signed, has been the target for both theoretical and *real* cancellation.) It is disingenuous, at the very least, when these established intellectuals (with the sole exception of Rushdie) with free and easy access to wide audiences include themselves in the "we" subject of the sentence that begins: "We are already paying the price in greater risk aversion […]." To critique the powerful, whoever they may be—even allies—in no way silences speech.[12] This confusion is the unfortunate but predictable consequence of all-too-hasty intellectual interventions in those all-too-rare cases when unlicensed minoritized voices suddenly get heard. The reactionary tenor of the letter ultimately undermines the rectitude of their lesson about free speech—however hackneyed it is. Nesrine Malik, who places the scare quotes exactly where they should be, has it about right, in my view:

> They have confused a lack of reverence from people who are able to air their views for the very first time with an attack on their right to free speech. They have mistaken the new ways they can be told they are wrong or irrelevant as the baying of a mob, rather than exposure to an audience that has only

---

[12]Cf. Jessica Valenti, "'Cancel Culture': How the Powerful Play Victim." *The Guardian*, July 8, 2020. https://gen.medium.com/cancel-culture-is-how-the-powerful-play-victim-e840fa55ad49 (accessed September 13, 2023).

recently found its voice. The world is changing. It's not "cancel culture" to point out that, in many respects, it's not changing quickly enough.[13]

What struck me first—even before I took the measure of the *Harper's* superciliousness—were the odd bedfellows among the signatories: Noam Chomsky, for example, alongside George W. Bush's former speechwriter? This letter endorsed by those specific personalities soon had me agreeing with one commentator who wrote that "'cancel culture' is […] a fundamentally elitist complaint."[14] This characterization helps understand how neoliberals and reactionaries could make common cause with progressives and anarchists.

"No one calls it a 'cancellation,'" that same commentator continues, "when a higher-up fires a lower-down worker, even when the reasons are obscure." The authority of this observation leads us right back to the distinction that I think would clarify so much of what separates the spuriousness of "cancel culture" and the vital seriousness of what can legitimately be named *cancel culture*. When the US Department of State rescinded Finnish journalist Jessikka Aro's International Women of Courage Award because she was found to have been a critic of Trump, *this* constituted cancellation—albeit one that didn't threaten the victim's life. When events where critics of Israel's genocidal war on Palestinians like Judith Butler or Masha Gessen or Ai Weiwei are "postponed for safety reasons" or cancelled, this is censorship. Sarah Hagi, who self-identifies as a Black Muslim woman, writes "frequently about racism and Islamophobia." Hagi points out that when her detractors "throw around terms like 'cancel culture' to silence [her] instead of reckoning with the reasons [she] might find certain actions or jokes dehumanizing, [she's] led to one conclusion: they'd prefer [she were] powerless against [her] own oppression."[15] Such is the force of actual cancellation—even if the cancelled individual is allowed to go on living.

---

[13]In "Is Free Speech under Threat from 'Cancel Culture'? Four Writers Respond." *The Guardian*, July 8, 2020. https://www.theguardian.com/commentisfree/2020/jul/08/is-free-speech-under-threat-cancel-culture-writers-respond?CMP=Share_iOSApp_Other (accessed September 13, 2023).

[14]Lili Loofbourow, "The Cancel Culture Trap." *Slate*, July 27, 2020. https://slate.com/news-and-politics/2020/07/black-lives-matter-me-too-cancel-culture-blacklash.html (accessed July 30, 2020).

[15]*Time*, November 21, 2019.

Yet, an alarming number of journalists lose not only their livelihood but, indeed, their lives for the noble work that they do. When Jamal Khashoggi met his atrocious death in Istanbul for daring to criticize the heir to the Saudi throne, this was *true* cancellation. When Shireen Abu Akleh was "accidentally" assassinated by the IDF for reporting from the West Bank, this was *true* cancellation. When Chauncey Bailey was bumped off in my beloved Oakland for his fearless reporting on graft, this was *true* cancellation. When record numbers of journalists perish as part of Israeli retaliation for Hamas's brazen 7 October attack, this is tantamount to the liquidation of witnesses—*true* cancellation. Whether as "collateral damage" in war, as in Ukraine or Gaza, or as targets of gangs, as in Haiti or Mexico, dozens of journalists every year lose their lives exercising their freedom to report fact. Taken together, the crimes exemplified here constitute a worldview that would be happy seeing journalism disappear altogether. I have no doubt that Thomas Chatterton Williams and his cosigners had unfettered freedom of the press in mind, but why not say so explicitly instead of grousing about threats to their own free speech. And what a strategic blunder for them to endorse one of the tropes that reactionaries use, namely, "to police the limits of social change while portraying themselves as victims of an organised assault on liberty itself."[16]

From these examples it is possible and, indeed, usefully instructive to extrapolate. Beyond assassinated journalists, who are some of the other victims of an actual cancel culture? In the first paragraph of this section, where I identified a handful of the people aggrieved by "cancel culture," I noted how *notable* they all are. Their visibility and their notoriety—their mere name— authorize them to intervene on subjects in which they have no expertise. And based on their fame, we give credence to the authority of those interventions: we believe that "cancel culture" is "a thing." But what about Trayvon Martin or George Floyd or all the others whose names we now know only because they were murdered? We, who know them now, only learned their names after it was too late, after they were cancelled. Any authority that their names now

---

[16]Billy Bragg, "'Cancel Culture' Doesn't Stifle Debate, but It Does Challenge the Old Order." *The Guardian*, July 10, 2020. https://www.theguardian.com/commentisfree/2020/jul/10/free-speech-young-people?CMP=Share_iOSApp_Other (accessed September 14, 2023).

carry is relayed by whoever still cares to do something about the culture that killed them.

And then there are all the peoples that have been liquidated or, more accurately, all the *cancellations of cultures*. In the United States alone, we have the litany of crimes—the Indian Removal Act, the Trail of Tears, all the massacres—that more than justify the labels of genocide and ethnocide to describe crimes committed against the humanity of Native Peoples; we have the four centuries of African slavery, identity denial, the rapes, the murders, the breeding, followed by a hundred more years of slavery by other means— lynching, convict leasing, myriad humiliation, mass incarceration. Racism cancels cultures: whole populations. Cancel culture, in this literal sense, has taken place elsewhere as well: we can think of the Irish under England, Cambodia under the Khmer Rouge, the Armenians in Turkey, the Aboriginal Peoples of Australia, Rwanda, Kosovo, Russians "adopting" Ukrainian kids. It would indeed appear that there is something we *can* and *should* call cancel culture without scare quotes and the list seems endless. Endless unless a critical reckoning be had.

We must learn to pirouette. But more about that in the last chapter. Suffice it to say for now, though, that whereas firing someone for committing offenses of discrimination or crimes of any sort is quite simply normal and justified, firing someone for opening young minds to their critical potential is a crime committed against generations coming up and to come. While the "victims" of the first category of action whine that they have been "cancelled," the victims— real victims—of a stunted education rejoin society as sexists, racists, and so on.

Short of genocide, rendering the other *invisible* is a common culture-cancelling strategy. This is what *nativism*—an offshoot of the eugenics movement—attempted with its distortion of the expression "native American." Most people today accept "Native Americans" as a descriptor for descendants of the aboriginal peoples of the continent—colonized yesterday and on which the United States rests today. This, however, is not the expression's referent according to *nativist racists*. We need only be reminded, for example, of what Washington congressman Albert Johnson, chair of the House Committee on Immigration and Naturalization, meant in December 1923 when he introduced legislation that would prevent "native Americans from mixing with lower types."[17] Earlier, in 1918, when Johnson's mentor, the arch-eugenicist Madison Grant (idolized, we recall, by Hitler), established the Galton Society, he did so specifying that membership would consist only of "native Americans, who are anthropologically, socially, and politically sound."[18] Not only is the claim of "native" status for people from Europe or descended from Europeans now living in America a patent absurdity, it denies any visibility to First Nations of so-called Indians.

Writers in the existentialist vein writ large well understood the erasure strategy of actual cancel culture and portrayed it vividly. When Gregor Samsa awoke transformed into a "monstrous bug" (*in einem ungeheueren Ungeziefer*),[19] he was no longer visible as the human whose voice only a reader of *The Metamorphosis* can "hear."[20] Similarly, the unnamed (perhaps because unnamable) narrator of Ralph Ellison's *Invisible Man* doubts he "really exist[s]" because, as he explains in the Prologue, "I am invisible […] simply because people refuse to see me."

The Israel-Palestine case is certainly one of the strangest examples of cancel culture that should appear without scare quotes. When Chaim Weizmann succumbed to the temptation of picking up the old *Christian* Zionist saw that Palestine was "a land without a people for a people without a land,"[21] he was setting the stage for a prophesy that is being fulfilled today, ever more blatantly, as Israel relentlessly expands. New settlements are built on land confiscated by fiat, houses, olive groves, and other crops of the West Bank's non-Jewish population are regularly bulldozed, leaving "Arabs"—the "othered" Semites—displaced, further impoverished, further deprived of water. The urban version

---

[17]See Sussman, 102. The nativist movement survived delegitimization after the Second World War. One need only think of the life and times of John Tanton and his Federation for American Immigration Reform (FAIR).

[18]See Sussman, 175. See also Aliya R. Hoff, "The Galton Society for the Study of the Origin and Evolution of Man (1918–1935)." *The Embryo Project Encyclopedia.* https://embryo.asu.edu/pages/galton-society-study-origin-and-evolution-man-1918-1935 (assessed September 14, 2023).

[19]For an interesting discussion of how most effectively to translate Kafka's designation into English, see Rochard H. Lawson, "*Ungeheueres Ungeziefer* in Kafka's 'Die Verwandlung.'" *The German Quarterly* 33, no. 3 (May 1960), pp. 216–19.

[20]I substitute "hearing" for "decipher through reading" to recall the tragic incommensurability between Gregor's stream of consciousness and the chirping his sister hears.

[21]For a pondered history of the phrase, see Muir 2008.

of the same process is the radical transformation of the demographics and economics of East Jerusalem. The statistics over the course of history since the Six-Day War can easily be consulted. They are eloquent: the settler movement, with Israeli support, is transforming the land from the Jordan River to the Mediterranean Sea into one single "historical homeland of the Jewish People" instead of the touted democracy.

If the plight of Palestinians (a term strategically absent from the Basic Laws of Israel) sounds so familiar to some North American readers, it is because the effects of Israeli settler colonialism are altogether homologous with those of Manifest Destiny in the United States. Just as rapacious expansionism—from one end to the other of the nineteenth century—destroyed much of First Nations cultures in addition to countless lives, so Israeli expansionism, which at present is only accelerating, cares not one whit about non-Jewish lives and wantonly cancels Palestinian culture.[22] Little wonder, in this case, that the United States remains Israel's most fervent ally. Little wonder too that critics of Israel are immediately labeled either "anti-Semites" or "self-hating Jews." When attempts to open discussion on the Middle East conundrum are shut down by essentialist defensiveness from an otherwise perfectly atheistic individuals, the trap in which adherence to a religious faith is conflated with "race," "ethnicity," or "nationhood" has completely closed in.

There is a weirdness in Israel's policy of cancelling Palestine that is, as Freud might have said, a strangeness of the *unheimlich* or uncanny variety. The principle human group that the Third Reich was bent on eradicating has slowly but surely built a state that resembles South Africa under apartheid: a state of affairs quite *estranged* from principles of justice and equality under democracy has become *familiar*. On multiple occasions, Victor Klemperer sensed that such a perverse dialectical upending could take place in the establishment

---

[22]See the remarks of Dima Khalidi, head of Palestine Legal, on the consequences of IHRA's definition of anti-Semitism during the USACBI webinar on April 6, 2021. Removed at some point from YouTube, the session was available on September 15, 2023, on Facebook, at https://www.facebook.com/USACBI/videos/weaponizing-anti-semitism-ihra-and-the-end-of-the-palestine-exception/804723197144689/. The events that have unfolded since October 7, 2023, have only exacerbated this reality.

of a Jewish state in Palestine. Long before Shlomo Sand,[23] Klemperer clearly perceived the creation of a single people out of a religion uniting disparate "ethnic" groups: "Hitler is the most important promoter of Zionism, Hitler had literally created the 'Jewish nation,' 'world Jewry,' *the* Jew'" (I:450; I:571). The planners and perpetrators of the Shoah had already succeeded in getting their victims to interiorize eugenicist definitions of "racial" essence. In June 1942, as Klemperer studies Herzl's *Der Judenstaat* and *Altneuland*, he writes: "Very great affinity with Hitlerism. Except that Herzl dodges the blood definition. To him a nation is a 'historical group, which recognizably belongs together and has a common enemy'" (II:85; I:115), and "Herzl's *Zionist Writings*. This is Hitler's reasoning, sometimes precisely his words, his fanaticism" (II:86; I:117).

statues removed, institutions renamed

It is expected that a person accorded the privileged of representing those who elected them play a role exemplifying the society's highest values. If in exercising that privilege, they fail that expectation and their removal from office is the consequence, only the most hypocritical or zealous could disagree and shout "cancel culture!"[24] It is expected that a regime promoting itself as a democracy not only extends all rights and privileges to all citizens but treats new migrants as potential citizens in the making. If, while benefiting from that designation, inequality of any sort comes to dominate their daily existence, who could seriously dismiss a movement to boycott that sham democracy as "cancel culture"? Both procedures arise from below, from beneath the seat of instituted power.[25] The pressure that both exert to rectify the behavior of those exercising instituted power is material. Another set of actions whose intent is to set things right in relations between humans, while mainly of

---

[23]I would refer the reader to the final chapter in Sand's excellent *The Invention of the Jewish People*, entitled "The Distinction: Identity Politics in Israel" (250–313).

[24]As James McAuley (2021) rightly observes, "people call out such tactics only when their political opponents use them, never when their allies do."

[25]As much as it maddens, Davis Polk rescinding offers to Harvard and Columbia law students (*The Guardian*, October 18, 2024) is their right as much as it is mine to boycott a colonial apartheid regime.

the order of the symbolic, is also condemned as an aberration of "cancel culture." Although defacing, unbolting, and removal are actions performed in the material world, when the statue of some historical figure or another is defaced, unbolted, or removed, the consequences are purely symbolic. It's a bit like flag- or effigy-burning in that when a monument to Robert E. Lee is dismantled, no one suffers physically or financially (although "lost cause" ideologists call Confederate statue removals "heritage attacks" on "hallowed locations"[26]—semantic elements in the vocabulary of "cancel culture"). A modest effort at correction of the skewed legacy of "race" is simply occurring, an acknowledgment that racism is not heroism, a sign that perhaps things *can* change for the better.

Commemorative naming of institutions and streets, statues in remembrance of historical figures: such onomastic symbols forcefully speak to the children learning to become citizens under the shadow of such letter combinations on façades. The secondary school that I attended for three years in Oakland bore the name of one of the military men responsible for multiple genocidal events perpetrated against Native people. He is remembered today certainly not by the names of any of the individuals massacred but only by the European names for the geographic locations of the crimes: Sacramento River, Klamath Lake, Sutter Buttes. Despite such actions—hardly considered heinous at the time of their occurrence or even for several subsequent generations—history was very kind to "The Pathfinder": John C. Frémont's murderous expeditions through the American West in the 1840s expanded significantly on the Lewis and Clark endeavors, triggering (enabling) the mass migrations of whites from the East and their settlement on "land without a people."

My alma mater is still known as Fremont High School—a fact that John C.'s marginally more egalitarian spouse, Jessie Benton, might have been proud of. But many places I knew then have been renamed in ways meant to enlighten youth about the ways things have been and about how they can become: East 14th Street is now International Boulevard; 9th Street between Peralta and

---

[26]"Manual Advises How to Stop Removal of Confederate Statues: Don't Mention Race." *History News Network*, July 4, 2021. https://historynewsnetwork.org/article/180656 (accessed September 20, 2023).

Mandela Parkway bears the name of Huey P. Newton; MacArthur Boulevard between Grand and Van Buren is now Tupac Shakur Way. In none of this was anyone "cancelled." Most importantly, these new names recognize and honor demographic realities by naming individuals whose work contributed to reversing the malignant legacy of "race."

In response to an editorial attempting to explain "Why cancel culture threatens our basic freedoms," the Canadian scholar Reuben Rose-Redwood, whose research and writing centers on the historical geography of cities and the cultural politics of place naming, replied forcefully that "the hypocrisy of these claims never ceases to amaze me." Rose-Redwood continues:

> If we want to talk about cancelling cultures, many of the historical figures who have been placed up on a pedestal in the public square were the quintessential culture-cancellers—promoting genocidal policies, banning Indigenous cultural practices, and so on.
>
> If we want to talk about the "narrowing of dialogue" and the "closing of minds," one need look no further than the tunnel vision of Eurocentrism that has produced commemorative landscapes in which the vast majority of honorifics are bestowed upon white, European men who build their reputations and legacies by cancelling the cultures of "others."
>
> The renaming of places and removal of statues is not a narrow-minded form of cancel culture. Rather, it is a means of reckoning with the legacies of historical injustice that continue to shape our present.[27]

Since this clearest of statements has brought us to Canada, let's stay there for a moment, for this story repeats itself across the border to Canada's south and, indeed, across the globe. When a statue of Egerton Ryerson was brought down at the university in Toronto that had previously borne his name, when bronzes of John A. MacDonald, Canada's first prime minister, who presided over the consolidation of the white-run confederation, were removed from

---

[27]*Times Colonist* (Victoria, BC), February 18, 2021. https://www.timescolonist.com/opinion/letters/letters-feb-18-cancel-culture-hypocrisy-container-housing-village-4687519 (accessed September 18, 2023).

parks and city halls, when churches were "vandalized"[28] in Calgary or when calls are issued to forego Canada Day, this does not occur in a vacuum: mass graves of hundreds of indigenous children had just been uncovered near "church-run residential schools" in Alberta, Saskatchewan, and British Columbia, proving forensically that, as in the United States, genocidal crimes had indeed been committed in the name of the constitutional monarchy known as Canada. In fact, it is estimated that at least 150,000 Indigenous children were taken from their families to attend such schools[29] where they were given new names, forcibly converted to Christianity, and prohibited from speaking their native languages. As historian Ned Blackhawk's essential book amply shows, the same crimes against humanity were committed south of the 49th parallel.

And yet we unflinchingly express righteous indignation when Russia abducts Ukrainian children to make them Russian. Such deafening hypocrisy should seem obvious to everyone. But is it? "We" don't hesitate a moment to condemn cultural cancellation when we see it perpetrated by one white European group on another white European group. Could that be because this "we" identifies, in this case, with *both* perpetrators and victims? But when survivors of ethnicities, groups, and "races" that white supremacy has attempted for centuries to stifle and eliminate "vandalize" churches, topple monuments to the "heroes" of genocide, or merely raise their voices, they are roundly and hysterically condemned for carrying out "cancel culture." Is it not that the "we" that cries "cancel culture" still fails to wrap head or heart around *their* hurt? Is it not so much easier to snidely accuse the descendants of the downtrodden of "group think" and "intolerance"?

No, this is worse still than hypocrisy: it is either the incapacity to imagine the other or a stubborn imperviousness to the lived experience of humans not of "our" gender, not of "our" "race"—persons from whom we are severed out of laziness, fear, and ignorance. The proposal to place a statue of

---

[28]The layers of hypocrisy in the use of the term here are multiple. For one, the "vandalism" consisted in a quite moving work of art: human handprints in red and orange—reminders of the indigenous victims—daubed on the church doors. Besides this "defacing" or "desecration," the indigenous vandalism was condemned because one of the churches had been used by African migrants who, according to Alberta's Premier, "came to Canada with the hope that they could practice their faith peacefully."

[29]The last residential school were only closed in the 1990s.

seventeenth-century philosopher Elena Lucrezia Cornaro Piscopia, atop just one of the several pedestals that have been vacant since 1797 on the Prato della Valle in Padua, was met with hysterical accusations of "cancel culture." The pedestals were erected to commemorate seventy-eight men—no women, whined, wide-eyed, the threatened males. Such socio-historical disability keeps us stuck in the childhood of our species. As we should have learned centuries ago, the path of evolution is paved in education. Honoring the natural impulse to inform ourselves, listening to others as well as we listen to ourselves, thinking before acting, and mobilizing such practices universally is to just possibly contribute to obviating the destruction that looms in the Anthropocene.

It behooves the Critical Watch to be careful and alert. It is one thing to send children to a school named after Jefferson Davis and quite another to have budding citizens attend a school called Thomas Jefferson. One led a renegade nation whose economy was massively dependent on the enslavement of Africans; the political thought of the other—despite his considerable personal flaws—set the foundations for universal democracy. It will and indeed *should* be pointed out that Jefferson, like Davis, owned slaves. Yet with the knowledge that the former was old enough to be the latter's grandfather, should the evolution of mentalities in regard to "race" and slavery factor into our comparison? While the jury is still out with respect to the founding father's position on human chattel, perhaps it would be most appropriate, in the meanwhile, to honor the memory of Sally Hemings. After all, removing the name of an unapologetic racist—US president or not—from the public policy school of a venerable university[30] or renaming a New York state park for Sojourner Truth instead of for the founder of "Truth Social" is not knee-jerk revisionism or "cancel culture": these are modest moves to gain a more fulsome grasp of the US past so that the future be just a little less unjust. Contextualizing names—whether used commemoratively or not—is one of the simplest and most honest ways for us to see where we have been, where we are now, and where we want to be sooner than later.

---

[30]Board of Trustees' decision on removing Woodrow Wilson's name from public policy school and residential college, https://www.princeton.edu/news/2020/06/27/board-trustees-decision-removing-woodrow-wilsons-name-public-policy-school-and.

It might be nice to fantasize that we could forego commemoration of historical figures altogether until we overcame the impulse to sacralize and fetishize. That seemingly impossible, however, we should at least be able to accept that culture is not just *like* an organism: culture *is* an organism. And, as a living thing, culture is sculpted out of both the appearance of the new and the disappearance of the obsolete.[31]

Illustrating that principle within the confines of the activity of book publication may clarify what some people think they mean by "cancel culture" and why the term is so slippery. Burning or banning books actually published could be accurately described as a species of culture-cancelling. Klemperer noted as early as April 1933 that "In Kiel the students have put un-German texts by their former and no longer acceptable teachers on the index" and that at his own university in Dresden, a notice had been posted on the Student House that read, "When the Jew writes in German, he lies" (I:15; I:21). We know where that led over the next twelve years of German history. When Khomeini issued a fatwa against Salman Rushdie for a book that the ayatollah had undoubtedly never read and when the most serious attempt to assassinate Rushdie was carried out thirty-four years later, these could indeed be characterized as cultural cancellation. Even something like the banning of Art Spiegelman's *Maus* by a Tennessee school board is a measure of the same ilk.[32] All of these acts are meant to deprive readers of access to cultural artifacts—components of and testimonials to what we are—and of the ability to judge critically for themselves as to the value of the works.

What these examples reveal is that book banning and book burning derive from decisions made by political regimes—governments or agencies of governments—and political actors, not by publishers. Unless prohibited by governmental censorship, publishers are free to choose what to publish and what not to publish. If publisher *X* decides not to publish novel *A*, the author or her agent can always turn to publisher *Y*: this is not book banning (or "cancel culture"), but rather one of the vagaries of the publishing world under

---

[31]Cf. Jean-Claude Ameisen, *La Sculpture du vivant: Le Suicide cellulaire et la mort créatrice*. Paris: Seuil, 2003.

[32]In their statement, the McMinn County School Board explained that *Maus* did not "reflect the values of the community it serves." All one can say is that one would *hope* not!

capitalism. However, when publisher *Z* decides that certain *words* in a work it published in year J should be deleted or modified as it prepares to reprint the work in year J+40, we enter the realm of expurgation and sanitization. It might be one thing for a publisher to issue modernized editions of, say, *The Canterbury Tales* or *Gargantua* in order to make them of easier access to readers unschooled in Middle English or *moyen français*, and it's quite another to try to "clean up" Sade or Céline or—perhaps more to the point of "cancel culture"—to bowdlerize Agatha Christie or Roald Dahl[33] in deference to individual sensibilities apparently ignored when the works first appeared and now of central concern.

Such concerns are not new. High school districts have for decades debated whether *Adventures of Huckleberry Finn*—despite its qualities as a novel and as a representation of a troubled moment in US history—should or can be taught. College film instructors balk regularly at using *Birth of a Nation* to study cross-cutting, flashbacks, dissolves, and parallel montage. But how difficult is it, really, to suggest for students' consideration that a virulent racist can also be an accomplished early filmmaker? How instructive might it be for young people in the early twenty-first century to enter the semantic world of a bold white boy from Missouri who in the 1830s befriends a fugitive slave? Sure, these adventures in humanity are told from the white boy's perspective, but so the misadventures of a Black woman are told by a Black male authorial voice in *The Blacker the Berry*. These identities—gender primarily here, race primarily there—in no way impede vividly powerful imagining of the other.

This rule seems not to have been lost on Oprah Winfrey. Fifteen summers before that of 2021, when the murder of George Floyd triggered mass protests and catapulted the Black Lives Matter movement, the "Queen of All Media" put her considerable influence to suggesting that her book club spend a summer reading Faulkner. Her wager was that her followers might discover glimmers of hopefulness through the bleakness in Faulkner's ambiguous, yet profoundly insightful, representations of the ruin that the false concept

---

[33]True to form, in a 1982 conversation with his friend, Francis Bacon, Roald Dahl declared that "I've warned my publishers that if they later on so much as change a single comma in one of my books, they will never see another word from me. Never! Ever! When I'm gone, if that happens, then [...] I will send the 'enormous crocodile' ['a horrid greedy grumptious brute'] to gobble them up."

of "race" has wrought. Her wager was that her fellow bibliophiles might see that the great-grandson of a slaveowner had developed a certain capacity to see the world through the eyes of other persons—even those "othered" by the social system that still reigned in his native Mississippi—and transformed that capacity into a monumental literary oeuvre. Predictably, a few snobs who maintain that difficult literature can only be *taught* (presumably by them) and not experienced or understood firsthand, blasted Winfrey for dumbing down the classics.[34] Yet fifteen summers before the rise of BLM, Winfrey had made a laudable and altogether plausible attempt to use the fiction of a modernist—who happened to be white and from the Deep South—to awaken empathy in *all* people.

Any overview of the commotion over "cancel culture" as it may impact literary creation, book production, and book circulation quickly exposes incongruities and drift of a political nature. While it is the conservative sector of US society that regularly regulates reading by banning books at the local and state levels and that cries bloody murder in the national discourse about "cancel culture" in a "culture war" they have been keen to fuel for decades, liberals, in the meantime, are overly concerned with policing printed language: they all too easily forget that art lends itself necessarily and naturally to historical contextualization. The first contradiction participates in the same twisted logic that moved the Nazis to amalgamate their predatory conquests and human annihilations under the label "the Jewish war."

from "woke" to "wok(e)ism(e)"

It would be useful, at this point, to stand back for a moment and examine the word "woke," considering whence it came, then grappling a bit with whither it's gone. So far as I've been able to determine, the first time that this vocable employed as an adjective with anything like its current meaning appeared

---

[34]For example, Max Fisher, "How Oprah Ruins Classic Literature." *The Atlantic*, December 14, 2010. More generally, a non-negligible number of so-called "progressives" are dismissive and quick to disassociate themselves from anything someone like Oprah Winfrey does. Why? A woman. Black. Influential. Arguably powerful. Appeals to segments outside the ivory tower.

in print was in an article by William Melvin Kelley that *The New York Times* published on May 20, 1962, provocatively affirming that "If You're Woke, You Dig It." The slang-inflected "to dig"—meant to mean to understand, to appreciate or to admire—hints at the social identity of Kelley's addressee, "you." A couple of decades before Kelley's article, "to dig" carrying these meanings had migrated from African American vernacular to infuse the lexicon of jazz aficionados and hipsters. Kelley's title assures his assumed mostly white audience (we're talking about *The New York Times*) that if they've attained a state called "woke," then they're well aware of lurking dangers, that they've understood and can appreciate the nexus of problems that plague people in the United States who, unlike them, walk around in black skin.

Kelley's article is a playful overview of a few terms that, by 1962, would have already been somewhat familiar to readers of the *Times* by dint of their use by mostly white beatniks. He speculates about why a linguistic code might come in handy to a harassed group of people and gently mocks his readers by inviting them into the alternate universe of the Black American. Invoking James Baldwin's analysis of the "double-think" that Blacks adopt as psychosocial coping mechanism, he boldly asserts that "The only time a Negro can forget he is a Negro is when he is with Negroes." But this axiom perhaps never hit home to white Americans until it was illustrated by a white man in *Black Like Me*, to which I have already referred. A key to the destiny over the past decade or so of the adjective "woke"—a destiny that brings us to our present moment and the wrangling over "cancel culture"—comes when William Melvin Kelley kids in his conclusion that "The Negro's pride in this idiom is that of a man who watches someone else do ineptly what he can do well." It is perhaps still only Black Americans who can say what it truly is to strive to be "woke" and why. It is perhaps still only Black Americans who can teach us the vital importance of being "woke" and the power that comes from calling out power from "below."

So much for "woke" in *written* form and a few thoughts thereupon. Well before Kelley's 1962 article, "woke" could be *heard* pronounced in a 1938 recording of Leadbelly's "Scottsboro Boys."[35] (When I write "heard," by the

---

[35]Nine teenagers, ranging in age from thirteen to nineteen, were falsely accused in 1931 of raping two white women on a train. Their first of many trials was heard in Scottboro, Alabama. The classic case

way, I don't mean merely on the street corner, but in a broadcast medium with the potential of being widely heard.) The lead line of each stanza of "Scottsboro Boys" clearly limns the necessity for the predisposition signified by the adjective "woke": "Go to Alabama and ya better watch out," Leadbelly warns. Why? Because merely being Black in Alabama is a threat to existence itself: "Don't ya ever go to Alabama / And try to live." Before the recording's close, after singing his simple, straightforward lyrics, Leadbelly speaks out a codicil: "So I advise everybody, be a little careful when they go along through there—best stay *woke*, keep their eyes open." In the *OED*, one of the examples preceding the famous Leadbelly one shows "woke" being used more generally to mean awake or no longer asleep[36]—less specifically, that is, than "woke" in the sense of being awake, aware, and wary in the social sense. More convergent, however, with Leadbelly's intended meaning, the *OED* also cites a 1920 edition of a Portsmouth, Ohio, newspaper that reports a "Stay Woke Ball," in what was at the time often called Harlem's "Black Belt." It is not unlikely that we will learn of earlier occurrences of "woke" when the *Oxford Dictionary of African American English* under Henry Louis Gates' direction is published in 2025. All this to say that "woke" was undoubtedly invented on one of those streetcorners where Black Americans somewhere in the racist country could feel momentarily safe from white supremacist violence, in one of those moments when, as William Melvin Kelly wrote, "a Negro can forget he is a Negro."

A variant of awake that draws attention by its very variance, "woke" thus originated at some point, presumably in the early twentieth century, possibly as early as the late nineteenth, as code among members of an oppressed group doing what humans so naturally do: viz. organizing themselves, in face of aggression and oppression, in mutual self-defense. Once it seeped out of the confines of Black America, it was taken up first, primarily, by less-than-Black allies savvy to and in agreement with the word's intent. Inexorably, however, it got picked up by *regressives* of all stripes—in particular those nostalgic for white

---

of racist railroading and legal miscarriage. By the time Leadbelly recorded his song, the infamous case was widely known. So, some whites will have surely made the connection between it and the need to stay "woke."

[36]"[He] dreamin', mon. He ain't woke good yit." J.C. Harris, *Balaam and His Master*, 1891.

supremacist order—as a tool to denigrate and mock anyone seeking justice and equality. Using our nomenclature here, in the hands and mouths of these forces, it would be fully justified to qualify the quotation marks around "woke" as *sneer* quotes. As if to insinuate ignorance in the term's coiners, Andrew Sullivan—one of hundreds of reactionary examples—denounces what he calls the "cult of social justice" in an article entitled "The Great Awokening."

This is where "woke"—the innocent verbal shield held by an oppressed people—stands today. Those who hysterically recoil from its source in Black vernacular snidely spawn grotesque neologisms, building "cleverly" on the root word, such as "wokeism," "wokery" (doubly racist for gaslighting another minority), "wokedom," and "wokeness," and phrases bandied about by the political class when in full electoral mode, such as "the woke mob" and "woke culture." Adding the -ism suffix to a word for an attitude that was (and remains) a pacifist survival strategy twists the term's meaning into that of some nefarious dogma or cult ideology. In addition, whatever "cancel culture" is (or is not), "wokeism" is conveniently and uncritically conflated with it. Even if we agree for argument's sake that they are both phenomena emanating primarily from progressive segments of society, a fundamental difference stands between them. "Cancel culture" necessarily involves action, whereas staying "woke" is a stance for survival. If "cancelling" entails calling out, shaming, seeking to remove the powerful from positions that allow them to oppress, putting one's being in a "woke" state is simply meant to protect that being from harm. By extension, positioning oneself as "woke" means facilitating voices from heretofore unheard perspectives.

Just who are the whiny denouncers of "wokeism"? What typifies their economic or political position in society? From what perch do they speak? In broad terms, they are the pundits: individuals whose ability to broadcast their opinions is well established. They are people from whom we have already heard on the subject of "cancel culture" and who are hypersensitive about losing those privileges. University professors and political players are prominent among them. The fact that being woke has spread from Black America to prove to be a compelling strategy for homologous social groups and their allies disrupts the assumed power and sense of unassailability of the mockers. The gatekeepers of culture have devised a simplistic game that consists of bashing the "woke"—

those beyond the pale—with grotesque derivatives of the peerlessly concise term. The fear trumped up over "wokeism" has come to a point where any second-rate scholar or bigot can scream fire with the term and get repaid in unwarranted attention. As James McAuley, writing about the "genuinely pathetic part" of the strained pathos driving the "war on woke" in both the United States and France, said, "being aggressively anti-woke is a last-ditch attempt at mattering."[37] Not only is such attention undeserved—McAuley and so many others are right to point out that it is "an outgrowth of entitlement," it comes at the expense of the very people who came up with "woke" to name a key instrument in their self-defense toolbox.

Politicians the likes of Sarah Huckabee Sanders and Ronald Dion DeSantis—to name only two of the dozens—built veritable cottage industries on being "anti-woke" champions. In her response to Biden's 2023 State of the Union address, the Arkansas governor asserted that Joe had "surrender[ed] his presidency to a woke mob that can't even tell you what a woman is." While the crass xenophobia driving the last part of the quote is so patent as to warrant no commentary, Sanders borrowed the association of Biden's progressive supporters with a riotous rabble-rousing crowd of indistinct lowlifes from DeSantis.

His position as governor of Florida and ephemeral presidential candidate amplified DeSantis' obsession with "wokeism" and the "mob" he sees everywhere promoting its decadent program. The governance of New College of Florida in Sarasota, a public liberal arts college, falls under the aegis of the state's governor. Determined to put an end to "woke activism," DeSantis authorized himself to curtail all diversity, equity, and inclusion (DEI) programs in Florida's state university system as well as any curriculum that could be construed as pertaining to Critical Race Theory (CRT). At New College, specifically, DeSantis dismissed the entire board of trustees, replacing it with a "landing team" (war semantics: check) including none other than Christopher Rufo. Doing what conservative "think tanks" do best—groups like the Heritage Foundation, of which Rufo is an active member, catapulted him to punditry in the worlds of Fox News and Donald Trump. (Lots else could be

---

[37]*Op. cit.*

said about the Heritage Foundation, but it's worth noting parenthetically that Roger Pearson, founder of the British neo-Nazi Northern League, was for a time one of the Heritage Foundation's illustrious board members.) Once he had the new governing board in place, DeSantis could announce in zealous military imagery the new phase in his "war on woke": "We are over the wall and ready to transform higher ed from within."

Once the ramparts of "wokeism" are breached, according to DeSantis' wildly imaginative plan, a "battle" on the model of the post-9/11 "war on terrorism" can be waged. To impress his allies and supporters, he has spewed grandiose mortiferous threats like "Florida is where woke goes to die," and he and his consultants appeal to the same kind of linguistic gimmicks deployed in the wake of the Twin Tower attacks. We may recall, again, that in order to ensure that the key buzzword of "patriot" was front and center in the laws of exception (cf. Nazi jurist, Carl Schmitt) passed in October 2001, John Ashcroft and his team coined the oh-so-clever acronym of USA PATRIOT Act out of the tortured programmatic phrase "Uniting and Strengthening America by Providing Appropriate Tools Required to Intercept and Obstruct Terrorism." Starting with his *cancellation* of AP African American studies meant to curtail "the state-sanctioned racism that is critical race theory"—yet another case of a pot calling a kettle black—DeSantis inaugurated the "Stop WOKE Act," where, in all caps, the word meant to raise hackles and hair stands for "Stop the Wrongs to Our Kids and Employees." If there be any doubt that this byzantine acronym has "Patriot Act" in its subconscious, consider this declaration of DeSantis' official rationale: "to give businesses, employees, children and families tools to fight back against woke indoctrination." All this smacks of the same deadly white backlash that followed on the heels of Reconstruction: the enemy behind the code word to be crushed is the "uppity" Black.

Few experiences can be more effective at revealing how embarrassing the insanity of reactionary behavior at home can be than to study the life of its homologue abroad. The specter of everything "woke" has sadly migrated outside the United States. Given the French penchant for being the first in Europe to pick up bad habits from the Land of the Free, it may not be surprising that the latest avatar of our "culture wars" reached there if not first, at least most spectacularly. Let us therefore briefly cross the Atlantic and visit our cousins in democracy. With France's reputation as a crucible of critical thinking, it is properly cringeworthy, as we say, that aversion to *wokisme* is rampant across France's political spectrum. The intensity of Gallic backlash at the phantom of "woke" rivals that of DeSantis' Florida.

French fear of threats to (white) Eurocentrism reached such a fever pitch by 2021 that Minister of Education, Youth and Sports at the time, Jean-Michel Blanquer, was authorized to establish a "think tank" dubbed "Le Laboratoire de la République," whose specific mission is to defend France's sacrosanct principle of *laïcité* against so-called new radicalities, of which the onslaught of what Emmanuel Macron calls (albeit without scare quotes) "woke culture" is seen as the most insidious. One of the first activities that Blanquer's "think tank" undertook was to organize (incongruously in collaboration with an obscure specialist in seventeenth-century French literature[38]) a colloquium entitled "After Deconstruction: Reconstructing Science and Culture." (First mistake— an elementary one that has been made for decades: since *deconstruction* has nothing to do with *destruction*, no *reconstruction* is required in the wake of its passage. And for another, no less elementary: in no way is the critical approach developed by Jacques Derrida out to undo science or destroy culture.) Speakers came to Blanquer's staid and righteous culture fest to attack "decolonial thought, otherwise called 'woke' or 'cancel culture.'" Initiated from the seat of governmental power, the colloquium which ran on January 7–8, 2022, was able to garner for its proceedings none other than the majestic Grand Amphitheater at the Sorbonne where doctoral dissertations, such as "Madness and Unreason" by a certain Michel Foucault, have been defended since 1889.

Speakers at Blanquer's "anti-woke" summit ranged from the essayist and pundit Pascal Bruckner, author of such essays as *Un coupable presque parfait* [*A Near-Perfect Culprit*], purporting to trace the history of how white people have been "constructed" as scapegoats for all the world's ills[39] and whose

---

[38]Emmanuelle Hénin is a professor of comparative literature at Sorbonne Université.

[39]Pascal Bruckner, *Un coupable presque parfait: la construction du bouc émissaire blanc*. Paris: Grasset, 2020. Bruckner is an editor with Grasset and a member of France's most prestigious literary organization, the Académie Goncourt. This book is only the latest in an obsessive string of Bruckner books including *The Tears of the White Man*, *The Tyranny of Guilt*, and *An Imaginary Racism: Islamophobia and Guilt*.

comments on who was to blame for the *Charlie Hebdo* massacre are, let us say at the very least, controversial, to the venerable expert on racism, Pierre-André Taguieff, who in 2002 coined the concept of *"islamo-gauchisme,"* to journalist Élisabeth Lévy, whose positions on migrants and race are, to put it as journalists sometimes coyly do, "ambiguous." Meanwhile individuals like entrepreneur and Macron advisor Mathieu Laine make no secret of his commitment to staving off the "fascistic [*sic*] drift of woke culture." Most of the speakers at the conference pointed their finger at social theories like CRT, queer theory, and postcolonial studies, developed or seen to have been developed primarily in the United States, as factors in having set the stage for *wokisme*.[40] If it might be properly said that the Cassandras that Macron and Blanquer gathered are situated in the middle (*grosso modo*) of France's political road, figures from both far right and far left also express outraged dismay and panic over an all-too-woke society à la US Xenophobic Vichy apologist and presidential candidate Éric Zemmour[41] associates "wokisme" with "islamisation," while general secretary of the Communist Party and another presidential candidate Fabien Roussel sugarcoats his disdain with juvenile jokes.[42] Even *Charlie Hebdo*, with interventions like "Those new 'fatwas' from the left," jumps regularly on the anti-"woke" bandwagon.[43] Blanquer's congress held at France's sanctuary of lay higher education did not go unchallenged. The event itself was heavily picketed by student and labor unions. Figures such as Élisabeth Roudinesco and Mathieu Potte-Bonneville expressed dismay in the press at the exercise. Exactly one year after Blanquer's "After Deconstruction," a three-day colloquium entitled "Who's Afraid of Deconstruction?," organized by Isabelle Alfandry, Anne Emmanuelle Berger, and Jacob Rogozinski, was held at the University de

---

[40]Norimitsu Onishi, "Will American Ideas Tear France Apart? Some of Its Leaders Think So." *The New York Times,* February 9, 2021. https://www.nytimes.com/2021/02/09/world/europe/france-threat-american-universities.html?referringSource=articleShare (accessed February 10, 2021).

[41]Zemmour's 2014 screed entitled *Le Suicide français*, in which he called for "deconstructing the deconstructors."

[42]"J'ai cru que les 'woke', c'était un plat" in an interview with Raphaël Enthoven.

[43]"Ces nouvelles 'fatwas' venues de la gauche." *Charlie Hebdo*, September 2, 2020.

Paris Sorbonne-Panthéon. Most of those proceedings with the eighteen eminent speakers have been gathered in a published volume.[44]

English-language publication undoubtedly holds first place for the number of books excoriating "wokeness," warning about the dangers of "cancel culture," and so on. The Goodreads website lists about 100 titles under the search terms "anti-woke books." *Woke Racism* by John McWhorter and *Woke, Inc.* by Vivek Ramaswami are among the better-selling ones. Rare is the book that favors a sober critical stance. One of these rare interventions—*Stay Woke*—looks favorably on the Black Lives Matter movement, suggesting strategies to extend the effort.[45] The French, on their side, are not far behind the anti-woke frenzy. (We must never forget a prevalent French self-perception that they are the leading experts on practically every subject.) There are scores of titles raising alarm at the specter of "wokeism." I've perused or plowed through a dozen or so. That translates to roughly as many "woke"-warning books per capita as in the United States. Two that I consulted compare *wokisme* (the "e" in the middle is usually dropped in French, making it read like a frying pan cult) to a contagious disease.[46] For heretofore repressed voices to make themselves heard would be reactionary for one author,[47] while for another this would more likely result in totalitarianism.[48] One, by an intrepid investigator who "infiltrated the land of woke," calls its proponents "the new inquisitors,"[49] while yet another identifies it as a religion.[50] (Religion and totalitarianism being kissing cousins, these authors cannot be reproached for inconsistency.) Two more attempts to confirm what Blanquer's summit tried to prove: that Derrida

---

[44]Isabelle Alfandry, Anne Emmanuelle Berger and Jacob Rogozinski, eds., *Qui a peur de la deconstruction ?* Paris: Presses Universitaires de France (Perspectives critiques), 2023.

[45]Tehama Lopez Bunyasi and Candis Watts Smith, eds., *Stay Woke: People's Guide to Making All Black Lives Matter.* New York: New York University Press, 2019.

[46]Anne Toulouse, *Wokisme: la France sera-t-elle contaminée ?* Monaco: Les Éditions du Rocher, 2022 and Gad Saad, *Les nouveaux virus de la pensée: wokisme, cancel culture, racialisme ... et autres ideologies qui tuent le bon sens.* Limoges: FYP Éditions, 2022 (note also, with the reference to "bon sens," how, being a good Frenchman, Saad holds Descartes up as a recognizable rampart against the siege).

[47]Alex Mahoudeau, *La Panique Woke: Anatomie d'une offensive réactionnaire.* Paris: Textuel, 2022.

[48]Nathalie Heinich, *Le wokisme serait-il un totalitarisme ?* Paris: Albin Michel, 2023. The paper ribbon that French publishers wrap around new issues reads "woke hell is paved with good intentions" ... Yes, they forgot that "road" is necessary for the metaphor to work.

[49]Nora Bussigny, *Les nouveaux inquisiteurs.* Paris: Albin Michel, 2023.

[50]Jean-François Braunstein, *La Religion woke.* Paris: Éditions Grasset, 2022.

and his ilk are incongruously at the root of all this. Marcel Kunz affirms that a sort of deconstruction-*wokisme* nexus is threatening nothing less than science itself,[51] while Philippe Forest, building on the colloquium's title, deepens the canard consisting of confusing deconstruction and destruction, calling for *reconstruction* after the storm.[52]

It would be inaccurate and unfair, however, to conclude that everything that has been published so far in France follows the lead of US reaction to the progressive initiative. At least two books focus usefully on the maddeningly uncanny capacity of capitalism to parasitically profit from anything, including the phenomena under scrutiny here.[53] Readers of French can find a somewhat more nuanced approach to the destiny of Leadbelly's call to "stay woke" in political scientist Pierre Valentin's recent study, *Comprendre la révolution woke.*[54] (Although, really, what actual *revolution* could come of simply being woke to systemic racism or sexism?) This rather supercilious study suffers nevertheless from insufficient historical contextualization. And although Laure Murat intervenes more often on "cancel culture" than on "woke" (with which it is not, moreover, homologous), she is one of the rare French voices to approach some understanding of how such movements emerge when it becomes clear that democracy under capitalism proves incapable of ensuring justice and equality in face of raw instituted power.[55] She has characterized "cancel culture" as the "last recourse of an exasperated and marginalized population."[56] I'm only speculating, but her professional position in Los Angeles may not be a negligible factor in her more nuanced thinking.

Vis-à-vis the bogeyman of "woke," France often presents itself as a grotesque caricature of the phenomenon in the United States. It should be clear from this short tour abroad that "wokeness" generally generates hysterical reactions

---

[51]Marcel Kunz, *De la deconstruction au wokisme: la science menacée.* Versailles: VA Éditions, 2023.

[52]Philippe Forest, *Déconstruire, reconstruire: la querelle du woke.* Paris: Éditions Gallimard, 2023.

[53]Audrey Millet, *Woke Washing: capitalisme, consumérisme, opportunisme.* Paris: Éditions Les Pérégrines, 2023 and Anne de Guigné, *Le Capitalisme woke: quand l'entreprise dit le bien et le mal.* Paris: Les Presses de la Cité, 2022.

[54]Pierre Valentin, *Comprendre la révolution woke.* Paris: Éditions Gallimard, 2023.

[55]See Laure Murat's astute pamphlet, *Qui annule quoi ?* Paris: Seuil (Libelle), 2022.

[56]I would have placed "marginalized first ... La « cancel culture », c'est d'abord un immense ras-le-bol d'une justice à deux vitesses" *Le Monde.*

at voices heretofore unheard or ignored rising up from the *center* of cultural and political power: like outrage at the removal of Confederate monuments, such reactions constitute yet another manifestation of white whiny panic over perceived threats to privilege. However that may be, adopting and maintaining what African Americans some hundred years ago identified as a woke attitude in one's social existence remains, as it was in the days of the Scottsboro Boys, a vital skill for survival and an affirmation of being—especially for heretofore stifled voices and existences.

what is to be done?

Returning then, once again, to the United States, where the terms "woke" and "cancel culture" first came to occupy, preoccupy, and finally obsess political opinion, the proverbial question must be posed: What is to be done?[57] When semantically perverse discourse feeds civil unrest, threatening to destroy polity, certainly *something* must be done. No amount of skirmish among eggheads in the arena of "culture wars" will dissipate the madness. That is the realm in which minds formed and fixed in their ways duke it out. Attention should be focused rather on all those millions of nascent humans hurtling at this very moment toward adulthood. As always, in other words, *education is the answer*. But without further detail, for the moment, the benchmark of education, of course, remains a commonplace without fuel to fire the future. Yet again, we know that exercising the mind to its fullest potential, intermingling and cooperating with other subjects who are committed to the natural inclination to learn, and using what we learn (and teach) to strive to ensure well-being everywhere sufficient to enable ever-renewed education will always be the only way this species can survive.

Left unspecific, though, the word for the mind-expanding activity remains inert, without programmatic content. What do we mean when we say "education"? To what types of learning do we aspire? We are not just animals

---

[57] The question forms first the title of 1863 novel by Nikolai Chernyshevsky, then a 1902 pamphlet by Vladimir Lenin. In *Notes from Underground* (1864), Dostoyevsky excoriated the utopian socialist ideas expressed in Chernyshevsky's novel.

who operate and cooperate by means of complex signifying systems that we call languages: the elements composing these systems are rich reflections of our actions and interactions. Bringing whatever critical skills we can acquire and develop to bear on those elements enables us to explore and, sometimes, find solutions to the problems that our actions and interactions create. The kind of work to which a Victor Klemperer devoted his life of the mind led his education in that practical direction. In turn, we who study his observations and findings come to a certain understanding how—through the prism of language—the twisted pseudo-concept of "race" could produce paradigmatic genocide. We call *that* kind of work linguistics. Klemperer carried that work out with the force of critique in LTI. For the present study, I have derived inspiration from Klemperer, by investigating a few salient cases of manipulative rhetoric and semantic perversion.

Linguistics deployed with a critical approach is, therefore, one avenue for enlightened improvement. But it is only one. Another promising method, an educational endeavor that envisions a more just immediate future, is education carried out under the aegis of Critical Race Theory. Here, as with critical linguistics, the adjective inflecting the name of the discipline is indeed that, at the very least: *critical* in the sense of clear-minded, unprejudiced, essential, and ineluctable. Yet, as employed in the phrase "Critical Race Theory," it remains unclear whether "critical" means that the theory under study or to be developed (yet another issue) is *just* critical (as in "crucial") or if it is impelled—as linguistics may be—by *critique*, that is, the analytical approach first elaborated in the realm of philosophy in the late eighteenth century. It is essential that it be so. Only the development and exercise of what Kant called *the faculty of judgment* has the power to get us beyond the damage caused by the ideologically driven transformation of "race" into a concept and beyond all the consequences of that transformation of which I merely scraped the surface in the previous chapter. Ever since the word was borrowed from ancient Greek, critique names the exercise of the power of the faculty of judgment. In this sense too, the onomastic sequence "Critical Race Theory" ultimately falls short of clearly conveying an understanding of the program's *critical* intention. However one parses the phrase, this name for what is an urgently necessary component of education remains nebulous and problematic. Presenting a critical approach to "race" as mere "theory," when ample evidence has existed for a century that "race" is a bogus concept, either conveys retrograde temerity or is an example of modish (i.e., thoughtless) invocation of "theory." No theory of "race," however critical in its deployment, can improve on an idea that is, a priori, bankrupt. And in any case, under such a label, Critical Race Theory signifies to the subject who lives to learn (the infant, the child) that the interpretation of events has somehow already been determined by the subject who claims to have already learned (the adult) before she enters the classroom. No better way to discourage and defeat a hungry mind than to declare the case closed, the problem solved.

Is the budding critic not left freest to invent, is she not most apt, that is, to dance and pirouette toward invention heretofore unknown, when introduced to and versed in the historical data from which theories and solutions to come may be built? (And by history, we must mean that which can already be written and that which is writing itself in the *now* moment.) If the answer to my rhetorical question is "yes," then education requires first and foremost contextualization. Or, in deference to the work yet to be carried out by those now in the early years of their learning (and since, inevitably, I have been speaking from the position of educator): *suggesting context*. It would be presumptuous and stifling for educators to assume and claim they already know *what theories will nourish what is to be done*: Those theories and those decisions will emerge from the imagination of their students who today are feverishly reassembling what has been and what is to set the groundwork for what will be. The more historical and cultural context students can load into their critical toolboxes, the more inventively informed will be their decisions on what to do with dangerous words and misplaced statues.

As I've said more than once, we must learn to pirouette. The strategy that African Americans invented and named "staying woke" is a form of such a move: the woke subject is apt to sidestep potential harm while not turning the other cheek and, in cases where this proves ineffective, apt to deploy self-defense by all means at their disposal, demanding and exercising equity where equality is denied. Highly effective for self-preservation, then, "staying woke" can feed self-affirmation. This dynamic wherein the subject can shift from mortal threat to peace of mind and flesh was of utmost interest to philosophers from Edmund Burke and Immanuel Kant through Jean-François Lyotard, who studied the phenomenon of the sublime.

The great epistemologist Gaston Bachelard contended that when what he called a "poetics of space" is at hand—that is, when two or more subjects are copresent in a resonant linguistic environment—there can be a sort of "communion through brief, isolated, rapid actions" (xvii). This aligns with Burke's view when he said that the empathy ("sympathy" in eighteenth-century vocabulary) precipitated by what Kant would later call the "experience" of the sublime "put[s us] into the place of another man, affect[ing us] in many respects as he is affected" (91). Thirty-three years later Kant put the inestimable inspiration he had derived from Burke's analysis of the sublime on display in the most challenging part of his *Critique of the Power of Judgment*.[58] What Burke thought of as empathy ("sympathy") connecting individuals and Bachelard would, 200 years later, see as communion. All took place within one subject according to Kant's description of the sublime.

This is where we do well to turn to Lyotard. To express things in terms aligned with the subject of this chapter, it can be put thus: between those who have awakened and vowed to stay woke and those who bristle at "wokeism," there exists what Lyotard termed a *differend*. Lyotard defines a differend as a "case where the plaintiff is divested of the means to argue and becomes for that reason a victim" (9). The wrong resulting from a differend entails "damage accompanied by the loss of the means to prove the damage" (5). On the surface, this may sound like a simple dialogue of the deaf. But, in practice, there is always an identifiable power that is unassailable and that enforces the divestiture. The Nazi decrees that the Jew is not Aryan. The party of slavery deems the African inhuman.

The most important work in Lyotard's varied oeuvre, *The Differend*, mounts a relentless and radical critique of contrived and forced homogenization. A major consequence of a differend is that any affirmation of a consensual mass of people under a collective "we" subject is necessarily a lie—one that causes mortal "damage," as Lyotard termed it. "We the people of the United States

---

[58]Kant's Third Critique appeared in 1790; Burke's *Philosophical Enquiry into the Origin of Our Ideas of the Sublime and Beautiful* was published in 1757.

[…]," for example, was a discursive death warrant for first people, slaves, and women. Without the right to vote, the federating phrase excludes women and children as well. Of course, the US Constitution is far from the only nation-founding document plagued by this problem—a problem which turns not only on an exclusionary use of the first-person plural pronoun but also on the all-important concept of the *person* which, as John Locke forcefully put it, is a "forensic term." If certain individuals (i.e., "people") implied by the "we" subject are deemed not to be persons ("people"), then the rights and privileges outlined in the document do not pertain to them. "We" thus, for Lyotard, harbors and dissimulates differends, that is, "damage accompanied by the loss of the means to prove the damage."

For Lyotard, who so often was seen as one of deepest pessimists among so-called post-structuralists, all, however, is not lost for the possibility of a plurality of subjects joined ethically in view of realizing social and political projects that ensure justice and equality. Pessimism does not necessarily win the day. Being no Cioran, Lyotard found slivers of hope for dissipating differends in abiding reflection on what Kant appeared to mean by the ethical implications embedded in the experience of the sublime and on what the father of modern philosophy might have done with those implications in a critique of political judgment.[59] Lyotard stakes provisional hope in some scrupulously careful reconstitution of a "we" subject following manmade human disasters. This minimal, provisional first-person plural—a near degree zero of community—subsists at the outer limits of precariousness. It hovers already at the threshold of the main body of Lyotard's text, in the tongue-in-cheek "Reader's Guide" at the beginning of *The Differend*, which plotted the coordinates of the relationship between a reader and an author. Then suddenly, 100 pages later, in introducing the key function of witness as third party, Lyotard states unequivocally that the singular, lone witness is a "*we* composed at least of *I* who writes and *you* who read" (1988, 103; my emphasis on "we"). As we might perceive, this minimal "we" subject is akin to

---

[59]Another fertile ground for thinking lies between Lyotard and what Hannah Arendt had to say about this in her late *Lectures on Kant's Political Philosophy*.

the dynamics at work in education. Importantly too, in Kant's description of what happens in the subject's experience of the sublime, this dynamic inhabits the same subject, the self-same person. As Kant describes it, the faculty of the imagination is alone capable of overcoming the initial dread experienced by the subject in face of the sublime, thus allowing the understanding (*Verstand*) to get a grip on itself, to take itself in hand and proceed with the faculty of reason reinforced. The imagination and reason thus cooperate as a minimal "we" subject.

Empathy, which blossoms in the rescue of reason by the imagination, may not be able to fully come to terms with and solve the differend that operates today between persons woke out of vital necessity, woke for self-preservation, and "wokeism's" naysayers and negationists. But we have seen examples of it doing something similar in cases like that of Ann Atwater and C. P. Ellis, both of Durham, North Carolina. The creation out of former mortal enemies of such an intimately minimal community that can legitimately speak using a minimal and intimate "we" calls to mind yet another key figure in Lyotard's exhaustive attempt to envision a world beyond pervasive and entrenched differends. I will thus conclude my brief excursus into the realm of the sublime with a few words on what Lyotard calls *le veilleur critique* or, as I like to translate it, the Critical Watch.

The Critical Watch and the role it (he/she/they) commit(s) to fulfilling are the most productively visionary extensions of the minimal "we" subject. The main reason why I have invited my readers down this path is that Lyotard's vision of the Critical Watch sounds to me to be quite homologous with the strategy adopted by the subject who must stay woke. Lyotard announces the role to be played well before naming the role player. In the final movement of the six-page programmatic preface to *The Differend*, he calls for reflection redoubled despite its being "thrust aside today not because it is dangerous or upsetting, but simply because it is a waste of time" (xv; 14). What, precisely, is reflection supposed to do in face of pervasive and entrenched differends? "Reflection requires," Lyotard writes cryptically, "that one watch out [*prendre garde*] for occurrences [and] that one doesn't know in advance what's happening" (xv; 14). If that doesn't exactly sound precise, it's because no one knows *now*, at this moment and in advance, just how and in what idiom (phrases, rhetoric, semantics) differends can be superseded. We simply have an inkling of this possibility.

Be wary, pay attention, take heed, and watch out: these are all valid English equivalents for *prendre garde*, the verb Lyotard uses here. And the object of this watchfulness?—Occurrences, occasions, opportunities, openings for movement beyond the impasse of the differend. However, staying woke is needed in face of threats, violence, mortal danger, injustice. We are thus in the same realm: one vigilance is defensive in the *present*, the other expectant of *some future*. In taking on the assignment of vigilance, nothing less than "the honor of thinking" may be saved, solemnly declares Lyotard in those first pages (xii; 10). As for the subject of such crucial and vital watchfulness, Lyotard lends it a name on four occasions over the course of the vast work. Clear from the first instance is that the status of the Critical Watch is equivalent to that of judge (123; 180). In the second, we understand that the Critical Watch takes on the role of judge in the realm of metaphysics (135; 196). "Critical watch" (*veilleur critique*) would, according to Lyotard, be an appropriate name for the subject performing judgment in Kant's aesthetics (168; 242). And, finally, uniquely qualified for detecting the referent that would support such an assertion, the Critical Watch is alone positioned to legitimate phrases such as "Progress is at hand" (171; 246).

With this excursus, my wager has been that I could lead my readers down the meanders of a path of critical thinking with the potential to be brought to bear on all the semantic and rhetorical problems I have limned in this book. Specific to this chapter are the very stakes involved in today's intense squabbling over "cancel culture" and "wokeism." It is beyond the scope of this book, however, to fully unpack Lyotard's intricate argument in *The Differend* knitted with yarn borrowed from Kant's political and aesthetic writings and yarn from Wittgenstein's *Philosophical Investigations*. I am confident, however, that my call for intensified efforts at free, inventive, and universal education— always with a critical valence—resonates with this interpretive opening.

Mastery of scare quotes in lieu of being mastered by scare quotes may be a micro-technique: it is nevertheless a crucial skill in the toolbox of critical thinking. Such mastery entails both the ability to identify and denounce their abuse as well as the ability to judiciously apply them. With the help of

Klemperer and others, I have tried to demonstrate how both components of the micro-technique can prove useful. By the same logic we applied to the handling of "cancel culture," the flap over "wokeism" raises the issue of *actual* cultural appropriation—the variety that should appear without scare quotes—as opposed to the trumped-up manifestations of it that would be most usefully written with the tiny tongs of punctuation: "cultural appropriation." By the same token, when imagining other lives proceeds in a disinterested way, gratuitously, it is a laudable and constructive attitude by which to approach the world. When profit of any sort is sought, on the other hand, "imagining others" is fake, false, regressive, and opprobrious. These two diametrically opposed outcomes allow us to consider what "cultural appropriation" can mean and just how actions falling under its aegis may be evaluated. The former, ancient, and reliable impulses with names like empathy and mutual aid advance the species.

Educational methods such as those few I have quickly sketched here enable individuals to see clearly into social phenomena that perpetuate injustice. Formed and informed by them, we may just see our way to the root of, and come to terms with, the deleterious effects of acts committed in the name of false and phantom ideologies under the guise of manipulated rhetoric. Through the twelve-year Nazi nightmare, Klemperer emerged bent over, but not beaten down: he was alive to return to the university from which he had been expelled for the sake of "race." After thirteen years under the Nazi jackboot culminating in the Dresden bombings that ironically saved him from the final deportations to Auschwitz, he still had the wherewithal to contextualize, to teach the tools of contextualization, to educate and be educated, to open minds and have an open mind, to develop and help develop the critical mind so that lifetimes now and in the future be spent questioning authority.

5

College, Inc.

Denouncing semantic perversion requires the mobilization of recognition. The eye that can see and the ear that can hear must be moved to shift to looking and listening in order for *manipulative mendacity* in action to be detected, denounced, and defused. In their merely passive mode, the ear and the eye are continually exposed to myriad speech acts. Lassitude easily leads to brain-based deafness and blindness. But even from a state of fatigue from the endless barrage of bullshit,[1] acquiring a taste for—even a fascination with— the work of language may arise. How language works and how language is worked take center stage for the Critical Watch. For such a passion to serve justice, honesty, and community, the organs that perceive it must be trained to discriminate among elements of language. Simply put, we are talking about schooling: learning together with others starting from the subject's very entry into language and, then, as far into adulthood as one can go.

For a viable world, for a human community to exist, an uninterrupted trajectory must be assured, for the sake of each mind, from the stage of development where the distinction between right and wrong begins to be mastered to the stage where the fully fledged *person* recognizes residual unethical or unjust behavior and works with other fully fledged *persons* to reason it away, disallowing it. Learning to share a toy and take turns in the playground and classroom must translate seamlessly into the will to preserve peace and prevent genocide. If kindergarten is the crucible of schooling,

---

[1] The best theoretical text on the subject is Harry G. Frankfurt's 2005 classic.

the University is its pinnacle. From first grade, all education emanates; the University sets education on the path of culmination. Given this status, the University must be unfettered by any interests other than the development of the critical mind.

Let us start, then, with a warning. The fate of the University under the Third Reich and, in particular, the fate of those sectors of the University most associated with "intellectuals" and "academics" will serve, as it has throughout this book, as cautionary tale. From the cell where he was incarcerated for several weeks in 1941, Victor Klemperer reflected lengthily on the Nazi "Hostility to Reason, emphasis and overemphasis on volition, action, hostility to scholarship" (I:404; I:513–14). At the inception of that regime, in 1934, Klemperer had already remarked that "they do *not want anyone to study*: intellect, scholarship are the enemies" (I:64; I:87), that "primary schoolteachers should no longer be 'academically' trained" and that only "total science" (I:85; I:116) could, according to the Reich masters, "avoid an academic proletariat" (I:88; I:120). "Hitler [and] National Socialism *despise* the 'intelligentsia,' scholarship, insofar as they do not produce any technological benefits. [...] whoever is not simplistic and not 'fanatical'—is 'liberalistic'" (I:261; I:341). In short, everything needed to be done to have done with what Bernhardt Rust, the Reich's Minister of Education, termed "insipid intellectualism" (I:116; I:157).

Resisting the forces that consider "the humanities" expendable, this final chapter will be an attempt to contribute to an unapologetic, full-throated defense of the vital need for these supposed softest of the soft disciplines. As rubrics for the educational fields that cultivate rational, historically informed, and ethical lives, "liberal arts" and "humanities," are unfortunately the weakest of terms. No wonder college administrators everywhere seek cynically to fund and support only those disciplines "that the world actually needs."[2] Not only must the Critical Watch be on the lookout for semantic perversion and manipulative rhetoric and denounce them wherever they may be found, so

---

[2]From an interview found in Anemona Hartocollis, "Can Humanities Survive the Budget Cuts." *The New York Times*, November 3, 2023. https://www.nytimes.com/2023/11/03/us/liberal-arts-college-degree-humanities.html (accessed November 5, 2023).

too must the Watch be keen to establish truthful semantic precision: adjusting language to express as truthfully and as precisely as possible what it is meant to refer to.

Science is the process—ever open to contestation, modification, adjustment—whereby knowledge is established through community consensus when research and experimentation have been deemed to have reached their limits. Although usually thought to be a purely objective endeavor, scientific knowledge may also be obtained by subjective means—for example, through speculation—so long as consensus is grounded in honest, thorough, and sound argumentation. What Victor Klemperer termed the "thinking stratum" of humanity consists of both "pure" and "impure" scientific endeavors.[3] The primordial task of educators is to see to it that this stratum not be stifled. Anti-intellectualism and the corporatization of everything, however, conspire against this task.

Doubts about the scientific validity of such work of the mind are underwritten by the fact that in the United States they are conducted under the aegis of "the liberal arts" or the "humanities"—labels that smack of approximation rather than precision, fantasy rather than fact, imagination rather than reason. In addition, the fields of inquiry under the "humanities" rubric have always been targeted for attack and, thus, suffer the brunt of consequences deriving from the congenital anti-intellectualism characterizing much of the US population's outlook. In light of their denigration and devaluation, "humanists" have every right to push—despite disdainful resistance even from within academia[4]— to demand and garner the same respect enjoyed by the "pure" scientists by claiming that very status in their name.

---

[3]Klemperer's diary entry for May 23, 1938, reads, in part, as follows: "I once wrote [...] that one should not separate intellectuals from the general population, but the popular stratum in the soul of each person, what is instinctive and in thrall to suggestion, from the thinking stratum. I now add to that: the aim of education in the Third Reich and of the language of the Third Reich, is to expand the popular stratum in everyone to such an extent that the thinking stratum is suffocated" (I:258; I:338).

[4]A recent example among dozens is an August 20, 2012, article in *Scientific American* entitled "Humanities Aren't Science: Stop Treating Them Like One," from which we might consider the following quote, which sounds like the unspoken drive behind certain television advertisements for medical treatments: "Every softer discipline these days seems to feel inadequate unless it becomes harder, more quantifiable, more scientific, more precise."

Examining the impulse behind and the consequences of physics, biology, mathematics, chemistry, medicine—in short, the ontology and epistemological thrust of every mode of scientific inquiry—is carried out not in those domains themselves but in the realm of the human sciences. Without Aristotle or Descartes or Foucault, how would we have even begun to examine why and, especially, how we strive to understand what we call a "world" or "life"? Without Chaucer or Rabelais or Proust, how could we have ever begun to think about the productive interface between the faculty of imagination and the faculty of reason?

Let us therefore—as is done in other cultural-linguistic spaces[5]—boldly and proudly scrap the milquetoast label of "humanities" once and for all and replace it with that of *human sciences*. Let us also, as we now move to describing and assessing the effects of the corporate university, bear in mind that the human sciences constitute the ethical nerve center of the institution. For this ethical spine to function healthily, we must have done, once and for all, with the remnants of anti-intellectualism that has retarded the US body politic for far too long.

the corporate university: the big picture

The body of teaching researchers—without whom there would be no University at all—have known for a long time that from sanctuary for the free development of knowledge, this institution has become a corporate enterprise. Because of this metamorphosis, everything down to the fundamental exchanges—between teachers and students, among teachers and among students—are tainted by clientelism, profitability, monetization, patronage, interest, and so on. The deal is done. No college or university functions independently from the corporate universe and its attendant semantics. Educators know this truth whether they have consciously realized it or merely sense it in dark hours of reckoning. All can be convinced of it by merely opening eyes upon the evidence.

---

[5]The name in France is *sciences humaines* and in Germany *Geisteswissenschaften*. Spanish, however, like English, all too modestly uses the term *humanidades*.

If our institution of highest learning has been turned into a vast business and if, as such, it functions at the whim and will of the corporate investors, it is because all the players in the reigning economic system have for decades been in their assigned positions and acquit themselves eagerly or at least willingly of their roles. This reality works within us just as we compose this reality, whether we choose to face it or not, whether we like it or not. And this reality should not be taken lightly, as we shall see. Some faculty deplore the corporate University; others, naturally, embrace it. Meanwhile, there are all the shades of ambivalence and indifference in between. While I admit that I have no statistics to bolster the assertion, I think it's safe to say that the majority of those who regret this development work in the *human sciences*. In the past thirty or so years, several articles and books have been published stating this as fact, deploring it as they analyze it.[6] Many of these writings are quite thorough and convincing; some of them are what one might call definitive. Some of them promote the process; others dissect and deplore it. Because this is so well-known, I will refrain from cataloging, summarizing the corpus or trying to one-up what has already been written.

Published posthumously in 1996, Bill Readings' *The University in Ruins* stands preeminent, however, among interventions focused on the decline of the University in the age of triumphant corporatization. It is also one of the first. Readings' study drives a provocatively ironic argument rife with potential to reenergize the Critical Watch. Applying what Kant termed the conflict (or strife) of (or among) the faculties (*der Streit der Fakultäten*)—specifically to those faculties that constitute the University on the Humboldtian model— Readings *celebrates* what the University had already become as the end of the twentieth century approached. "The ruins of culture's institution," he wrote as he neared his conclusion, "are simply there, where we are, and we have to negotiate among them" (171). This assessment of the given situation resonates with Foucault's analysis of *discipline*, a plurality of which the faculties in the University are composed. To the extent that "discipline" came to be the

---

[6]In addition to Bill Readings' book and Chris Lorenz's article, to which I will now briefly turn, other useful and canny studies are Jennifer Washburn's *University Inc.* (2005) and Wendy Brown's *Undoing the Demos* (2015).

term indicating mastery of a faculty—this time in the metaphysical, rather than institutional, sense—then the set of disciplines constitutes, according to Foucault, "the ensemble of minute technical inventions" (220). Instead of the egalitarian emancipation that Kant envisioned, strife between disciplines modulated by corporate money and management results in what Foucault sees as definitive disciplinary inequality (222). However, for Readings, recognition of this ruination of the faculty meant to uphold the University's cultural function would be the first task in the Critical Watch's program to rebuild that faculty on adaptable scientific foundations.

Today's synonym for *marchand,* or "mercantile"—that adjective that Molière's Magdelon disdainfully hurled at her father[7]—is "neoliberal." It is a term that another perceptive critic, Chris Lorenz, places at the heart of his trenchant analysis of how New Public Management has been applied to and now grips the University. The term first occurs when the historian and historiographer[8] (a "soft" scientist, as it were) sets the parameters for his project: "This essay analyzes how neoliberal ideology conceives of the public sector in general and, in particular, how this translates to an economic higher education sector" (600). Barring the rare exception when it is used in strict accordance with its actual meaning, as it is by Lorenz, "neoliberal ideology" is a term that demands scare quotes. In all other cases, as Daniel Rodgers argued in the Winter 2018 issue of *Dissent,* "neoliberalism" stands as "the linguistic omnivore of our times, a neologism that threatens to swallow up all the other words around it" (78).[9] As a point of departure for presenting his thoughts, Rodgers first poses, then interrogatively answers, the acerbic rhetorical question, "Does the term 'neoliberalism' clarify our understanding of capitalism today, and efforts to overcome it? Or does it only bring more confusion?" (86). The implication of Rodgers' second question is clear

---

[7]Cf. Chapter 2.

[8]Chris Lorenz teaches history and historiography at Vrije Universiteit Amsterdam and is a senior research fellow at the Institute for Social Movements Ruhr.

[9]"Debating the Uses and Abuses of 'Neoliberalism': Forum." Julia Ott, Mike Konczal, N.D.B. Connolly, and Timothy Shenk respond to Daniel Rodgers. *Dissent.* For an acerbic analysis of how the term "neoliberalism" perpetuates not so much white supremacy but rather more acutely Black disenfranchisement, see N.D.B. Connolly's response, "A White Story." Thanks to Daniel Levy for pointing me to this discussion.

enough: if the term and its relatives were meant—starting in the Reagan-Thatcher era—to designate the mantra of finance capital's inevitability, it has, like a spent metaphor, lost much of its power to signify precisely. And by "gluing too many phenomena together," Rodgers continued, the term "may make it harder to see both the forces at loose in our times and where viable resistance can be found" (78). It doesn't help that a prevalent US understanding of the word conflates politics and economics, transforming "neoliberal" into a strictly political epithet. For the purposes of the present discussion of elusive scare quotes, and despite the term's origins in the late nineteenth century, let us agree that "neoliberal" designates the amplification, in the era of Thatcherism and Reaganomics, of manipulative rhetoric and policy whose obsessive goal was the establishment, as sole possible economic reality, of the so-called free market. To the "liberal" element in the term attaches such a market and to the recrudescence of the concomitant ideology in the 1980s attaches the intensified "neo-" prefix.

The very institution that ostensibly stands as the preserve of critical thinking, the very haven and center from which public practitioners of honest speech are formed, itself suffers from a stultifying strain of semantic perversion. Corporatization is no longer a menacing horizon for institutions of higher education: colleges and universities are now full-fledged business enterprises. They are, in every sense of the term, corporations. The nomenclature used for and by all the players in this sector has been consequently modified. Instead of research-driven educators stimulating young minds, professors have become *service providers* and students their *customers*. Where once a handful of humble administrators tended budgets generously nourished by federal and state tax revenues, now droves of CEOs, managers, branding "experts," and gatekeepers (paid far more than teachers) overtly ensure the implementation of corporate oversight and endless waves of government regulation. Where once there were a few selfless benefactors rectifying shortfalls in public support of higher education, there are *shareholders*, external *stakeholders*, fundraisers, and a proliferation of ego-endowed professorial chairs. If performance, evaluation, and control quizzes, surveys, and algorithms—all written in perfect "qualispeak" (Chris Lorenz)—were not enough to deaden the senses of faculty of good will, the human sciences appear to be on their last leg. It is vital, as

Jean-François Lyotard pled already in 1983,[10] that a last-ditch effort be made to save the dignity of thinking for the sake of the work of reflection and judgment to be carried out by the Critical Watch that we can all potentially be.

Given the priorities and management style of today's University administrators, it may be fair to assume, having studied them assiduously, that many of them have handbooks like Thomson Reuters' *Principles of Corporate Governance: Analysis and Recommendations* sitting in prominence on the shelves of their spacious mahogany offices. If reviewing this classic proves too dry to them, they may choose to leaf through how-tos like *Corporate Rebels* to delude themselves into thinking that they're staying relevant and hip ("8 radical [*sic*] lessons") while "boosting performance and success" at their beloved institution.[11] "They may not teach corporate in college," as the title of another book for neoliberal go-getters strains to enticingly proclaim,[12] but the University is definitely corporate to the core. One of the precursors of NPM, former SS-Oberführer Reinhard Höhn, to whom we will have occasion to turn before the end of this chapter, published dozens of such handbooks in the 1950s, 1960s, and 1970s.[13]

When used correctly and bolstered by solid exemplification,[14] elaboration, and argumentation, the systematic application of scare quotes to "neoliberalism" results in a critical force that discloses the naked term as stagnant and stultifying academic conceit. As someone wrote with pithy scare-quoted example in a January 1980 issue of *Time Magazine*: "The air is thick with devalued buzz words, including 'buzz words.'"[15] Populating the doublespeak lexicon are otherwise positive (though hopelessly nebulous) attributes such as

---

[10]"Preface" in *The Differend*.

[11]Joost Minnaar and Pim de Morree, *Corporate Rebels: Make Work More Fun*, Eindhoven: Corporate Rebels Nederland B.V., 2019.

[12]Alexandra Levit, *They Don't Teach Corporate in College*. 3rd edition. Newburyport, MA: Career Press (Redwheel/Weiser), 2014. "The book every graduate and young professional needs on how work actually works!"

[13]Cf. Chapoutot, 88–91.

[14]In responding to four *Dissent* editors who commented on piece cited, Daniel Rodgers pointedly stated that "Words gain political traction when they resonate with immediate experience. 'Neoliberalism' does not."

[15]Stefan Kanfer, "Time Essay: 80s Babble: Untidy Treasure" *Time* v. 115, no. 4 (January 28, 1980), pp. 90–1. The example I've quoted is given in the *OED* at the rubric "buzzword."

"efficiency," "accountability," "excellence," and "quality" that become corrosive weasel words by dint of their rote imposition by the neoliberal program known as New Public Management (NPM). The perfectly airtight cynicism of NPM hegemony is maintained by a whole lexicon of keywords whose meaning has been forgotten in proportion to their relentlessly repeated usage.

To retool a rhetorical question that Wendy Brown posed at the beginning of *Undoing the Demos* into a statement, when "neoliberal rationality saturates political life" we can kiss "the constituent elements of democracy—its culture, subjects, principles, and institutions"—goodbye (27). When every aspect of the University comes under the sway of New Public Management, "the decline and treachery of the intelligentsia"[16] is sealed by the complicitous faculty members who remain as its ready foot soldiers. These warnings recall to mind the discoveries that Johann Chapoutot recently shared in a book, to which I shall soon turn, that boldly and shockingly outlines "how the Nazis invented modern management."

the corporate university: the fine print

If it is primarily political discourse that comes under analysis when we have Fighting Words in mind, when it comes to academia, it is corporate discourse that comes to the fore. As patently visible as the commercial character of the University is, what is less visible, less audible, and, consequently, far more insidious and corrosive is the manipulative semantics of this reality. A mere nine months after Hitler's ascent to the chancellorship, Victor Klemperer committed this chilling observation about linguistic contagion to his notebook: "The philological journals, the journal of the university association have adopted the opinions and jargon of the Third Reich to such an extent that every page makes one feel sick" (I:38; I:53). As managerial vocabulary and discourse become second nature, infecting everyone in the institution, so the wisdom behind such language goes unquestioned. Only when human

---

[16]Klemperer on March 21, 1945, referring to a former Dresden colleague: "[Harms] is a perfect representative of the decline and of the treachery of the German intelligentsia, of German morals" (II:435; II:574).

scientists *come to critical terms with the critical terms* that we and our fellow educators far too readily (uncritically) interiorize can we have any hope of extirpating the University from the grips of the corporate world, from its dependency on the illusory fruits of capitalism for its existence.

As usual, the crux of the problem is semantic perversion. Certain words and expressions are lodged so deeply in the collective psyche that nothing can improve without exposing and extirpating them. To save his own skin under the Third Reich, Klemperer had to confine exposure of linguistic manipulation to his secret journal. We can, for the time being, count ourselves fortunate enough to not live under such constraints. Since they are pronounced and published constantly, the verbal symptoms of the problem are already fully exposed! Yet it's almost as if their very ubiquity were the cause for our lazily ignoring them.

When Ludwig Wittgenstein affirmed that "problems are solved, not by giving new information, but by arranging what we already know," he was referring to the need for us to engage in what Jacques Derrida would, for better or worse, call "deconstruction." Yes, that vilified term to describe the process consisting of not merely gazing at oneself in the mirror but *seeing* what one can see is fundamental to critical practice. "Philosophy," Wittgenstein concluded, "is a battle against the bewitchment of our intelligence by means of language" (47). Like any other language user, the person committed to educating himself and others is susceptible to "bewitchment." When the terms and phrases of corporate management become second nature to educators, when they have incorporated them into their everyday parlance and, thereby, practice, when they become interiorized, as Freud would have put it, and no longer subject to question and critique, then the actions they describe are carried out willingly, eagerly: the ideology sustaining them triumphs. This is what is called *compliance*—a form of voluntary servitude. Compliance is what the corporate management of the University wants first and foremost from its troops.

When administrators boast about the institutions that they are so highly paid to steward, they spew standardized, predictable, clichéd adjectives, sometimes absurdly strung together, delaying arrival at the all-important noun: the university they head is a "world-class top-tier research-intensive flagship [deep breath] institution." Some faculty in the human sciences scoff at and muse about how it can be that there are any students or their financial sponsors gullible enough to still be taken in by such fluff. Yet those same faculty members, priding themselves for their putative critical acumen, adopt this terminology, readily using the same empty hyperbole found in promotional brochures and on department mastheads. As is so often the case when a new vernacular gets introduced to a community, addictive too is the corporate lingo. As the addiction settles in, it begins to cultivate in the minds and wills of the individual users a type of conventional wisdom that can only be qualified as blinkered thinking.[17]

Out of the mouths of administrators, such signifiers are not only empty (in the Saussurian sense) but they are also "knowingly mendacious," as Klemperer tirelessly qualified declarations made by the totalitarian regime he managed to survive.[18] The vocabulary in such a lexicon are the tools of a politics that has nothing to do with elevating the minds of citizens, preparing a population of critical free thinkers. It is the vocabulary of hucksters hawking a product in the marketplace. The big lie is that thinking is not some good, some bit of merchandise to be bought or sold. Out of the mouths of faculty, on the other hand, corporate jargon is the sign of their having capitulated, succumbed to, and interiorized the code of the "mass dressage [*Massenzurichtung*]" (II:310; II:412) meted out by the corporate overlay. Wittgenstein's principle that "to imagine a language means to imagine a form of life" (8) can be applied here: the form of life that emerges from the fog of such language is not humanity at the pinnacle of its critical capacities but, rather, exchange for profit.

What remains after the exposure and excoriation of the metamorphosis are of course the practices, which are more or less conscious, if not avowed. Sustaining the practices and far more difficult to critique and scour is the lexicon. On the threshold of a micrology of the semantic perversion that undergirds the corporate University, it is useful to familiarize ourselves with the four theses that Chris Lorenz set out to guide his study:

---

[17]We have seen this phenomenon analyzed before. It is not unlike what Sartre vividly described in *Being and Nothingness* and named bad faith (*mauvaise foi*). It is also akin to the "goodthinkful" behavior of compliant subjects in George Orwell's dystopian *1984*. Today, in France, it's called "la pensée unique."
[18]See, e.g., II:362; II:380–81.

[1] neoliberal policies in the public sector [...] are characterized by a combination of free market rhetoric and intensive managerial control practices; [...] NPM policies employ a discourse that parasitizes the everyday meanings of their concepts [...] and simultaneously perverts all their original meanings; [3] the economic NPM definition of education ignores the most important aspects of the education process and therefore poses a fundamental threat to education itself; and [4] the NPM discourse can be termed a bullshit discourse.

(Lorenz 600)

Connecting all this to the ever-perceptive, visionary Klemperer once again, be it noted that regarding his third thesis, Lorenz sees "extremely interesting similarities to the type of managerialism found in former Communist states."

So, let us begin our micrological review with the most vulnerable stratum of the University: doctoral candidates. Graduate faculty have been trained by the corporate trend to, in turn, train their charges to "market themselves." The "marketability" of PhDs has become an unquestioned keystone of sessions held annually in the months leading up to professional congresses where preliminary interviews for tenure-track positions are held. It is taken for granted that "newly minted" doctors have to make themselves attractive critics who critique, but as *products expected to produce*, to be invested in by other corporate colleges. Meanwhile, undergraduates now also, with increasing frequency, express to teachers and advisors their keen desire to be transformed into "marketable" items through their four-year college experience. They too have sadly interiorized this key dimension of neoliberal "reason." More recently even than the drive to sell educated humans as if they were branded goods offered on the market, all the University's key players have been cajoled into adding "entrepreneurship" to set of skills that they must deploy in order to move up in the academic ranks, please bosses and patrons, be good citizens, and gain peer recognition. As a result, for many, entrepreneurial activities can tend to occupy their work time more than their teaching and research. Workshops on how to become "successful faculty entrepreneurs" can be found offered in institutions across the nation. One program, conceived ostensibly to celebrate alumni (which is always also a scheme to elicit donations), asked faculty and staff to "Help us celebrate our most innovative, service-oriented, and entrepreneurially spirited graduates." That these qualities are the ones that the institution promotes as foremost among those that it sees itself embodying is clear from the end of that long sentence: "… who exemplify [the university's] mission."[19] "Building bridges" with extramural businesses and industries or even moonlighting in intramural money-making enterprises hatched while ostensibly teaching and doing research is not only tolerated: it is encouraged to the point where, if they could, the University's managers would make it mandatory.

Back in 1996, Bill Readings was already able to report that "excellence" (as opposed, for example, to any goal with actual substance, like "culture" or "critique") "is rapidly becoming the watchword of the University" (21). What was a mere watchword in the University of the late twentieth century has been assumed as pivotal criterion in the twenty-first. What hasn't changed one iota, however, is the utter emptiness of the term. Readings, again, was prophetic:

> The point is not that no one knows what excellence is but that everyone has his or her own idea of what it is. And once excellence has been generally accepted as an organizing principle, there is no need to argue about differing definitions. Everyone is excellent, in their own way, and everyone has more at stake in being left alone to be excellent than in intervening in the administrative process.
>
> (33)

Thus, today, just as they do as political subjects, teaching, and research faculty are content to develop their own individual "excellence" rather than challenging a system, with its atavistic semantics imposed from above, to keep them working busily while living precariously. Meanwhile, sensing that "excellence" is after all a rather vacuous term, the University's CEOs fall over themselves to expand and elaborate. We already saw "top-tier" and "world-class" among the adjectives marshaled by the hyperventilating Administrator. "Premier," "acclaimed," "distinguished," and "outstanding" are only a few more of the nebulous alternates. But, of course, no one should forget the

---

[19] "40 Under Forty" is a program administered by the Alumni Association of Stony Brook University to "celebrate 40 individuals under 40 who have made an impact since graduating." https://www.stonybrook.edu/40underforty/.

simple mathematical fact that the product of zero and any number is always zero. Regarding the hyperbolic adjective "world-class," our touchstone from Dresden once again comes to mind. Klemperer had occasion to observe that "the epithet 'historic' applies to all, even the most natural actions of the Nazi leaders in peacetime and of the generals, and the super-superlative '*welthistorisch*' is on hand for Hitler's speeches and edicts" (*LTI* 227).

To become such excellent institutions, industrial "efficiency" becomes an absolute *must*—one that quickly supplants educational effectiveness among priorities.[20] In university administrative meetings, the call to "do fewer things better" that one might expect to see in the Amazon warehouse or on the microchip shop floor translates as "get ready, everyone, for the elimination of the 'softest' disciplines."[21] Do the corporate administrators obsessed with this current mantra of academic management actually believe that, if implemented, such disciplinary eliminations will authorize them to continue with straight faces to qualify their institutions as "universities"—havens, that is, for education across the spectrum of human knowledge and investigation? To put it in their terms, such "leadership by subtraction"[22] only cheapens the product offered to the consumers. To put this in *my* terms, such corporate realism confirms the undervaluation of human potential. But what about the student hungry and ready for everything? What about the future polymaths in the wake of the likes of Einstein, Nietzsche, or Adorno?

Once the student comes to be considered (and to consider himself) primarily a customer rather than a young intelligence to be encouraged, informed, and nurtured, the real and perceived demands of the consumer take precedence over education. Care and concern for the "customer's satisfaction" loom. Questions in the student's mind like "Through what I have learned here, have I expanded my role as a person or my qualities as an evolved ape?" become secondary in

---

[20]Cf. Lorenz, 604.

[21]The weasel formula has become a cliché. It was used by Greg Summers, who is provost at the University of Wisconsin, Stevens Point in defense of eliminating "soft" disciplines in favor of majors leading to what the journalist termed (without scare quotes) "clear career paths." Mitch Smith, "Students in Rural America Ask, 'What Is a University Without a History Major?'" *The New York Times*, January 12, 2019. https://www.nytimes.com/2019/01/12/us/rural-colleges-money-students-leaving.html (accessed January 18, 2019).

[22]Sharon L. Gaber, "Leadership by Subtraction." *Inside Higher Education*, May 23, 2023.

importance to "What has this experience done to help me slip into a cushy job?"—in other words, "Was the lemon worth the squeeze?" Satisfaction is only guaranteed when education can be monetized.[23] Meanwhile, the obverse of the grading coin—student evaluation of "instructors" (notice the corporate-driven shift from *educators* in this context)—is nothing more than "customer feedback" by consumers rating the cogs of a businesses. It should be noted further that although prone to deep flaws, student evaluations of "instructors" are a non-trivial variable in the algebra used in tenure and promotion decisions. They are, in any case, an eloquent component of the University's commitment to "quality control." The University's adoption of the stratagems bundled as "total quality management"—also borrowed from NPM—was thoroughly analyzed by Readings, Lorenz, and others.[24] Controlling quality raises questions of both a theoretical and a practical nature. Who, first of all, defines quality? Are the criteria, categories, and intensities of quality decided at the top or by consensual decision? And, of course, there is the perennial question as to how quality can possibly be subjected to quantification which is patent in the adoption of quality management of education.

Traditionally, the three pillars of tenure and promotion are publishing, teaching, and service. Ostensibly university administrators ratify this as being the case. However, in practice, one must add the ability of the faculty member to garner grants. While it might seem natural, given the importance of education for nurturing democracy, that all funding for research would come from taxes levied on the income of the nation's citizens so that new, ever more educated citizens may be formed, this ideal is far from actual practice. The pressure to garner grants is a non-trivial component in the educator's ability to hold her job, be promoted, and remunerated fairly for her work training critical minds. In principle, there is nothing wrong with the obtention of funds from outside the University for a research project. But when the source is a corporate entity, that entity's temptation to impose their "vision" on the project becomes irresistible. Meanwhile, the University's eagerness to convert every grant

---

[23]The following are pages in *The University in Ruins* where Readings discussed academic consumerism: 11, 22, 27–8, 53, 130–1, 137, 172, 174, 176–7, as discourse, 19, 149; logic of, 132, 134, 141, 143, 146; as self-victimization, 116.

[24]Cf. e.g. Readings, 21–23.

obtained by a laboratory or individual researcher (a "PI") into an item on their public brag sheet is creepy. Instead of spending dozens of hours on a grant proposal that—because it comes from the "soft" sector of the University—is unlikely to even get past the institutions internal filter, the faculty member could accept an offer to lecture at a conference or a public venue or not have to turn down an enticing request to write an article or contribute an essay to an anthology or even review a book manuscript for publication.

Preparing critical minds for world citizenship, as the human sciences tirelessly strive to do, if not entirely beside the point, has strictly no relevance for corporate management. To justify their continued existence, faculty departments, programs, research institutes, and so forth must regularly produce self-studies at the behest of the administrative class followed, normally, by external reviews. These typically begin with "mission" statements, modeled after documents that are the pride and joy of the top administration. Guided presumably by such texts, the "missionaries" can go back—for a while—and resume their selfless work of proselytization of the "savages." Sarcasm aside, such exercises factor into the calculations that produce coveted institutional rankings[25] and, even more importantly, they can and are used by corporate management in their "strategic planning" which can (and quite often does) result in "restructuring," which, in turn, leads with some regularity to the elimination of programs and, hence, of faculty with—and especially without— tenure. For administrators busily ensuring that their role in the University is essential, most anything can be construed as "strategic," so long as it serves the "advancement" (i.e., making profit, meeting costs) of the institution. In lieu of all these "excellent" exercises, in the time that it takes to perform them, "line" faculty could be devoting all their time to educating the students, helping them to become citizens with critical minds: by increasing intellectual contact with undergraduates by offering extra office hours; by organizing an archive or gallery or cinematic visit for them; and by proposing an additional seminar on some key philosophical work or another to motivated graduate students. Rather than pandering to bosses who need costs cut, scraping for funding, and

---

[25]*U.S. News & World Report*, Shanghai Ranking, *Times Higher Education*, Quacquarelli Symonds, *The Princeton Review*, *Forbes Magazine*, and so on.

helping administrators impress the public, these are just some of the initiatives for the benefit of *students* that could be implemented were so many of our ninety hours of work per week not consumed participating in largely petty managerial functions.

Meanwhile there is the steady stream of seemingly all-important dispatches—analog and digital—from the top. One must imagine the care and time managers devote to crafting what they term, with solemnity, "white papers" announcing policy adjustments, many of the details of which they have usually siphoned from the brains of sycophantic faculty all too willing to brainstorm for them. One must imagine the vague attempt at marshaling authentic feeling required to emit text, for example, that wrings its hands over "tragedies" like mass shootings or hate crimes that hit sister institutions. One can only imagine the backroom fretting over reception by the rank and file at the next memo announcing the creation of yet another vice-provostial position. Or perhaps they are more shameless than we think. All of this of course constitutes ample justification for faculty frustration and cynicism as well as for the large and ever-growing disparities between administrative salaries and those of the plebes. Verification and confirmation of the fact that administrator salaries outstrip faculty and staff salaries by ratios that are increasing every year are easily obtainable by the curious.[26]

A great many bulletins and emails are secreted to faculty from the offices of the vast corporation's noncommissioned officers: vice-presidents, vice-provosts, associate deans leading (or at least overseeing) a myriad of sectors: budget, finance, procurement, media relations, research compliance, human resources, vendor management … the divisions and subdivisions are seemingly infinite. These dispatches request or require from faculty (and, sometimes, staff) a multitudinous array of exercises—some required by state or federal law, others concocted by administrative bodies anxious to appear relevant. To understand whence comes this madness, we must remember that in the corporate world, ensuring the "accountability" of line workers is of paramount importance to justify bureaucratic existence. Under such conditions, reading essays, evaluating experiments, attributing grades to students become

---

[26]AAUP, Glassdoor, SeeThroughNY, etc.

secondary in importance to producing ethics declarations, as only one example.[27] Ensuring "accountability" involves a baroque array of procedures with which faculty and staff are "requested" to comply. With few exceptions, these procedures are mandatory and carry material consequences—such as withheld salary—for negligence or noncompliance.

Now, few will dispute the need to obviate corruption in *any* of society's institutions, be they political, legal, educational, or so on. However, the annual "disclosure" of external interests and commitments is yet another time-consuming exercise imposed (on penalty of withheld paychecks) on the faculty member and designed in such a way as to consume the maximum amount of time on the part of the subject under scrutiny while asking many irrelevant questions vis-à-vis the purpose of the exercise. Answering yes or no to the question "Have you used any university resources to promote a political candidate?" should be as easy as it used to be with the infamous United States Citizenship and Immigration Services (USCIS) questions, "Have you ever been a member of a Communist Party?" The type of verification that disclosures of external interests belong to could easily saves everyone a lot of time by astutely tethering IRS information to the state's ethics committee database. Ethics declarations and their concomitant certifications come under the rubric of "compliance." Compliance names the act of yielding to a condition or order. So firmly implanted is this meaning in our linguistic culture that the *OED* points out the actual shift in English etymology from seeing the word's source in *complere* (to complete) to associating the word's second syllable with *plicare*, hence "bending to the will of another." In requiring various types of compliance, the corporate University overtly demands obedience, allegiance, fealty.

"Surveys" of various sorts are one example of such docile body training, as Foucault might have called it. One would think that deleting a call to fill out something labeled a "survey" would be as simple and routine as a "skip this" button allowing you to get to the desired YouTube video. Yet participation in some surveys circulated at the University has somehow gone from voluntary ("if you have time" or "could you please help us?") to mandatory, with enforcement ensured, again, by pulling the paycheck tether. If such

---

[27]Cf. Lorenz, 609.

paper shuffling didn't require us to scrimp on our time devoted to education, we could consult with advanced students and collaborate more often with colleagues to adjust existing or develop new curricula.

Given the burgeoning of administrative positions, the plethora of personnel, and the concomitant labor hours this represents, it is quite simply mindboggling that the University has not yet figured out how to implement Title IX and DEI policy without infantilizing faculty and staff. At the conclusion of compulsory online courses like one dubbed "ReportIt," whose subtitled purpose is "ending sexual conduct for [*sic*] faculty and staff,"[28] faux "certifications of training" or "certificates of achievement" are doled out like gold stars in kindergarten for each unit successfully completed. Another mandatory program (same noncompliance consequences as above) issues from cybersecurity educational entities like "KnowBe4," which offers (no doubt at considerable cost to the University strapped for money) a course entitled "Security Moments Series: Social Engineering 101." (The deleted spaces, here and there, mimicking digital-age branding, the weird association of safety with sappy "moments," and the hair-raising notion that *people* can be "engineered" by such programs, as if they were inanimate objects.) While it is probably no more possible to know how effective such programs are in preventing harassment, discrimination, malware than it was for Iraq under Saddam to prove it *did not* have WMDs, what *is* certain is that highly qualified educators and researchers who are typically averse to being infantilized in this way are compelled to suck all this up.

Perhaps if less faculty time were consumed by bureaucratic exigencies, we could help the public better understand the incontrovertible centrality of education in the construction of a just and peaceful society. Perhaps we could find ways, means, and time to invite the "outside world" in to hear what we have to say and, thus, break down barriers, reduce alienation, diminish divides, attenuate the atavistic anti-intellectualism that has kept the United States back since the country's founding. To paraphrase Nick Lowe (via Elvis Costello), What's so funny about socioeconomic seamlessness?

---

[28]Not quite certain what preposition to use—for, with, among …—the author chose the one that leaves undecidable whether the lessons are meant to prevent sexual misconduct or to promote it.

All this busywork can easily lead to "a state of organizational insanity in which academics can no longer function as scholars" that has been dubbed "academentia."[29] Worse still, rare is the professional educator who takes stock of this anesthetizing lexicon that so many of us passively interiorize, lulling us into serving as compliant soldiers of the corporation. Priorities are no longer set based on what might truly be good for students or might advance knowledge (yes: science); instead, they are set by management fiat and deadlines. Bureaucratic busywork siphons time away from curriculum preparation and carefully critical reading of essays. As a result, papers get returned to students with unacceptable delays and, instead of renewing and reinventing courses, teachers are reduced to repeating old ones with identical readings and assignments. This time-saving strategy is boring for the educator and the boredom shows in the classroom. Nonacademic demands not only devour time but they also sap the energy required to carry out the educational mission—one fixed expression with which I can agree, despite the tinge of religion in it. Just as the taxed scholar ends up cutting corners in delivering on his passion—teaching—he is forced to cancel or postpone scholarly activities due to simple, raw fatigue. Not only is bureaucratic busywork debilitating but it is also, as I have tried to show, demeaning and infantilizing.

We sometimes forget that pronouncing the "pledge of allegiance"— whose history runs parallel with the early twentieth-century rise of fascism in Europe—is still mandatory in schools in several parts of the country. In the same vein, although *loyalty oaths* per se are employment conditions from a bygone era,[30] procedures theoretically tied to the same consequences exist today, here and there—even in academia—albeit under new guises. Failure to swear to one's non-communism was once routine ground for unemployment. Today, in their zeal to belatedly inculcate Diversity, Equity, and Inclusion across the institution, University administrators, executing mandates from state governments, have begun to require incoming faculty to sign and swear their agreement to the policy as part of their hiring package on pain of being

---

[29]Thomas Klikauer and Meg Young, "Academentia: The Organization Insanity of the Modern University." *Counterpunch*, July 28, 2021. https://www.counterpunch.org/2021/07/28/academentia-the-organization-insanity-of-the-modern-university/ (accessed October 20, 2023).
[30]Keyishian v. Board of Regents of the University of the State of New York.

rejected for declining to do so. While that might smack of sheer McCarthyism, we must be careful. While we need to be woke to the fact that the expression "loyalty oath" has also become dog-whistle code among far- and alt-right critics of Title IX training and mandated language in faculty search descriptions, the spirit of DEI is as noble as it is belated.[31] Hence, we must be vigilant to distinguish between "thought police" ("Marxist" infiltrators) and thought police (corporate overseers) who make it their job to "manage risk." When the University adopts DEI policy based on recommendations by management consulting firms like Bain & Company, it is wise to be skeptical at the very least and probably suspicious of their intentions.

It would be inaccurate and perhaps a little unfair, however, to imply that the highly paid class of college administrators do nothing but impose busywork on faculty and staff. Since it is the public's image of the institution more than the quality of world citizens it forms that is of utmost concern to the managers, they periodically embark on "branding" or rebranding programs that deeply encumber the budget. After all, as Donald Trump is wont to remind everyone, "I became president because of my brand."[32] Millions of dollars are shelled out to hire consulting firms to redesign logos, letterhead, and apparel or adorn the campus with creepily Nurnbergesque banners displaying feel-good imagery and uplifting prose costs millions. After the dust settles, faculty and staff are "encouraged" to promote "our brand" by wearing lapel pins, donning the college colors on designated rah-rah days, and generally "talking us up." Obsessing over the institution's brand, pledging allegiance to it, is the campus-level equivalent of the bellicose patriot syndrome on the national level.

For teaching and research faculty, perhaps the clearest proof of the corporate coup perpetrated on the University is the transformation, since the turn of the twenty-first century, in the role played by college deans. From allies of departments and advocates for faculty in dealings with the higher administration, they have become the henchmen of the corporate bureaucrats who govern the University as if they were wannabe CEOs. As such they are

---

[31]"The University's New Loyalty Oath." *Wall Street Journal*, December 19, 2019; J. Scott Turner, "The New Loyalty Oaths: DEI Statements Are a Failure of Priority." *CounterCurrent*. https://www.nas.org/blogs/article/the-new-loyalty-oaths (accessed October 18, 2023); the Heritage Foundation …
[32]Stated after testifying in New York on November 6, 2023.

tending more and more to be disdainful of faculty concerns, diffident toward ideas that the underlings who teach have for running the place. In many colleges, well after it was clear that Covid-19 had become an epidemic and before surgical masks become fixtures, deans ignored the alarm sounded by faculty about the dangers to everyone of continuing to meet in crowded classrooms. For the sake of their students and themselves, ad hoc groups of faculty in many places took it upon themselves to shift their teaching to online platforms days and weeks before administrations finally issued "stay-at-home" directives, thus demonstrating the cooperative wisdom of independent rational thinkers. What is more, as what Klemperer observed with the "favor [shown to] non-professors and lay healers" (I:55; I:74) in 1934 Germany or as in the replacement of doctors with "doctors" during the Chinese Cultural Revolution as shown in Zhang Yimou's 1994 film, *To Live*, in decanal, provostial, and even presidential hiring, there is an increasing trend to recruiting nonacademics or scholars whose research careers are lackluster or stagnant. This widens the rift separating them from the ranks of faculty.

Concomitantly, *faculty governance* has become largely illusory, the expression surviving only as a semantic scrap tossed at professors to keep their sense of autonomy on life support: a toy, a vain exercise we're allowed to pretend we play—an empty principle with no legislative heft. A department chair can well be elected unanimously by the voting faculty, and the college dean will superciliously receive it as "the department's recommendation" and assure the popular incumbent chair that he'd "be glad to discuss this possibility"—slick circumlocution, weasel words equipped with an escape hatch. In academia, "recommendation" is the degraded, attenuated, supposedly palatable form of what was once autonomous democratic decision with legislative legitimacy. But for the well-trained dean today, this kind of euphemism is standard practice. As much a symptom of varying degrees of cowardliness in individuals, this rhetorical device drips managerial disdain for the faculty, who are the mainstays of the institution. Instead of telling an employee that she has been fired or even replacing that word with "let go," today's boss will "suggest" that she is now "free to seek other opportunities."

The fate of education sealed by slippery semantics was not lost on the linguist from Dresden, who noted in March 1934 that "There has already been talk of pensioning off the Whole Humanities Section" (I:60; I:81) and that by fall "Our whole Humanities Section [has been] destroyed (*Unsere ganze Kulturwissenschafliche Abteilung zerschlagen*)" (I:135; 183). Toward the endless end of the Third Reich, in the fall of 1944, he reported that "no more 'belletristic' [*schöngeistigen*] and 'related' [*verwandten*] books may be printed anymore. Only natural science and technology!" (II:351; II:464) and "new 'totalization' decrees [*Totalisierungs-Bestimmungen*] have come out: University departments have largely been closed down (theology and philosophy completely), the senior classes of secondary schools have been dispatched to factory work, all periodicals apart from those 'important to the war effort' [*kriegswichtigen*] have been suppressed" (II:355–56; II:470). Klemperer's diaries thus relentlessly remind the reader patient enough to plow through them what can never be repeated too often: when totalitarianism is the order of the day, the "soft" disciplines—deemed "hotbeds" of critical thinking—are the first to be eliminated from institutions of higher learning.

Meanwhile, to *cut costs* without negatively impacting their own bloated salaries, college management has a whole bag of strategies applied to personnel and infrastructure alike. Replacing tenure-track professors with adjunct faculty—especially in the human sciences—is a well-known and long-established measure. Highly qualified instructors on stipends that are a fraction of what "line" faculty[33] need to be paid and who can be renewed or let go on an annual basis are a boon for the corporate managers focused solely on "the bottom line." One adjunct can teach twice as many classes as a faculty member required to produce research. And since research in the human sciences is treated with disdain anyway, the fact that adjuncts are not expected to produce any at all makes them ever more attractive. (Meanwhile, these scholars all of whose time is consumed in teaching see their hopes for

---

[33]I set "line" off with scare quotes to draw attention to an actual term that the university uses in relation to its workers and also to similarities that exist in the area of job security between professors and factory workers. Tenure-track positions are pegged to faculty salary "lines," referring to lines on an accountant ledger. Thus, tenure-track faculty are sometimes referred to as "line faculty." Once on those "lines," similarly to a worker on the shop floor, professors must meet performance standards keyed to expectations of customers and investors as well as to academic requirements (teaching, research, service) to have a shot at tenure. Like the notorious arbitrariness of expectations to which factory workers are held, all such standards for faculty are nebulous.

a tenure-track job fade as their production of publications is put on hold.) Cost-cutting measures are visible in quite disparate corners of the University. Take office furniture, for example. In lieu of the fancy mahogany fixtures found in presidential and provostial digs, faculty offices and cubicles can be furnished with bookshelves and desks manufactured in state penitentiaries by nominally remunerated prison labor[34] and delivered to campus by low security inmates. Such equipment is not only dirt cheap but arranging to buy it enables the University's PR division to boast its support for carceral "correction" and "rehabilitation."

Now that we have arrived at the magic kingdom of cutbacks, personnel trimming, and other human resource "strategic planning," we should circle back to the start of this overview to the strategies university administrators use to garner revenue to make up for the paucity of government funding. Pressure on faculty to cultivate and establish ties to industry is constant and multifarious. Once an institution receives an endowment, payback is invariably expected. Thus, buildings come to bear the investor's name, educational policy becomes subject to inflection by the investor's will, students who voice unpleasant political opinions may be doxed and blacklisted for future employment. Those, on the other hand, able through this system to pull ideological strings are invariably referred to as "stakeholders." A stake is a fist full of money deposited (or guaranteed) to be taken by a game, a race, or some contest. Big donors with big stakes wield outsized influence. They are likely to sit on executive boards. Alumni, community donors, "partners" of nebulous or dubious origin, communities, parents, industry investors, project sponsors, suppliers and vendors, "policy makers"—so long as they stay clear of ethics breaches—also hold stakes of various magnitudes in the game of keeping the University afloat. But while teaching faculty too are small-time punters in the free-for-all competition between colleges, the educators are usually at the bottom of the list, as they wield the least power in the monetized environment.

---

[34]According to one New York State inmate, "The current wage scale for people incarcerated here, [...] ranges from $0.10 an hour to $0.65 an hour and is determined by your program or assignment. The majority of the prison population earns $0.25 per hour or less." Walter Ball, "Increasing Prison Wages to Dollars Just Makes Sense," *Vera*, February 7, 2023.

Another important hook for high stakes is sport. The US University is rather unique in the world for the ubiquity of sports and, concomitantly, the money involved. The pervasive and massive presence inside these institutions of proto-professional football, basketball, and virtually every other team sport played for huge profits and salaries outside the University can be explained by one reason: they stimulate rah-rah nostalgia in alumni with deep pockets. Graduates of X or Y university who have gone on to lucrative jobs are often more than willing to lavish endowments in exchange for being thrilled at an NCAA final while they grouse about the radicals in the classrooms and libraries. Meanwhile, it is generally only from the cynical ranks of the human scientists that arguments against what is seen as the oversized role played by athleticism in the institution for higher learning are heard.

With Christmas 1936 approaching, Klemperer noted that language was revealing a collapse of any difference between competition among retail stores, competition among service providers, and militarization. "Last summer," he wrote, everyone spoke of the "battle of production [*Erzeugerschlacht*]— Now in the Christmas advertisements: battle of customers [*Käuferschlacht*]" (I:202; I:267). US colleges and universities compete with the same ferocity. Investment in team sports, whose expected tenfold returns in the form of alumni donations is the core pretext, is one visible tip of the battle for customers iceberg. Although a few anodyne complaints are occasionally voiced (invariably by human scientists) about how the University's resources could be better invested in education, much like the suggestion that a sliver of the enormous US defense budget could easily finance universal healthcare, these are brushed off as pinpricks from the "intelligentsia." The vast majority of faculty fall in lockstep, in an "appalling degree of toadying [*ungeheure Kriechen*]" (I:202; I:267), with the University's strategies to fight for customers.

Cultivating endowments, fundraising competition with other corporate colleges, and simply paying the bills require a catalogue of strategies among which one of the most spectacularly cringeworthy is the "gala fundraiser." These are predictably modeled on corporate fundraisers: people in the public eye whose celebrity is deemed proportional to the prestige of the institution are begged to host, glamorous evening wear is donned, one vacuous "rousing" toast follows upon another, and so on. The Covid years rendered such events even more ludicrous. Forced to be held virtually, "reduced" price tickets were offered for modest sums like $250 a head to see glamourous celebrities and entertainers perform in Zoom® rectangles. The attendees could sip virtual (BYOB) cocktails in lounge pajamas instead of evening wear. In its determination to excel, the "university of excellence" sometimes converges perilously with the "excellence" of Bill and Ted's adventure.[35]

As if the University were some church or a charity organization, faculty receive frequent if not downright relentless requests, bolstered by good old American peer pressure, to *give back* to the institution where they try to carry out their work. Colleges and universities all over the country organize Giving Days ostensibly for everyone to donate to the institutions, but very much pointed at the ranks receiving far less on their paychecks than the administrators who come up with these schemes. Regular appeals in the form of "gift giving facts" memos go out to faculty and staff explaining how they can participate in funding what the government, through tax revenues, should be funding but don't. "If you're 70.5 or older, you can give through your IRA," as one goad goes, "This is called 'qualified charitable distribution.'" Giving tithes and offering alms are, of course, reflexes so engrained in our deeply puritanical roots that many individuals find this perfectly natural.

A pulldown menu extracted from a typical survey form designed by administrators to pigeonhole the University's employees stands as testimony to just how buried (and, thus, insignificant) the educational function of the institution is beneath the vast and ever-growing array of activities (to which I have added my sarcastic editorial remarks) that contribute little or nothing to (in)forming young minds and citizens:

Admissions/Enrollment

Business Affairs/Operations [A spade called a spade: after all, it *is* a business]

Competency/Assessment [How can we quantify the qualitative?]

---

[35]"Kant thought we could find ourselves as entirely reasonable. The German Idealists thought we could find ourselves as an ethnic culture. The technocrats of today think we can find ourselves as 'most excellent,' to cite *Bill and Ted's Excellent Adventure*—a film which is an interesting attempt to understand the impossibility of historical thought once knowledge has itself become commodified as information" (Readings, 53).

Development/Alumni Affairs [Who to tap for funding that the State holds back and how]
Diversity/Inclusion [How to ensure compliance with state and federal guidelines]
Executive Leadership [The corporate elite, the highest salaries]
Faculty/Researcher
Human Resources [What a euphemism!]
Learning Design/Digital Learning
Marketing/Communications [Where the semantics really goes wild and infects everyone]
Strategic Planning/IR [AKA, the bullshit incubator]
Student Affairs
Technology
K–12/College Counselors
Other [staff, who are mainstays]

All of this echoes the brilliant and prescient analysis of what Michel Foucault termed "disciplined bodies" in *Discipline and Punish*. Not only does the University, by means of an array of micro-techniques, normalize the students: now that it has become a fully corporate entity, the administrative *will to compliance* seduces teaching faculty into normalized behavior as well. As Foucault was predicting already in 1975 regarding the hallmark exercise of normalization,[36] "We are entering the age of the infinite examination and of compulsory objectification" (189).

Even more disturbing and more specific is the genealogical link between New Public Management—as implemented now across the entirety of academia— and rightwing totalitarianism. In an essay published in 2020, historian Johann Chapoutot advances the suggestive, enlightening, and frightening argument that the hugely successful management of human resources that typified the postwar "German miracle" (*Wirtschaftswunder*) was refined into a system applicable to all sectors of a society during the Third Reich. In 1956, what would become the management training center for two decades of "miraculous" economic

---

[36]"At the heart of the procedures of discipline, [the examination] manifests the subjection of those who are perceived as objects and the objectification of those who are subjected" (1975, 184).

recovery, the Akademie für Führungskräfter (Management Academy), was opened, as Chapoutot puts it, "under the direction of the man who, eleven years earlier, was still 'SS-Oberführer Professor Dr. Reinhard Höhn'" (73), the brilliant Nazi jurist of public law close to (and in rivalry with) Carl Schmitt. In historical retrospect, the theories Höhn had been developing as early as the 1930s can be seen as prophetic for the emergence of "NPM, which," as Chapoutot writes, "has become the new religion in Western countries" (117). For deans in today's US University who prove not quite up to their tasks, higher management willingly hire professional coaches to bolster their confidence, lending them tips on how to deal with frustrated faculty, and on how to manage their stress. Höhn was an early proponent of such remedial measures to keep the managers "excellent" by managing themselves (90). In eagerly and uncritically adopting the manipulated and manipulative rhetoric of the management class, the educators participate body and soul in the corporatized way of running everything as envisioned by Höhn. Together, the administrators and their administered teachers form a *Betriebsgemeinschaft*—a happy "community of bosses and workers" (50), of leaders and the led.[37] Through self-study, strategic planning, and surveys, faculty in academic departments freely feed ideas to the management class, who then freely turn the findings against the teaching class in the form of reorganization, reassignment, and receivership. Thus, the title that Chapoutot leant his essay perfectly encapsulates the voluntary servitude that results from the University's line workers falling in lockstep with the semantic perversion of the corporate administrators: *Libres d'obéir*, or, *Free to Obey*.

Klemperer's cautionary chronicle and the corporate university

As educational anthropologist, Rosemary C. Hense aptly points out that "once we have accepted a particular metaphor into our discourse, it becomes difficult

---

[37]The German term for management is *Menschenführung*. I have added the adjective "happy" in allusive reference to the program of Kraft durch Freude (Power through Joy) modeled after the Italian fascist Opera Nazionale Dopolavoro, whose idea was that "productive power was sustained by joy, a joy produced by pleasure and leisure" (61ff).

to think of the concept otherwise" (246). This and the preceding chapters may allow us to amplify the warning by stating that, once the manipulation of metaphor has been become naturalized, thinking the corresponding concept otherwise becomes well-nigh impossible. The same goes—even more importantly—for action and practice based on the concept.

In the case of the University, failing to free the institution from the corporate maw would have profound consequences. We are experiencing some of them already. The interiorized semantic veil blinds us and the din of that language deafens us. Worse still, blind to the veil, we remain mute rather than resisting and opposing it. The imagination, the inventive engine that drives reason, becomes stunted and risks ending up altogether tetanized. Recoiling from the task of carrying out the critique that would reverse this process will only make it virtually irreversible. Are we willing to let ourselves and our children descend into the state that Klemperer lamented in 1942 and again, in 1944, in the form of a rhetorical question? As then, what seems to be happening today is the slow execution of "an intellectual death sentence, enforced illiteracy [*Geistiges Todesurteil, Analphabetismus erzwungen*]" (II:84; II:115). At the end of the nightmare, he wondered, "How long will it take to remove the National Socialist filth [*Unrat*] from these children's heads?" (II:294; II:391)? Such filth sullies far too many heads today.

Though far-fetched to infer an equivalence between today's situation of the University in the United States to that of higher education in Nazi Germany, it behooves us to consider the consequences of total fealty to Capital. These consequences return us to the subject of the first chapter of this book: the pervasiveness of the language of war in general culture. It is no secret that the discourse of college administration is rife with military metaphors and that these metaphors take root in the way faculty members speak as well. We have seen that *strategy* is so important that it tends to supplant thinking. *Campaigns* are waged to *recruit* students as they are to garner donations. Planning proceeds in *war rooms* where *briefing* and *debriefing* set the tone, while teachers *maneuver* through *mine fields, in the trenches* or *on the front lines* (as if students were so many enemies to be conquered). In teaching, some *battles* are won, some are lost. Adjustments in *tactics* are sometimes required. Faculty and academic units—especially in "soft" fields—*under fire* for one failing or another are subject to *attrition*. The list seems endless. We wield these metaphors mindlessly.[38]

As the University threatens to forgo the human sciences altogether, such semantic perversion would be free to proliferate, blurring the fragile divide between language and action, naturalizing the worse instincts of the species. The correlate of the obsessive "cancel culture" formula would be the cancellation of endeavors humans have developed for training and exercising the critical faculties of the brain. Important here is to recall that when Klemperer noted, in the first year of the Nazi régime, that "military sports [*Wehrsportübungen*]" were being prioritized over study, "A series of lectures was simply canceled. Scholarship," Klemperer lamented, "is no longer essential" (I:37; I:50). Were the critical firewalls made possible by human sciences to fall, not only would the language of war—already pervasive—persist in a myriad of peaceful contexts, making nothing but war the norm, but the faculties ostensibly destined to thrive—science, technology, medicine—would become massively willing contributors to the extinction of peace. In the process, the qualities and capacities of our minds that—according to us—place us highest among the animals currently walking the planet—qualities and capacities whose development and expansion are the domain of the University—would continue to be starved, staved, and stunted.

I wrote earlier in this chapter that "Certain words and expressions are lodged so deeply in the collective psyche that nothing can improve without exposing them." And I wrote in this book's first chapter about what could be the most massively egregious example in the twenty-first century of just such denial due to semantic perversion. Short of exposing the first implementation of the expression "Ground Zero" not in Manhattan in 2001 but at Hiroshima in 1945, we perpetuate the lie of our unique and aboriginal victimhood to justify the wanton murder of millions and we go on supporting only regimes that do likewise.

---

[38]Many articles have been written concerned with the language of war in academia. "War Metaphors in Public Discourse" by Teenie Matlock, "Education Debates Are Rife with References to War" by Mark Hlavacik, and "War Metaphors Are Damaging Our Schools" by Tim Price are a few examples.

In the truly free university, fully funded by democratic institutions, as it should be, unfettered by corporate totalitarianism, all forms of science—including those pertaining to the faculty of imagination—would flourish. No longer would "disciplines" be set in stone. No prejudice or presupposition—ideological or religious—would fetter or impede the free flow of inquiry and thought. Only then would the belief that "race" is a theory or even a concept be set to rest.

Bibliography

Abbott, Barbara. "Some Notes on Quotation." In Philippe de Brabanter, ed. *Belgian Journal of Linguistics* 17 (2003): 13–26. Amsterdam: John Benjamins, 2005 ("Hybrid quotations" issue).

Adorno, Theodor W. "Punctuation Marks." Translated by Sherry Weber Nicholsen. *The Antioch Review* 48, no. 3 (Summer 1990): 300–5.

Alburger, James R. *The Art of Voice Acting: The Craft and Business of Performing for Voiceover*, 4th edition. New York & London: Focal Press, 2011.

Anscombe, G.E.M. "Aristotle and the Sea Battle." *Mind—A Quarterly Review of Psychology & Philosophy* 65, no. 257 (January 1956): 1–15.

Antelme, Robert. *L'Espèce humaine* [1947]. Paris: Gallimard (Tel), 1978. Translated by Jeffrey Haight and Annie Mahler as *The Human Race*. Marlboro, VT: Marlboro Press, 1992. Reprint Northwestern University Press, 1998.

Asim, Jabari. *The N Word: Who Can Say It, Who Shouldn't, and Why*. Boston: Houghton Mifflin, 2007.

Bachelard, Gaston. *La Poétique de l'espace*. Paris: Presses Universitaires de France, 1957. Translated by Maria Jolas as *The Poetics of Space*. New York: Beacon Press, 1994 [see Chapter 4, page 27.].

Barthes, Roland. "Dominici, or the Triumph of Literature." Translated by Richard Howard. *Mythologies* (1957): 48–52 [*Œuvres*, t. 1, 592–94.].

Bataille, Georges. "The Notion of Expenditure" [1933]. In Allan Stoekl, ed. *Visions of Excess. Selected Writings, 1927–1939*: 116–29. Minneapolis: University of Minnesota Press, 1985.

Bazin, Hervé. *Plumons l'oiseau*. Paris: Grasset, 1966.

Bernasconi, Robert. "A Most Dangerous Error: The Boasian Myth of a Knock-Down Argument against Racism." *Angelaki* 24, no. 2 (2019): 92–103.

Black, Edwin. *War against the Weak: Eugenics and America's Campaign to Create a Master Race*. New York: Four Walls Eight Windows, 2003.

Black, Jay. "Semantics and Ethics of Propaganda." *Journal of Mass Media Ethics* 16, nos. 2–3 (June 2011): 121–37.

Black, Jay and Chris Roberts. *Doing Ethics in Media: Theories and Practical Applications*. New York: Routledge, 2011.

Blackhawk, Ned. *The Rediscovery of America: Native Peoples and the Unmaking of U.S. History*. New Haven, CT: Yale University Press, 2023.

Blum, William. *Rogue State: A Guide to the World's Only Superpower*, 3rd edition. London: Zed Books Ltd., 2006.

Boas, Franz. "Race." In Edwin R.A. Seligman and Alvin Johnson, eds. *Encyclopedia of the Social Sciences*, v. 13: 25–34. New York: The Macmillan Company, 1934.

Brody, Jennifer DeVere. *Punctuation: Art, Politics, and Play*. Durham: Duke University Press, 2008.

Brown, H. Rap. *Die Nigger Die!* Westport, CT: Lawrence Hill Books, 1969.

Brown, Michael K. et al. *Whitewashing Race: The Myth of a Color-Blind Society*. Berkeley: University of California Press, 2023.

Brown, Wendy. *Undoing the Demos: Neoliberalism's Stealth Revolution*. New York: Zone Books, 2015.

Cappelen, Herman, Ernest Leporc, and Matthew McKeever. "Quotation." In *Stanford Encyclopedia of Philosophy*. Revised edition. 2019. https://plato.stanford.edu/entries/quotation/ [accessed May 24, 2019].

Catach, Nina. *La Ponctuation (Histoire et système)*. Paris: Presses Universitaires de France (Que sais-je ?), 1994, 2018.

Chait, Jonathan. "Scared Yet?" *The New Republic*, December 31, 2008. https://newrepublic.com/article/64702/scared-yet.

Chait, Stéphanie. "Foucault, Deleuze, Derrida … Aux origines françaises du 'wokisme.'" *Le Monde*, February 26, 2022. https://www.lemonde.fr/m-le-mag/article/2022/02/26/foucault-deleuze-derrida-aux-origines-francaises-du-wokisme_6115308_4500055.html [accessed June 15, 2024].

Chapoutot, Johann. *Libres d'obéir: Le management, du nazisme à aujourd'hui*. Paris: Gallimard (Essais), 2020. Translated by Steven Randall as *Free to Obey: How the Nazis Invented Modern Management*. New York: Europa Compass, 2023.

Charteris-Black, Jonathan. *Politicians and Rhetoric the Persuasive Power of Metaphor*. New York: Palgrave Macmillan, 2005.

Charteris-Black, Jonathan. *Fire Metaphors: Discourses of Awe and Authority*. New York: Bloomsbury Academic, 2016.

Chomsky, Noam. "International Terrorism: Image and Reality." In Alexander George, ed. *Western State Terrorism*: 12–38. New York: Routledge, 1991.

Chomsky, Noam. "Simple Truths, Hard Problems: Some Thoughts on Terror, Justice, and Self-Defence." *Philosophy* 80, no. 311 (January 2005): 5–28.

Darwin, Charles. *On the Origin of Species* [1859]. London: Collector's Library, 2004.

Davidson, Osha Gray. *The Best of Enemies: Race and Redemption in the New South*. Chapel Hill: The University of North Carolina Press, 1996.

Dawes, James. *The Language of War: Literature and Culture in the U.S. from the Civil War through World War II*. Cambridge, MA: Harvard University Press, 2005.

Dawkins, Richard. *The Selfish Gene* [1976]. New York: Oxford University Press, 2006.

Derrida, Jacques. *Politiques de l'amitié*. Paris: Galilée, 1994. Translated by George Collins as *The Politics of Friendship*. New York: Verso Books, 2006.

Derrida, Jacques. *Voyous*. Paris: Galilée, 2003. Translated by Pascale-Anne Brault and Michael Naas as *Rogues: Two Essays on Reason*. Stanford, CA: Stanford University Press, 2005.

Douglas, Susan J. and Meredith W. Michaels. *The Mommy Myth: The Idealization of Motherhood and How It Has Undermined All Women*. New York: Free Press (Simon & Schuster), 2004.

Dovring, Karin. *Road of Propaganda: The Semantics of Biased Communication*. New York: Philosophical Library, 1959.

Drillon, Jacques. *Traité de la ponctuation française*. Paris: Gallimard (Collection "Tel"), 1991.

Eagleton, Terry. *Sweet Violence: The Idea of the Tragic*. Oxford: Blackwell Publishing, 2003.

Ellison, Ralph. *Invisible Man* [1952]. New York: Vintage Books, 1995.

Emmert, Scott D. "Jack London and the Great White Hopes of Boxing Literature." In Gerald Early, ed. *The Cambridge Companion to Boxing*: 246–57. New York: Cambridge University Press, 2019.

Evans, Gavin. *Skin Deep: Journeys in the Divisive Science of Race*. London: OneWorld Publications, 2019.

Fairclough, Norman. *Language and Power*, 2nd edition. London & New York: Routledge, 2013.

Fallada, Hans. *Jeder stirbt für sich allein* [1947]. Translated by Michael Hofman as *Every Man Dies Alone*. Brooklyn, NY: Melville House Publishing, 2009.

Fanon, Frantz. *Black Skin, White Masks* [1952]. New York: Grove Press, 2008.

Finnegan, Ruth. *Why Do We Quote? The Culture and History of Quotation*. Cambridge: Open Book Publishers, 2011.

Flusberg, Stephen J., Teenie Matlock, and Paul Thibodeau. "War Metaphors in Public Discourse." *Metaphor and Symbol* 33, no. 1 (January 2018): 1–18.

Foucault, Michel. *Discipline and Punish: The Birth of the Prison* [*Surveiller et punir. Naissance de la prison, 1975*]. Translated by Alan Sheridan. New York: Vintage Books, [1977], 1995.

Foucault, Michel. *Power/Knowledge: Selected Interviews and Other Writings, 1972–1997*. Edited by Colin Gordon. New York: Pantheon Books, 1980.

Fowler, Roger. *Language in the News: Discourse and Ideology in the Press*. London & New York: Routledge, 2013.

Fowler, Roger, Bob Hodge, Gunther Kress, and Tony Trew. *Language and Control*. London, Boston, & Henley: Routledge & Kegan Paul, 1979.

Frankfurt, Harry G. *On Bullshit*. Princeton, NJ: Princeton University Press, 2005.

Friedlander, R.A. "Terrorism and National Liberation Movements: Can Rights Derive from Wrongs?" *Case Western Reserve Journal of International Law* 13, no. 2 (1981): 281–9.

Galtung, Johan. "Language and War: Is There a Connection?" *Current Research on Peace and Violence. War, Peace & Culture* 10, no. 1 (1987): 2–6.

Garber, Marjorie. *Academic Instincts*. Princeton, NJ: Princeton University Press, 2001.

Garber, Marjorie. *Quotation Marks*. New York: Routledge, 2003.

Garber, Megan. "The Scare Quote: 2016 in a Punctuation Mark." *The Atlantic*, December 23, 2016. https://www.theatlantic.com/entertainment/archive/2016/12/the-scare-quote-2016-in-a-punctuation-mark/511319/ [accessed January 10, 2019].

Gates, Henry Louis, Jr. "Editor's Introduction: Writing 'Race' and the Difference It Makes." *Critical Inquiry* 12, no. 1 (Autumn 1985) ("Race," Writing and Difference): 1–20.

Gates, Henry Louis, Jr. and Andrew S. Curran. "Inventing the Science of Race." *The New York Review of Books* 52, no. 54 (December 16, 2021): 56–7.

Gould, Stephen Jay. *The Mismeasure of Man* [1981]. Revised and expanded edition. New York & London: W.W. Norton & Co., 1996.

Gregory, Dick and Robert Lipstye. *Nigger: An Autobiography* [1964]. New York: Plume (Penguin Random House), 2019.

Griffin, John Howard. *Black Like Me* [1960]. San Antonio, TX: Wings Press, 2004.

Harvey, Robert. "Of Incredibility in the Need to Believe: A Philosophical Exploration." In Sara G. Beardsworth, ed. *The Philosophy of Julia Kristeva*: 513–28. Chicago: Open Court Publishing Co., 2020.

Hayakawa, S.I. "General Semantics and Propaganda." *Public Opinion Quarterly* 3, no. 2 (April 1939): 197–208.

Healy, Maureen. "Mission Accomplished: Karl Kraus and the Abuse of Language in Wartime." *Contemporanea* 17, no. 4 (October–December 2004): 647–53.

Hense, Rosemary C. "Metaphors of Diversity, Intergroup Relations, and Equity in the Discourse of Educational Leaders." *Journal of Language, Identity and Education* 4 (2005): 243–67.

Hitchins, Christopher. *The Trial of Henry Kissinger*. London & New York: Verso, 2001.

Houston, Keith. *Shady Characters: The Secret Life of Punctuation, Symbols, and Other Typographical Marks*. New York: W.W. Norton, 2014.

Howard, Marc Morjé. *Unusually Cruel: Prisons, Punishment, and the Real American Exceptionalism*. Oxford & New York: Oxford University Press, 2017.

Jones, Robert P. *The Hidden Roots of White Supremacy and the Path to a Shared American Future*. New York: Simon & Schuster, 2023.

Kelley, William Melvin. "If You're Woke You Dig It." *The New York Times*, May 20, 1962, Section SM: 45.

Killens, John Oliver. *Black Man's Burden* [1965]. New York: Pocket Books (Simon & Schuster), 1969.

Klemperer, Victor. *LTI–Notizbuch eines Philologen*. Berlin: Aufbau Verlag, 1947. Translated by Martin Brady as *The Language of the Third Reich: LTI: A Philologist's Notebook* [1957]. London: Bloomsbury, 2013.

Klemperer, Victor. *Ich will Zeugnis ablegen bis zum letzten. Tagebücher* 1942–1945 (v. 2). Berlin: Aufbau Verlage, 2022. Translated by Martin Chalmers as *I Will Bear Witness. Diary of the Nazi Years* (v. 1, 1933–1941 [1998]; v. 2, 1942–1945 [1999]). New York: Modern Library Paperback, 1999 (v.1), 2001 (v. 2).

Kropotkin, Peter. *Mutual Aid: A Factor in Evolution*. New York: McClure, Philips & Company, 1902. As arranged and edited by Jonathan-David Jackson.

Lebron, Christopher J. *The Making of BLM: A Brief History of an Idea*. New York: Oxford University Press, 2018.

Lorenz, Chris. "If You're So Smart, Why Are You under Surveillance? Universities, Neoliberalism, and New Public Management." *Critical Inquiry* 38, no. 3 (Spring 2012): 599–629.

Lyotard, Jean-François. *Le Différend*. Paris: Minuit, 1983. Translated by Georges Van Den Abbele as *The Differend: Phrases in Dispute*. Minneapolis: University of Minnesota Press, 1996.

Marcus, Greil. "Notes on the Making of *a New Literary History of America*—Part I—Scare Quotes Are the Enemy." *Harvard University Press Blog*, May 10, 2010.

Marks, Jonathan. *Human Biodiversity: Genes, Race, and History*. New York: Aldine de Gruyter, 1994.

McAuley, James. "Europe's War on Woke." *The Nation*, November 29, 2021. https://www.thenation.com/article/politics/murdoch-fox-dominion-election/ [accessed December 12, 2021].

McIntyre, Lee. *Post-Truth*. Cambridge, MA: MIT Press (Essential Knowledge), 2018.

Memmi, Albert. *The Colonizer and the Colonized* [1973]. Boston: Beacon Press, 1991.

Molière, Jean-Baptiste Poquelin. *Les Précieuses ridicules* [1659/1660]. *Œuvres complètes, I*. Paris: Gallimard (Bibliothèque de la Pléiade, 8), 2010: 1–30. *The Precious Damsels* in *Eight Plays by Molière*: 5–29. Translated by Morris Bishop. New York: The Modern Library, 1957.

Muir, Diana. "A Land without a People for a People without a Land." *Middle East Quarterly* 15, no. 2 (Spring 2008): 55–62.

Nietzsche, Friedrich. *Beyond Good and Evil: Prelude to a Philosophy of the Future* [1998]. Translated by Marion Faber. Oxford & New York: Oxford University Press, 2008.

Nietzsche, Friedrich. *Über Lüge und Wahrheit im außermoralischen Sinn* [1873]. Translated by A.K.M. Adam as "On Truth and Lies in the Extra-Moral Sense." Oxford: Quadriga, 2019.

Orwell, George. "Politics and the English Language." *Horizon* 13, no. 76 (April 1946): 252–65.

Painter, Nell Irvin. *The History of White People*. New York: W.W. Norton & Co., 2010.

Parkes, M.B. *Pause and Effect: Punctuation in the West*. Berkeley: University of California Press, 1993.

Pêcheux, Michel. *Les Vérités de La Palice*. Paris: François Maspéro, 1975. Translated by Harbans Nagpal as *Language, Semantics, and Ideology*. Paris: St. Martin's Press, 1982.

Perlman, Merrill. "'Scare tactics': Quotes around Single Words." *Columbia Journalism Review*, January 28, 2013. https://archives.cjr.org/language_corner/scare_tactics.php [accessed January 24, 2019].

Pratkanis, Anthony R. and Elliot Aronson. *Age of Propaganda: The Everyday Use and Abuse of Persuasion*. Revised edition. New York: W.H. Freeman and Company, 2001.

Predelli, Stefano. "Scare Quotes and Their Relation to Other Semantic Issues." *Linguistics and Philosophy* 26, no. 1 (February 2003): 1–28.

Ranger, Graham. "Quotative Like in Contemporary Non-Standard English." *Arts et Savoirs* 2 (2012) ("Les théories de l'énonciation: Benveniste après un demi-siècle"). https://journals.openedition.org/aes/513 [accessed July 2, 2019].

Rattansi, Ali. *Racism: A Very Short Introduction*. Oxford & New York: Oxford University Press, 2007.

Recanati, François. "Open Quotation." *Mind* 110, no. 439 (2001): 637–87.

Rée, Jonathan. "Funny Voices: Stories, Punctuation, and Personal Identity." *New Literary History* 21, no. 4 (Autumn 1990): 1039–58.

Rodgers, Daniel. "The Uses and Abuses of 'Neoliberalism.'" *Dissent* 65, no. 1 (Winter 2018): 78–87.

Romano, Aja. "A History of 'Wokeness': 'Stay Woke'—How a Black Activist Watchword Got Co-opted in the Culture War." *Vox*, October 9, 2020. https://www.vox.com/culture/21437879/stay-woke-wokeness-history-origin-evolution-controversy [accessed September, 9 2023].

Ryan, Marie-Laure. "Truth without Scare Quotes: Post-Sokalian Genre Theory." *New Literary History* 29, no. 4 (Autumn 1998): 811–30.

Sand, Shlomo. *The Invention of the Jewish People*. Translated by Yael Lotan. London & New York: Verso Books, 2009.

Sarraute, Nathalie. *Over Nothing at All [Pour un oui ou pour un non, 1982]*. Edited by Philippa Wehle. *Dramacontemporary: France*: 43–60. New York: PAJ Publications, 1986.

Scheible, Jeff. *Digital Shift: The Cultural Logic of Punctuation*. Minneapolis: University of Minnesota Press, 2015.

Sinclair, Upton. *100%—The Story of a Patriot*. Pasadena, CA: Published by the Author, 1920.

Snellings, Quincy Elizabeth. "White Privilege: A Study of White Students' Racial Awareness at a Predominantly White, but Historically Inclusive Institution" (2015). Bates College Honors Theses. 133. https://scarab.bates.edu/honorstheses/133/ [accessed June 23, 2023].

Sontag, Susan. "Notes on 'Camp.'" In *Against Interpretation and Other Essays* [1966]: 264–80. New York: Farrar, Straus and Giroux, 2013.

Srigley, Ron. "Whose University Is It Anyway?" *Los Angeles Review of Books*, February 22, 2018.

Stanley, Jason. *How Propaganda Works*. Princeton, NJ: Princeton University Press, 2016.

Steuter, Erin and Deborah Wills. *At War with Metaphor: Media, Propaganda, and Racism in the War on Terror*. Lanham, MD: Lexington Books, 2008.

Stove, David. *Popper and After: Four Modern Irrationalists*. Oxford: Pergamon Press, 1982.

Sussman, Robert Wald. *The Myth of Race: The Troubling Persistence of an Unscientific Idea*. Cambridge, MA: Harvard University Press, 2014.

Szendy, Peter. *Of Stigmatology: Punctuation as Experience*. New York: Fordham University Press, 2018.

Tattersall, Ian and Rob Desalle. *Race? Debunking a Scientific Myth*. College Station: Texas A & M University Press, 2011.

Teichman, Jenny. "How to Define Terrorism." *Philosophy* 64, no. 250 (October 1989): 505–17.

Thorne, Steve. *The Language of War*. London & New York: Routledge, 2006.

Truss, Lynne. *Eats, Shoots & Leaves: The Zero Tolerance Approach to Punctuation*. New York: Gotham Books, 2003.

Ture, Kwame [Stokely Carmichael] and Charles V. Hamilton. *Black Power: The Politics of Liberation* [1967]. New edition. New York: Vintage Books, 1992.

van Dijk, Teun A. *Ideology: A Multidisciplinary Introduction*. Thousand Oaks, CA: Sage Publications, Ltd., 2000.

van Dijk, Teun A. *Antiracist Discourse: Theory and History of a Macromovement*. New York: Cambridge University Press, 2021.

Varoufakis, Yanis. *Technofeudalism: What Killed Capitalism*. Brooklyn & London: Melville House, 2023.

Washburn, Jennifer. *University Inc.: The Corporate Corruption of Higher Education*. New York: Basic Books, 2005.

Weller, Shane. *The Idea of Europe: A Critical History*. New York: Cambridge University Press, 2021.

Wise, Tim. *White Like Me: Reflections on Race from a Privileged Son*. Berkeley, CA: Soft Skull Press, 2007.

Wise, Tim. *Between Barack and a Hard Place: Racism and White Denial in the Age of Obama*. San Francisco: City Lights Publishers, 2009.

Wise, Tim. *Colorblind: The Rise of Post-Racial Politics and the Retreat from Racial Equality*. San Francisco: City Lights Publishers, 2010.

Wittgenstein, Ludwig. *Philosophical Investigations*. Translated by G.E.M. Anscombe. London: Basil Blackwell, 1953.

Young, John Wesley. "From LTI to LQI: Victor Klemperer on Totalitarian Language." *German Studies Review* 28, no. 1 (February 2005): 45–64.

Index